Library
Undergraduate
Collection
Initiative

 University of Pittsburgh

University Library System

Dismembered Rhetoric

Dismembered Rhetoric

English Recusant Writing, 1580 to 1603

Ceri Sullivan

Madison ● Teaneck
Fairleigh Dickinson University Press
London: Associated University Presses

Associated University Presses
440 Forsgate Drive
Cranbury, NJ 08512

Associated University Presses
25 Sicilian Avenue
London WC1A 2QH, England

Associated University Presses
P.O. Box 338, Port Credit
Mississauga, Ontario
Canada L5G 4L8

The paper used in this publication meets the requirements
of the American National Standard for Permanence of Paper
for Printed Library Materials Z39.48-1984.

Library of Congress Cataloging-in-Publication Data

Sullivan, Ceri, 1963–
  Dismembered rhetoric : English recusant writing, 1580 to 1603 /
Ceri Sullivan.
    p. cm.
  Includes bibliographical references and index.
  ISBN 0-8386-3577-6 (alk. paper)
  1. English prose literature—Early modern, 1500–1700—History and
criticism.   2. Christian literature, English—Catholic authors—
History and criticism.   3. English prose literature—Catholic
authors—History and criticism.   4. Catholics—England—
History—16th century—Historiography.   5. Devotional literature,
English—History and criticism   6. English language—Early modern,
1500–1700—Rhetoric.   7. Rhetoric—Religious aspects—Christianity.
8. Hagiography—England.   I. Title.
PR428.C3S85   1995
828'.30809382—dc20   94-30701
                                                                CIP

Contents

Acknowledgments

I would like to thank the Bodleian Library, Oxford, for permission to reproduce the photographs on pages 78, 105 and 122. The staff were unfailingly courteous and efficient in helping me obtain research materials.

This book started as a D.Phil under the inspiration of Avril Bruten from St. Hugh's College, Oxford. Several people were good enough to read and comment on some of the ideas and drafts: Mary Hodder, Catherine Kenwood, Christopher Smith, and Kerry Sullivan. Peter Stoneley, of Queen's University, Belfast, has been most generous with knowledge, time, and detailed advice on writing and revisions.

A. D. Nuttall and David Crane gave helpful suggestions on its transfer into book form. Thanks also to the editors Michael Koy and Marilyn Silverman for their detailed work on the manuscript.

I would like to dedicate the book to my mother, landlady, and partner, for their warm interest and practical help—to Janet, Lois, and Tom.

Textual Apparatus and Abbreviations

The following printing conventions have been changed: long *s* has been replaced by *s;* contractions and ligatures have been expanded; the use of *vv*, *v*, and *u* has been modernized.

Abbreviations used include:

AR   Allison, A. F., and D. M. Rogers, *A Catalogue of Catholic Books . . . 1558–1640.*

CRS   Catholic Record Society.

NCE   *New Catholic Encyclopedia.*

Npp   No place of publication.

Npm   No publisher's name.

NT   Rheims New Testament.

RH   *Recusant History.*

ERL   *English Recusant Literature, 1558–1640* series of facsimiles.

[ ]   Conjectural publishing dates and names as suggested in *AR*.

Dismembered Rhetoric

1

Introduction

Father Luis de Granada described his *Memoriall of a Christian Life* to his reader in sacerdotal terms:

> it may serve thee for a preacher, to exhort thee unto good life . . . for an confessionall, to instructe thee, how thou oughtest to confesse thy sinnes, and to make due preparation, when thou intendest to communicate.[1]

The 1586 English translator of this popular Dominican also saw Granada's work acting as a silent preacher. Texts like Granada's would protect a Roman Catholic reader from heterodoxy, linking him with the body of his Church in prayer. They provided him with inspiration, with devotional formats, and even with a time schedule for prayer: all the practices which the Catholic Church would normally channel through its clergy.

Such texts were necessary because many recusants were without access to a Catholic priest, in the latter part of Elizabeth's reign. Two acts in particular enforced this literary dependence. Statutory measures had been passed early in her reign to encourage recusants to take the Oath of Supremacy and to attend Established Church services, but it was only with the reviving danger from a European Catholic enterprise against England, that stringent penalties were laid down. The 1581 "Act to retain the Queen's Majesty's subjects in their due obedience" made it treason to reconcile anyone to Rome, or to be reconciled. The fine for refusing to attend the Anglican Church service was increased from twelve pence to twenty pounds per person for each month of recusancy. In 1585, a further act declared that all ordained priests, other than those ordained under Mary, were guilty of treason if they came to Britain.

With insufficient numbers of missionary priests, the Catholic Church was forced to function through the Word more than through the sacraments. At the start of the period, with the exception of the aging Marian clergy, there were fewer than one hundred priests working secretly in Britain. John Bossy uses records from colleges and seminaries to suggest that even by 1600, twenty years after the start of the Jesuit mission to reconvert England and Wales, there were only around three hundred priests operating here. On the basis of the number of families that a priest could visit in a monthly circuit, Bossy calculates that the Catholic population numbered over forty thousand at this point.[2] His figure assumes that all priests were equally accessible to the laity, whereas in fact, many were confined to serving one family or patron. All of these Catholics comprised a potential audience for recusant texts; to them must be added those who fail Bossy's test for Catholicism, of habitual recourse to a priest, but who were still in sympathy with the devotional methods of the Roman Church. This group would include some Protestants and the infamous "church-papists." Thus, despite their prior commitment to the sacraments before the Word, Roman Catholics during the late sixteenth century had to become energetically involved in the anxious business of religious rhetoric. This book examines how the rhetoric in recusant devotional prose is used in the conflict between inclination and necessity.

Rhetorical theory at the center of Elizabethan writing circles around three elements of any speech: the speaker's ethos, the subject material, and the attitude of the audience. All three can be manipulated, with the object of changing the audience's opinion. However, the subject which a Catholic text discusses is fixed; the material of the faith is, in terms of rhetoric, a series of commonplaces. Nor can the speaker's approach be altered, since an interpretation provided by the Church is regarded as immutable. Thus in recusant prose of the three elements of the speech described by rhetoric, only that of the audience can be adapted. The reader is urged to become engrossed in the works, taking on their points of reference. Vernacular meditations, hagiographies, and catechisms were produced in order to persuade the reader to true devotion, to change himself rather than the texts.

Concentration on the Word and on the solitary prayer modes encouraged by reading are features usually seen as Protestant modes of worship. Catholic devotional texts have not received the same critical attention as have Protestant works demonstrating such features. In the 1930s, Helen White described a coherent and artful group of sixteenth-century Protestant texts. Recognition of these has been extended, by such critics as Barbara Lewalski, to an understanding of the influence which this native body of work had on poetry of the early seventeenth century. However, despite this interest in Elizabethan devotional work almost nothing has been published about recusant authors. In 1950, A. C. Southern's *Elizabethan Recusant Prose 1559–1582* clarified the existence and authorship of recusant texts from the early part of Elizabeth's reign, and gave brief descriptions of their polemical and devotional content. His book remains the definitive introduction to early secret-press publications. However, Southern's work did not expand into a literary appreciation of recusant work before 1582, nor is there a full-length study on English Catholic texts for the remainder of Elizabeth's reign.

Instead, discussion about Catholic prose has centered on Continental Counter-Reformation texts, looking at versions of the Ignatian meditation. The debate asks whether this or the native Protestant meditative tradition influenced seventeenth-century poetry in Britain. Louis Martz started the argument in 1954 with *The Poetry of Meditation,* which suggests that works by Southwell, Donne, and Herbert owe much to Continental Catholic spirituality. Given that Southern was engaged in exploring the native recusant prose tradition, it is startling to find Martz abducting Southern's work to prove that "the channels of communication between England and the Catholic Continent were ample to carry the meditation methods of the Counter Reformation into England." Martz uses an Ignatian model of meditation to analyze metaphysical poetry. This method of meditation he describes as being in three stages, initially with the meditator remembering the facts of a scriptural event or theological point, and applying each sense to imagine the scene. The meditator then puts himself in the scene, and realizes its moral significance. Finally, in a colloquy with God, he wills to apply this meaning to his own life. Martz believes that the first stage, the technique of "composition of place," lies behind the "vividly dramatized, firmly established, graphically imaged openings" of metaphysical poetry. He goes on to point out parallels between the aim and techniques of meditation and poetic self-scrutiny. In effect, Martz substitutes the influence of meditative habits of thought for the idea of a "school of Donne."

Battle-lines are drawn up where Martz sees problems in Puritan meditation, which would make this meditative influence specifically Catholic. "It was the doctrine of the 'real presence' which made possible that delicate sense of 'presence' which characterizes Catholic meditation on the life of Christ," one which he feels is impossible to retain in a Puritan mode of meditation. In Martz's view, Puritan meditations such as those by Arthur Dent, Joseph Hall, and Richard Baxter function as handbooks which show the evidence of grace but which are unable to produce it.[3]

This suggestion gets a frosty response from patriotic Protestants, who want to claim a British influence on such a valuable group as the metaphysical poets. Barbara Lewalski's *Protestant Poetics and the Seventeenth-Century Religious Lyric* of 1979 sternly insists that "the major seventeenth-century religious lyrists owe more to contemporary, English, and Protestant influences than to Counter Reformation, continental, and medieval Catholic resources." She proposes two origins to this Protestant poetic: the Bible, as "source and model for the presentation of sacred truth," and a "painstaking analysis of the personal religious life" in seeking out scriptural history within one's own soul.[4] Her claim does not demolish Martz's suggestion, that Protestant meditation texts function as measuring rods rather than as tools to create grace. However, it gives a poetic function to these meditations, justifying lyric self-contemplation and apotheosizing the parochial salvation of a single soul into the creation of a scriptural antitype.

Lewalski criticizes Martz for failing to deal with the developing native Protestant meditation genre she demonstrates. However, the limits of her work meant that she had to restrict her comments on the well-established native Catholic meditation genre. She repeats Richard Rogers's self-congratulatory preface in *Seven Treatises, Containing Such Direction as is Gathered out of the Holie Scriptures* of 1603.

> Offering his own massive work as a Protestant counterpart to the two Jesuit manuals, Parsons' *Christian Directory* and Gaspar Loarte's *Exercise of a Christian Life*, [Rogers] denounced their mechanical methods of meditation and devotion as a "ridiculous tying men to a daily taske of reading some part of the storie of Christs passion, and saying certaine prayers throughout the weeke."[5]

In her afterword, she does recommend further exploration of a "Tridentine aesthetic" based on "the senses, the liturgy and the lives of Christ, the Virgin and various saints."

Critics other than Martz and Lewalski also neglect the domestic Catholic texts of this period. Literary analysis has tended to follow Helen White's description of Elizabethan books of devotion and hagiography, which states that while "the works of the Recusant exiles deserve some attention for their own very high degree of interest as well as for their influence on the home [devotional] literature," she will make no effort "to do them the justice they deserve, because, for the most part, they remain outside the main stream of the development of English literature."[6] Lily B. Campbell's analysis of divine poetry and drama from the period confines itself to Protestant devotional texts, even when analyzing Robert Southwell's poetry.[7] Isabel MacCaffrey, commenting on the ideas of Martz, combines Augustinian and Ignatian meditation to construct a "meditative paradigm." This "journey towards a paradise within" recognizes the divine image in man by a discipline using the three powers of the mind: the memory, the understanding, and the will.[8] Once again, this model is produced with the intention of applying it to English poetry in the seventeenth century; there is no consideration of native Catholic prose itself. Pierre Janelle simply slots Robert Persons's *Christian Directorie Guiding Men to their Salvation* of 1582 into the Ignatian tradition, without any analysis of the work.[9] J. R. Roberts's *Critical Anthology of English Recusant Devotional Prose, 1558–1603* follows the excellent example of descriptive bibliography given by Southern, but chooses to consider recusant texts historically, as part of the main mission effort, rather than examining their style and structure.[10]

Why is this? Materials exist for such a study. The "Catalogue of Catholic Books in English Printed Abroad or Secretly in England 1558–1640" by A. F. Allison and D. M. Rogers conveniently lists every extant recusant text published in the period.[11] Nearly two hundred were published between the start of the Jesuit mission in 1580 and the end of Elizabeth's reign—about a tenth of the production by the licit press of devotional material.

The small amount of literary analysis on sixteenth-century recusant work which does exist, is partisan. Southern viewed recusant authors as literary "martyrs" of the Reformation, complaining that "since in the religious division of the kingdom the Catholics were of the weaker side," their prose had been ignored by scholars.[12] His wistful tone was taken up by other Catholic critics. Successive numbers of the journal *Recusant History* suggested that

> the domestic writers have been studied and duly praised. The exile writers . . . have been virtually unnoticed. Eclipsed for reasons that had nothing to do with their literary merit, sixteenth-century English Catholic authors gradually faded out of the national consciousness.[13]

This simmering resentment could reduce literary analysis to hagiography. About a style of prose he dislikes, Southern says hastily that its purpose is "first and last, to lead souls to Heaven . . . [and it is] beside the point to call attention to the methods employed by the two writers to give force and vividness to their message."[14] There is uncritical reverence for work by J. J. Dwyer's "shining band of young recusants . . . altogether fitted to embody the Spenserian dream of chivalry," the priests and martyrs of the English mission.[15]

Not that there is a lack of historical and biographical work on the recusant mission. At first, John Bossy pointed out, historical studies were handicapped by

> martyrology [which] pointed the subject, historiographically speaking, up a cul-de-sac; a lack of contact with universities left too much scope for

imitation of Hilaire Belloc and too little for influences which might have
enlarged an over-clerical conception of the community and its history.[16]

When reviewing the first ten years of *Recusant History* in 1961, its
editors had to enjoin the Catholic historian, austerely, to

> submit the view which, moved by feelings of loyalty to his Church, he
> would prefer to see vindicated, to the same objective scrutiny as every
> other, and if the facts warrant its rejection . . . reject it.

By 1976, however, the same editors realized that their warning had
been heeded. Indeed, they were now forced to caution against an
overenthusiastic historical ecumenism which ignored facts or attitudes
which could embarrass the reformed faiths.[17] In the literary sphere
also, setting aside ideas about exclusion and a receptive martyrdom
is a prerequisite for increasing critical interest in the literary aspects
of the mission.

To compensate for widespread neglect, grandiose claims for recusant prose have been made by a few critics. In 1913, J. S. Phillimore
stated that where Thomas More left the language, "there it remained
until Dryden definitely civilized it." He expanded on this in a letter
to Southern in 1921: "the main stream of scholarship and culture was
in the Catholic exiles . . . the commonsense unaffected English Prose
that reappeared in Dryden was the English Catholic tradition re-
vived."[18] Southern claimed to echo a 1920 lecture of R. W. Chambers,
who examined the "plain and open style" of Thomas More and suggested that such Catholic authors as More carried the English language through the dangers of Euphuism and rhetorical flourish.[19]
In 1950, Southern endorsed this view, saying that "what passed for
traditional in English prose of the Elizabethan epoch must be regarded
in the nature of a sport. . . . To trace correctly the history of that
prose tradition we must fix our attention on the prose of the Catholic
exiles."[20] Twenty years on, and very little more cautiously, J. X.
Evans considered

> that the prose of the Tudor recusants is often comparable in skill and
> sophistication to the prose we associate with Dryden and the great stylists
> of the eighteenth century. Furthermore, these remarkably well-written
> books appeared at a time when England had little reason to boast about
> its prose.[21]

These claims are unsupported by any detailed analysis of the style of
the recusant authors they wish to see canonized.

Perhaps more damagingly, critics of recusant prose have unwittingly discouraged a wider study of the works by praising "a simple and straightforward exposition of their themes, such as would appeal to the unlearned . . . [in other words] good sense in plain language."[22] Not that this emphasis is new: the *Tatler* was one of the first to praise the style of a recusant, "Parsons the Jesuit," in terms of being "simple," "clear and intelligible."[23] Critical fear that discovering rhetoric in these texts could subvert their purity appears to be based on two reasons. Firstly, recusant critics nurse the Ramist insistence that rhetoric is composed only of schemes and tropes, is merely *elocutio*. In Southwell's poetry, for instance, W. R. Maurer sees a "burdensome need to sugar-coat the sermon to make it more palatable for the weak and fickle reader, [which] all but stifles originality."[24] Similarly, Pierre Janelle concludes a vivid description of the integrated nature of the literary and spiritual aspects of the mission by lamenting the "crust of conceits and oratory" of Southwell's prose meditation, *Marie Magdalens Funerall Teares* of 1591. This misapprehension about rhetoric ignores the long-standing recognition, by critics such as Brian Vickers, Terence Cave, and Walter Ong, of the rhetorical nature of invention and judgment.

The second basis for this fear of rhetoric is its appeal to the reader through artifice. Rhetoric moves away from that chaste and virile morality, Barthes's "castrating ethic of 'purity'" with which Catholic analysts credit recusant writers.[25] Brian Oxley notes that critics "have tended to deprecate the mannerism or artifice of [Southwell's] work as somehow detracting from his sanctity."[26] C. S. Lewis, one of the few to discuss Cardinal William Allen's writing, praises him for a dignified, "virile" style, which goes to the heart of a subject.[27] Again, Janelle complains that he sees in Southwell's *Saint Peters complaint* a "conscious effort of the literary craftsman . . . to please his readers [which] diverts him from the true channel of his poetic inspiration."[28] Nor is this anxiety about rhetoric confined to the twentieth-century observer. Luis de Granada's Christian style, he said, was "like unto water, the which when it is good, it hath no maner of tast at all."[29] "No manner of taste," "clear," "good sense in plain language"—with such a forbiddingly austere press, it seems clear why studies of these texts have been confined to the historical and bibliographical.

A few recent articles have recognized the rhetorical bias of the texts. They have traced the rhetorical architecture of the Catholic *ars moriendi* (handbooks on how to die with grace), of work by Southwell, and in the poetry of William Alabaster. J. X. Evans succinctly describes the literary training which recusant writers and translators received at the universities in Britain, and in the Catholic colleges abroad. He shows that rhetorical schemes learned in youth reappear in treatises on the preparation for death by the living, by Thomas Stapleton, John Fisher, Southwell, and Persons. David Crane suggests that, in Southwell's verse, "disciplining of one's will to virtue and of one's mind . . . to subtly-measured words are properly aspects of the same activity."[30] R. V. Caro examines the work of recusant Thomas Wright, *The Passions of the Mind* written in 1598, which deals with arousing affections by the use of language. Caro shows how this strategy is employed in the sonnets of William Alabaster, converted by Wright in 1597.[31] Unfortunately, this angle of study has not been followed up, nor extended to a technical analysis of the rhetoric of recusant works. Confined to a few works, such analysis could not expand on the tension between Catholic practice and rhetorical theory.

Yet recusant authors do rise to Augustine's challenge:

should [the wicked], influencing and urging the minds of their listeners to error by their eloquence, terrify, sadden, gladden, and passionately encourage them, while [the good], indifferent and cold in behalf of truth, sleep on?[32]

They had no choice. For practical reasons, the recusant texts had to use rhetoric. To a large extent, books took the place of the priest in consoling, admonishing, and teaching the beleaguered group of Catholics. Such works met a diverse audience which needed to be persuaded to read. The term *recusant* originally covered anyone who refused to attend the Anglican service. In the later sixteenth century, it was confined to describing Catholics. "Church-papist" was the derogatory label used by both sides about those who maintained they were Catholic but who attended Established Church services often enough to avoid being cited for recusancy. Catholic texts had to reassure recusant readers that they were part of a viable devotional and political group. At the same time, authors had to reproach the infamous church-papists, encouraging them back to prison and scaffold. In the latter years of the century, especially after the publication of the 1570 Bull excommunicating Elizabeth, *Regnans in excelsis*, even the compliance of the recusant audience could not be guaranteed. This increased the pressure for authors to provide pleasurable and persuasive texts.

Since many Protestants were reading the recusant books, there was a second group to be satisfied. Enjoyment of the fierce controversy between the two faiths certainly made up some of their interest. However, it was not only polemical works on the English succession or dogmatic works on the Sacraments, but also devotional works that

were bought by Protestants. Recusant prefaces to devotional texts
address themselves to an audience of "Catholikes, protestants, and
demi-Catholikes." The rhetoric coaxed a Protestant audience to carry
on reading, letting the recusant author appeal to the tolerant reader.
William Allen adopts a superb tone of reconciliation on such
occasions:

> our pen (God willing) shalbe so tempered herein, that it shal displease no
> reasonable reader, nor surelie skarce them (if it may be) against whom in
> our inculpable defence we are forced to write.[33]

The small, close-knit and submissive audience, such as Catholic
preachers had hitherto enjoyed, listened to Robert Southwell's admo-
nitions on

> reading good bookes, hearing sermons, and such like godly exercises, not
> lightly runing over them, thinking it enough to have red or heard good
> things, but pawsing upon such thinges as move my affection, & printing
> them well in . . . mind & memory.[34]

The Protestant audience was not so humble. An entertaining or at
least attentive tone, acknowledging the reader's liberty to ignore the
writer, was necessary to tempt this second audience to peruse, let
alone possess, tracts which were enough to imprison them if found
by the authorities.

Catholic authors recognized the need for literary conciliation. Persons wrote to the General of the Society of Jesus, Claudio Acquaviva,
insisting that any confessors sent on the mission were well versed
in "polite letters."[35] Francis Bacon passed on Southwell's *Humble
Supplication to Her Maiestie*, written in 1591, to his brother Anthony
with the judgment that it was worth copying for its artistry, even
though he thought its argument wrong-headed.[36] Indeed, in 1601
Anthony Copley said that Jesuit authors had succeeded so well in
adapting their work to English taste that it passed "currant & ap-
plauded not onelie amongst the vulgar, but (which is a shame)
amongst the upper sort of Catholickes."[37]

Care over style got more than literary praise, as the *responsa scholarum* of the English College at Rome show. When Robert Persons
became Rector of the College in 1597, he introduced a system for
questioning each applicant for admission about their family, upbring-
ing, education, health, and religious history. Of the fifty-seven responses which survive from 1597 to the end of Elizabeth's reign,
twelve give recusant books as a determining factor in their conversion.

Since many students did not adequately answer the question about what brought them to Rome, the proportion of men converted by these books may have been higher.[38]

A diverse readership meant that authors found a style which let them ignore the destruction of the coherent audience of one faith. They had also lost the advantage of sound: "that *viva vox* word of mouth [which] hath incomparably more force, then the dead pen, whether it be to edifie, or to destroy," says Richard Bristow.[39] Gregory Martin agrees that

> men can not lightly learne the Christian religion by reading Scriptures, but by hearing, and by the preference of their teachers, which may instruct them . . . as cleerly & breefely by letters they could not doe.[40]

These writers had lost the audience's compulsion to listen, which any speaker can lay on it, let alone an audience which is commanded by divine precept to heed the preacher. A reader controls the pace of reception, enhancing his ability to criticize the material, as Quintilian points out. Thus, recusant texts were forced into a fundamentally rhetorical appreciation of the audience's point of view. While standard Protestant works on composing devotional prose, such as Andreas Hyperius's *Practice of preaching; Otherwise Called the Pathway to the Pulpet* (translated by John Ludham in 1577), could assume an exalted and energetic role for the preacher, who "chargeth, commaundeth, sharply rebuketh, threateneth, pronounceth, as one in place of authoritie," the Catholic preacher had to revert to the ignominious position of the rhetor, who, as Hyperius says, "supposeth none of these thinges to bee lawfull unto him, but rather he is compelled nowe and then fowly to flatter and fawne upon the Judges."[41]

A thorough use of rhetoric in these Catholic texts would be expected, given the courses which recusant students followed, before coming to and while at the colleges at Douai or Rheims, Rome, Seville, and Valladolid. Allen's realization that the Marian priests would have to be replaced as they aged inspired him to set up a seminary and college at Douay in 1568 (located at Rheims between 1578 and 1593), followed by those of Persons at Valladolid and Seville in 1589 and 1592, and the creation of the English College at Rome in 1579 from a former hospice for English pilgrims. The education here was fundamentally rhetorical, as appendix 1 shows. Spontaneous writing without due preparation of *res* and *verba* ('things' and 'words') was inconceivable. As Walter J. Ong notes, "Tudor exuberance of language and expression was not accidental, but programmed."[42]

I have suggested that, with the exception of a few recent critics, writers about recusant prose refuse to notice the rhetoric in these texts. This distaste for rhetoric has helped the paucity of literary comment on recusant writing. It is based on a concept of rhetoric as rule-based, asiatic, and emasculating. My examination, which acknowledges that the texts faced a sensitive double audience and that their writers were trained in rhetorical strategies to convince this audience, produces a theory of recusant rhetoric. It studies the effect of theory, in rhetoric manuals used in the education of these recusant writers, on practice, in the style of Catholic devotional texts in English secretly printed between 1580 and 1603.

In response to Martz's work, past criticism of Catholic writing has tended to concentrate either on polemic or on meditation. The term *devotional* should be used in a wider sense than Martz does, covering not only meditation but also hagiography and catechism. Admittedly, distinctions are hard to make between the genres, since recusant authors will mix all three in a particular text. The most learned example of this, Persons's *Christian Directorie Guiding Men to their Salvation,* encompasses meditations on the Passion, dry disquisitions on articles of the faith, hearty reasons for resolving to be Catholic, and moving "examples of true resolution," persecuted by past heretics and pagans.[43] Even the more humble texts, however, such as *A Manuall, or Meditation, and most necessary Prayers* of 1580–81, give both concise meditations on biblical events, and "a Memoriall of Instructions right requisite.".[44] Thus, I have had to make some rather specious definitions for the purposes of argument. Catechisms are assumed to be those which appeal primarily to the intellect rather than the will; meditations the reverse—though all recusant texts are didactic. Hagiographies come close to polemic at times, since they resent the state's definition of the executed man as traitor and not martyr.

The thrust of the literary aspect of the Catholic Church's mission to reconvert England was to provide vernacular texts. Indeed, many letters by William Allen, who was the Prefect of the mission, describe the preparation of priests for the mission in terms of using the English language. In the Catholic college at Douay which he set up, while Latin was used both in and out of the classroom, students regularly used to

> preach in English, in order to acquire greater power and grace in the use of the vulgar tongue, a thing on which the heretics plume themselves exceedingly, and by which they do great injury to the simple folk.[45]

Thus, sixteenth-century translations of Continental authors, and works by British authors in languages other than English, are used for reference only.

This study starts in 1580, the terminal date of Southern's work, and the beginning of the Jesuit mission. Nearly two-thirds of the authors studied here were Jesuit, or had studied at the English Catholic colleges which had close connections with Jesuit educational methods. As Helen C. White notes, members of the order had certain advantages in missionizing: a "deliberate and calculated worldliness," and an "understanding of the resources of the new age, particularly of the consequences of the invention of printing for the art of propaganda."[46] Although many attacks directed against Catholics focused on the Society of Jesus, there were never more than about ten Jesuits working simultaneously in Britain before the end of the century.[47]

As yet, there is no extended description of Catholic manuals of rhetorical theory to match Deborah Shuger's analysis of Protestant manuals, in *Sacred Rhetoric. The Christian Grand Style in the English Renaissance* of 1988. Shuger touches on what she calls Tridentine rhetorics, a group of rhetoric manuals written in the sixteenth and early seventeenth centuries by Counter-Reformation preachers. She describes them as "rhetorics in the Classical sense," in their "willingness to accept the legitimacy of deliberate rhetoric." She distinguishes them from Protestant manuals by their concentration on "the subject matter, structure, and style of sacred discourse" rather than on the life of the preacher. She finds that they encourage a greater emotional expressiveness than Cicero's *De partitione oratoria* or the *Rhetorica ad Herennium*, supplementing discussion of the traditional five parts of rhetoric (*inventio, dispositio, elocutio, memoria,* and *pronuntiatio,* or inventing matter, arranging it, clothing it in words, memorizing the speech and delivering it) by a section on amplification.[48] I use one of the most widely read of these Tridentine rhetorics to comment on the classical texts used in the schools and colleges which the recusant writers attended. The *De arte rhetorica* of 1562, by the Jesuit Cyprian Soarez, was used by thousands of Renaissance schoolboys in the quarter-century studied here.

There is a caveat to this study. As the *Rhetorica ad Herennium* says caustically,

> any one at all who has heard more than a little about the art, especially in the field of style, will be able to discern all the passages composed in accordance with the rules; but the ability to compose them only the trained man will possess.[49]

There is danger in using a theory of composition, rhetoric, for an analysis of the result of writing. However productive it may be for literary criticism, misusing rhetoric can be punished by misinterpreting its rules of composition. The enormous degree of quantification and description suffusing each rhetoric manual is often decried by twentieth-century critics as coming from a deadeningly hubristic wish to anticipate every discursive situation with a predetermined response.

It is true that all the rhetoric manuals say eloquence cannot be wholly taught; it is better absorbed by listening to the speeches of others. For the manuals, ironically, literary criticism is a means to teach rhetoric. However, this does not engender in them disrespect for method: "rules are helpful," says Quintilian, 'so long as they indicate the direct road and do not restrict us absolutely to the ruts made by others."[50] Laying down scripts for occasions with different speech, orator, and audience, rhetoric manuals encapsulate a series of minute dramas. In practising taking a role in such scenes, the rhetor's mind is made flexible and ready, not stolid as an accountant's with taxonomic regulation.

This study is split into four, starting with an extension up to 1603 of Southern's introduction to the range of recusant texts from 1580. This is followed by three sections of analysis. The first looks at the relationship between meditation texts and deliberative rhetoric. It establishes a theory of meditation, using some of the popular Continental devotions translated in this period, then turns to the way in which a reader's will is influenced in the English texts by rhetorical techniques of *inventio* and *memoria*. The next section looks at hagiographies and catechisms. Saints' lives are read as rhetorical examples, written to prove and then to clarify the faith. These hagiographies are held up by the catechisms for the reader to imitate. However, the link which one would expect between the demonstrative *causa* and these descriptions of saints' lives is not there. It appears that an emphasis on artificial and inartificial proof, as defined in the rhetoric manuals, joins recusant catechism and hagiography. Finally, catechisms are described as a means of producing a saint by rules, crafting characters. Repetition, induced by the texts' rhetoric, removes initial duplicity in acting out these rules, and a submissive reading technique allows their absorption. A short appendix traces which rhetorical textbooks the recusant writers encountered as students in Britain and at the Catholic colleges. The whole study works toward the conclusion that far from being innocently and solely concerned with their ostensible subject—the faith, the saints, prayer or meditation—recusant texts speak with one wily eye on the audience. In other words, I think these works are deeply rhetorical.

2

Producing Recusant Devotional Texts

Problems of bringing recusant texts to scholarly notice have been compounded because the original editions, issued through secret presses in small quantities, were hard to consult. A. C. Southern was one of the first to clarify what texts were printed by whom and where, during the early part of Elizabeth's reign. Scolar Press facsimiles of many recusant texts followed from the publication of the Allison and Rogers's "Catalogue of Catholic Books in English Printed Abroad or Secretly in England 1558–1640" in 1956, and access to the texts is no longer a problem. Nonetheless, there is no comprehensive survey of all recusant devotional texts published between 1580 and 1603, so this chapter deals with all such texts, and with how they were produced.

MEDITATIONS, HAGIOGRAPHIES, AND CATECHISMS

The first thirteen years of the Jesuit mission saw little new writing on meditation. Of the fourteen works on prayers from the English secret presses, half were reprints. Most were simply translations of influential Spanish and Italian devotions, by Luis de Granada, Lorenzo Scupoli, Gaspare Loarte, and Diego de Estella. The Dominican preacher and university lecturer, Luis de Granada, produced two meditation texts which were translated into English. *Of Prayer, and Meditation* (first translated in 1582) is in three parts, giving matter for reflection followed by advice on how to meditate and to fight hindrances to prayer, then linking works of prayer to works of fasting and alms. His meditations are based on doctrinal points and passional events. The book was extremely popular in Britain, receiving four secret press editions, and a number of Protestant adaptations for the licensed press.[1] Granada also produced an abridgment of *Of Prayer*, translated in 1599 as *A Spiritual Doctrine, Conteining A Rule To live wel*. This included additional material on the importance of vocal prayer and appended many new prayers to be recited after meditation.[2] The Theatine friar, Lorenzo Scupoli, produced a set of meditations which warned the reader to be wary of the life of the world. This *Spiritual Conflict*, which Janelle calls one of the most influential devotions of Elizabeth's reign, appeared in three editions in English from 1598 onwards.[3] It is an ascetic text, urging the reader to use force against himself to fashion a creature which pleases God. *The Contempte of the World and the Vanity thereof* by the Franciscan Diego de Estella, and translated in 1584, is almost as forbidding as Scupoli's meditation, giving a series of quiet statements on the difference between the divine and human perspectives.[4] The works of Gaspare Loarte were awarded the same importance as those of Persons, by Protestant writers such as Richard Rogers. Loarte's *Exercise of a Christian Life*, first translated into English in 1579, gives detailed, formal advice on meditation techniques, and lists matter on which to meditate for each day of the week. His concentration on a discursive style of meditation and one which uses the senses, was informed by his Jesuit training. Loarte ends the *Exercise* by pondering on temptations to be expected at certain points in life, suggesting that an awareness of how sin operates, helps defeat it.[5] His *Meditations, of the Life and Passion of our Lord and Saviour Iesus Christ*, translated in 1576; explore the variety of ways in which an event can be considered: in historical terms, with compassion, with admiration, with compunction. Once again, the meditations are on the Passion and on elements of the faith.[6]

Against this array of frequently reissued Continental writing, stand only a handful of indigenous manuals published before 1592. When Persons began to translate Loarte's *Exercise*, as a spiritual resource for the English recusants, he realized that a more ambitious text was needed for those who had not made the final election to the Christian life. The result was the *Christian Directorie*, expanded from a catechism for the faithful on how to live well, to an explanation for the doubtful, about God's existence and about why one should live well. The *Christian Directorie*'s evidence for belief includes affections, which are to be initiated through meditations given by Persons. Deducing a duty to serve God, his descriptions of saints exemplify this, as they follow the faith which is laid out by Persons in the Creed and which he expands upon in the catechism. The *Christian Directorie* was published six times by the secret presses, but was popular with non-Catholics also: in 1584 Edward Bunny put it into a form suitable for Protestant use as *A Booke of Christian exercise .... Perused, and accompanied now with a Treatise tending to Pacification*, running to over thirty licensed press editions. The second text from this period, *A Manual of Prayers Newly Gathered Out of Many and divers famous authours*, was also highly popular with recusants, with twenty-six editions following the first in 1583. This text has a short prayer for almost every occasion in daily life, and includes the Jesus Psalter, brief meditations on the Passion, and the Golden Litany.[7] *A Manuall, or Meditation, and most necessary Prayers* was printed three times, first in 1580–1581. Like the *Manual of Prayers* it gives prayers for specific situations, and a short catechism with points to meditate on for each day of the week. Two of the four texts by British writers were simply collections of prayers, not new devotional writing. The final text before 1592, John Bucke's *Instructions for the use of the beades, conteining many matters of meditacion*, was published only once in 1589. Bucke runs through the logic of worship: why the reader should love God, why he should use the rosary, why be grateful for blessings, why think often on the Passion. Bucke includes a pullout illustration of doctrinal points connected with the rosary at the back of the work, to gaze on while saying the rosary.[8]

It was only after 1592 that any quantity of meditations were published by English authors. Of around thirty meditation texts produced by the secret presses up to the end of Elizabeth's reign, over half had never been printed before and these were only printed once.

The first group of new texts, all by English authors, deal with the rosary. As in Bucke's work, these rosary texts provide only a framework for prayer; they are anxious not to be expansively affective. *A Methode, to meditate on the Psalter, or great Rosarie of our blessed Ladie* of 1598 has a long preface explaining the devotional attitude which the meditator should adopt before he reads its short and factual lists of points on each decade.[9] Thomas Worthington's *Rosarie of our Ladie* of 1600 follows the same format of elaborating on a method of remembering each decade of the rosary, before giving a point-form description of the gospel facts and verses and a picture to gaze on as the rosary is recited.[10] The single English text of this period to be reprinted was by Henry Garnet. In *The Societie of the Rosary* of 1593–94, Garnet describes how to become a member of the sodality, despite political constraints. His tone is legalistic and the meditations he gives on the mysteries of the rosary are simply terse lists of events.[11]

The theme of reflection on female scriptural figures is continued in three texts exploring reactions to the events of the Passion. C.N.'s *Our Ladie Hath A New Sonne* of 1595 describes the mute communication between the crucified Christ and his mother, urging the reader to examine his conscience for signs of compunction at this poignant sight.[12] I.C.'s *Saint Marie Magdalens Conversion*, issued in 1603, is designed less to raise compunction than to arouse the reader's curiosity about sacred matters. It is a long verse narrative which asks Mary for the reason why she repented and describes how she feels at the moment of the Crucifixion, since it is caused by her sins.[13] *Marie Magdalens Funerall Teares* of 1591, by Robert Southwell, also amplifies the passionate guilt of the Magdalen, before asking the reader to emulate her as she redirects this feeling toward Christ.

The next group of texts, secret-press verse meditations, transfer secular forms and expression to devotional subjects.[14] The printer Richard Verstegan produced a collection of *Odes. In Imitation of the Seaven Penitential Psalmes* in 1601. This translates the penitential psalms, relates the facts of the rosary events, puns on the names of the Virgin, celebrates the female saints of the Church, and complains of church disunity. In *Palestina* of 1600, Robert Chambers produces an allegory of a wicked Enchanter, a frail Lady and a handsome young Prince to explain the Fall and Redemption.[15] Although never published by secret press, the poetry of the Catholic converts, William Alabaster and Henry Constable is used to illuminate meditation texts. These authors' avowed aim is to use lay arts to good purpose, rescuing them.

Occasional devotional texts published in this period include Thomas a Kempis's *Imitatio Christi* in the William Whytford translation, republished in 1585 as *The Folowing of Christ*.[16] *A Breefe Collection Concerning the Love of God towards Mankinde* of 1603, follows the same format as the *Manual of Prayers* and *Manuall, or Meditation*, of the decade before 1592.[17] *A Breefe Collection* provides highly schematized meditations and prayers, giving reasons why the reader should love God rather than affective descriptions of his goodness. In 1599, Verstegan got papal privilege to produce the first English translation of the post-Tridentine *Officium Beatae Mariae Virginis*. *The Primer, or Office of the Blessed Virgin Marie* contains the penitential and gradual psalms, the litany of the saints, the office for the dead, and the hours of the Virgin Mary.[18] Most importantly, permission was granted for an English translation of the Bible. The heavily annotated *New Testament of Iesus Christ* appeared from Rheims in 1582, and the Old Testament (*The Holie Bible Faithfully Translated into English*) from Douay in 1609–10, both translated by Gregory Martin.[19]

The quantity of new work shows a resurgence of interest in producing English works, toward the survival of the Faith in Britain. About four books of all types of recusant work were published each year between 1583 and 1593, while the count for the following decade almost doubles. Devotional works kept pace with this trend. The increase may have some correlation with the political periods of resistance and compromise charted by Peter Holmes and Alan Dures. What Holmes calls "enthusiastic non-resistance" was advocated by recusant polemical texts until about 1583.[20] The missionaries were instructed not to "mix themselves in the affairs of States, nor . . . recount news about political matters in their letters . . . [to] refrain from talk against the Queen and not allow it in others."[21] Even in Campion's "Bragge" and Persons's *Confessio fidei* there is an almost defiant stress on not reacting to the persecution.[22] Such non-resistance was made possible by Gregory XIII's good sense in suspending for Catholics the operation of the 1570 Bull, allowing them to maintain their temporal obedience to the Queen.

Holmes suggests that the following decade saw the idea of resistance to government measures developing among recusants. The possibility of an armed invasion by European Catholic powers gave impetus to English persecution of the recusants and, in turn, to an attack on such action by Catholic polemical writers. This was reversed, however, after 1593. There was a dawning realization among Catholics that they would have to look to Elizabeth's successor for toleration. This recognition, coming at the same time as Spain's withdrawal from her North European commitments and the conversion of Henry of Navarre in 1593, returned Catholics' thoughts to nonresistance. It is possible that in the last decade, recusant writers moved toward relying on texts rather than on overt political resistance to keep the faith alive into the next reign. As a solitary prayer form, meditation must have become particularly useful after the 1591 Proclamation, which further inhibited access to priests.[23]

Although the need for recusant devotional texts to take a sacerdotal role was created by this political situation, Catholic authors rarely refer to the persecution. Manuals of prayer and meditation pass over the opportunity of praying for peace, for the souls of the martyrs, or for the conversion of Britain. The *Manual of Prayers* continues to give preparations for communion and confession as though the sacraments, necessarily obtained through a priest, are freely available. Describing how a priest created the "Crown" of Mary from a new rosary combination, Worthington casually mentions that this was done in the Tower but says no more of the circumstances.[24] Perhaps the most open discussion of these is in Garnet's arrangements for getting members of the Society of the Rosary registered: preserving anonymity by tearing out ledger pages as soon as the names had been written in. The texts move above their circumstances of production, serenely.

Unlike the meditations, there is no particular pattern to the publication of recusant accounts of martyrdom in English. There are three recusant texts published first in English which concentrate on Elizabethan martyrs. Thomas Alfield's eyewitness report of the *death & martyrdome of M. Campion Iesuite and preiste, & M. Sherwin, & M. Bryan preistes* appeared in 1582. It was plagiarized by William Allen as part of his breathless recounting of a dozen martyrdoms up to 1582, in *A Briefe Historie of the Glorious Martyrdom of XII. Reverend Priests*. Thomas Worthington displays the constancy of the martyrs of 1601, in *A Relation of Sixtene Martyrs*.[25] All three authors accuse the government of turning martyrdoms into political rather than religious occasions. They concentrate on the end of each martyr, giving his last speech, his final letters, and a brief summary of the career which has culminated in such glory. None of these texts were printed more than once in English; they were snap responses to recent martyrdoms.

However, these three hagiographies are in the minority. Most recusant authors ignore Elizabethan saints and honor those of the ancient Church. In *A Treatise of Three Conversions of England* of 1603–04, Persons answers John Foxe's *Acts and Monuments* of 1563, by displaying the earlier Christian missions to Britain, proving that she has always been Catholic. The Anglican Church is an intruder which cannot benefit from Christ's promise to protect his Church. One way in which Persons proves this, is by contrasting the mighty saints of the early Roman Church with the pseudomartyrs of the Anglican Church. Displaying Catholic saints against Foxe's, in the last two volumes of *Conversions,* Persons calendars only one Catholic saint after 1500 (Francis de Paul, canonized in 1507). Conversely, the majority of Protestant saints which Persons lists from Foxe are martyred after 1500. Gregory Martin's *Treatyse of Christian Peregrination* of 1583 cites the Church fathers only on martyrdom and *dulia*, when he justifies pilgrimage as honor given to the physical residue of the Church's past.[26] In 1593, in *A Treatise of Christian Renunciation*, Henry Garnet repeated sonorous exhortations to martyrdom from Jerome and Augustine and Chrysostom.[27] Garnet collects sayings from the fathers and saints on how to renounce all temporal objects of affection. Ostensibly a devotional text, it is aimed at stiffening resistance in recusants to government religious policies, and especially to the enforced presence at the Anglican service. Both Martin and Garnet exemplify their loci from the early Church period rather than from the lives of sixteenth-century saints.

Meditation texts display the same lacunae as the hagiographies. The *Directorie* gives examples of true Christian resolution from the actions of early rather than latter-day saints. Only martyrs of the primitive Church are extolled in Richard Verstegan's lines on the "Triumphe of Feminyne Saintes" in the *Odes In Imitation of the Seaven Penitential Psalmes,* of 1601. The *Manual of Prayers* has a section "contayninge Christian Catholicke prayers to Saintes & citizens of the glorie of heaven."[28] These prayers work down the celestial hierarchy, from Our Lady through to the angels, then John the Baptist, the apostles, the martyrs, and finally, the virgins. At no time is there intercession about the present troubles, nor appeal to a recent martyr.

It is hard to see why modern saints are excluded from English devotional texts, given that the twentieth-century Catholic martyrology includes the conservative total of nearly two hundred Britons executed between 1580 and 1603.[29] Perhaps the enormous excitement generated by the rediscovery of the Roman catacombs in 1578 simply threw contemporary saints into the shade. Perhaps the restrictions imposed by the Council of Trent on informal canonization by popular acclaim made writers chary of anticipating the decision of the Church. Prior to the Council, while formal canonization could only be given in Rome, an informal *cultus* could grow up. However, in 1563 the twenty-fifth session of the Council discussed 'the invocation, veneration and relics of saints, and . . . sacred images." It stated that new miracles and relics could only be venerated after the approval of the bishop. Recusant writers took heed of this. Even while he enthusiastically rooties among the relics of the catacombs, in the *Roma sancta*, written around 1581, Martin points out to the reader the caution which Trent requires.[30] When Persons deals with canonization in *Conversions*, he emphasizes that the decision is taken by indifferent men, who cannot be "carryed away eyther with passion, or deceyved by ignorance" because "great and long search is made about the matter first, and many hundred persons examined; many records also are sought out, of the life and actions of the person, of his vertues and miracles."[31] In fact, there were no canonizations between 1523 and 1588, when the Congregation of Rites took over canonization procedures at the request of Sixtus V. Not that such prudence meant that the exhortatory potential of hagiography was ignored. Gregory XIII, for instance, made preaching on the lives of the saints and the history of the Church the main task of the influential lay congregation set up by Philip Neri at this time.

Moreover, the Church was cautiously appraising the accuracy of records of past saints. Gregory brought together a commission which included Caesar Baronius, to consolidate and revise the many local adaptations of the commonly used martyrology by Usuard, from the late ninth century. This commission produced an official Roman martyrology in 1584, standardizing names, dates, and events. It was republished under Sixtus in 1586, with full annotation by Baronius. The Bollandists showed a similar determination to purge the canon of apocryphal detail. Leribert Rosweyde's *Fastes des saints*, published in 1607, outlines the scientific way in which saints' lives within the new *Acta sanctorum* would be examined, annotated with all available information gathered on a saint. Each volume of the *Acta* would have an index and table of reference, making it more of a textbook and less a day-by-day devotional manual. In this atmosphere, casual sanctification of contemporaries may have seemed to be impious or impolitic.

Such reserve is not in the Latin works which celebrate contemporary British martyrs. There are three main texts by Britons. Persons's *De persecutione Anglicana libellus* of 1581, purporting to be an outraged letter to John Gerard, defines the persecution of the Catholics as religious, not political. Despite wistfully sighing 'it is (I suppose) skant woorthe the laboure, to put [the executions] downe here in writing," Persons energetically marries gory engravings to vivid description of the suffering of the martyrs.[32] Verstegan produced the *Theatrum crudelitatum haereticorum* in 1587, a manual of pictures of martyrdom designed to stir repulsion.[33] About half of Verstegan's text and pictures show the executions of Catholics under Henry and Elizabeth; the other sections depict Huguenot and Genevan persecutions. The third text, the *Concertatio ecclesiae Catholicae in Anglia*, was edited by John Gibbons in 1583 as his contribution to the mission. (Gibbons admitted to his superiors that he did not feel he had the strength to resist torture, if he was captured.) The first edition of the *Concertatio* brings together Latin and English texts published elsewhere, including Campion's *Rationes decem*, *De persecutione*, Allen's *XII. Reverend Priests*, and an answer to William Cecil's *Execution of Iustice Against Certaine Stirrers of Sedition, and Adherents to the Traytors and Enemies of the Realme, Without Any Persecution of Them for Questions of Religion* of 1583.[34] All three texts were frequently reprinted in other languages, including French, Italian, and Spanish.

I use these hagiographies only incidentally, as they were not written to further the aims espoused by the English works. They serve other purposes. Recruits to the mission were encouraged by the way in which the martyrdoms were related to the students during meals in recusant colleges, and chapter 7 looks at the theatricality involved in this. The texts were advertisements to European Catholic countries also, of the efforts made in Britain to keep the faith alive.[35] Financing the English mission, as well as providing it with well-educated priests and laity from the English schools abroad, was costly. Rome and Spain were to be assured that their money could not be better spent on conversions in the New World, or on other ways of reinforcing their power in the Old. In the *Historia missionis Anglicanae societatis Jesu* of 1660, Henry More details Allen's complaint to Gregory about 'the poor distribution of labour involved in sending people who could do good work in their own country to the other ends of the earth';

the same complaint was made about other resources.[36] Therefore, Persons sends *De persecutione* to Jesuit Provincials to help a public collection for the support of the college at Rheims, "that all may realize that they are bound to grudge neither any kind of effort nor even money on behalf of God's honour."[37]

Another reason for the production of these works is suggested by A. G. Petti, who thinks that the *Theatrum* was written to stir Catholic princes to avenge the murder of the faithful. He sees a political motive in these texts—a warning not to allow a heretic to rule—and suggests that English martyrologies were used in attempts to exclude Henry of Navarre from the throne of France.[38] William Cecil highlighted this political aspect as the prime purpose of Catholic texts. In *The Execution of Iustice* of 1583 he warns other princes that if they admit the authority of the Pope in Britain by succoring the "martyrs," they will have to admit the same about their own rule.[39] Petti's suggestion reminds us of the international character of the Counter-Reformation. British priests were concerned with the success of the Church on all fronts, not just at home.

Many catechisms were published in this period. These are divided between books intended for beginners in the faith, and more detailed "rules for life," which apply the basic catechism to moral situations. The former type is epitomized by the 1568 *Catechisme or Christian Doctrine necessarie for Children and ignorante people* of Lawrence Vaux.[40] Vaux runs through the three theological virtues by linking them to articles of the Creed and to commandments of the Church, then recites common prayers and explains the rite of the Mass. His catechism was printed at least eight times up to the end of the sixteenth century.

The only other such question-and-answer catechisms of the period are translations of texts by Bellarmine and Canisius. Much effort was put into translating these Continental catechisms as a means of passing on the faith uncorrupted, and of overcoming the shortage of priests. Writers of the stature of Verstegan and Garnet spent time translating Bellarmine and Canisius.[41] The English version of Cardinal Robert Bellarmine's *Shorte Catechisme illustrated with the Images*, translated in 1614, was not so well known as Vaux's, though similar in purpose. It was the first response to Trent's request that the post-conciliar catechism produced for teachers, the *Catechismus Romanus* of 1566 (itself borrowing heavily from Canisius's *Summa doctrinae christianae* of 1555) should be adapted for use by pupils. The *Shorte Catechism* received only two English editions before 1640, even though it makes a particular effort to attract the reader. Plates dramatize the moral predicaments of man, giving an exciting feeling that the reader is there at the very moment of election to good or evil. The typeface changes like a tone of voice. Loud and large when it proclaims the commandments, daintily italic when it describes the Virgin Mary, it is a silent lesson in delivery. Like Vaux, the preface emphasizes that the catechism is to be learned by heart.[42] The translation of Bellarmine's catechism for teachers, *An Ample Declaration of the Christian doctrine*, went into seven editions. Once again, each clause of the Creed is extended into a bare bones description of the faith. The work is more sedate than the *Shorte Catechism*, however. The emphasis is on attaining knowledge of an objective and unchanging faith, rather than making this faith personal.[43] Its cool didacticism is matched by *A Summe of Christian Doctrine*, translated by Henry Garnet from the catechism by Peter Canisius, and published between 1592 and 1596. Starting, rather forbiddingly, with a quotation from 1 Cor.14.38 ("if a man know not, he shall not be known"), its questions are formal and do not urge the reader to apply what is learned or to visualize the moral problems discussed.[44]

British writers developed these question-and-answer catechisms into directories to apply dogma to common situations in life. This movement was foreshadowed by the appearance of casuist manuals written for the confessors and used in teaching casuistry twice-weekly to students at the English colleges. Southwell's *Short Rule of Good Life* of 1596–97, starts by analyzing the reasons for the belief in a God and what this entails about the way to live. This is a shorter version of the first book of Persons's *Directorie*, and Southwell's printer refers to it as preliminary reading before the *Short Rule*. Southwell's catechism ran through five editions between 1597 and 1622. Luis de Granada's *Memoriall of a Christian Life* of 1586, his most frequently reprinted text after *Of Prayer*, uses the same extension of logic. Reasoning first about the existence of God and then about the way he must be served because he exists, these texts share with the simple catechisms an appeal to the intellect to apprehend the duties of the faith.

Not that all the rules for life are as intellectually strenuous as those of Persons, Southwell, and Granada. When the English writer T.H.D. produces a text on the practical knowledge of virtue and the speculative knowledge of evil, he uses Aristotle's distinctions between the two. Nonetheless, the *Nine Rockes To Be Avoided, of those which sayle towards the Port of Perfection* of 1600 are simple lists of "evagation of the mind," "proprietie of wil, judgement or counsayle," and bitterness of heart.[45] Similarly, the translation of Alphonso de Madrid's *Breefe Methode or Way Teaching all sortes of Christian People, how to serve God in a most perfect manner* of 1602–5 rejects those texts which deal with 'heaven, hell, Iudgment, death, sinne, vertue, and the rest: Perswading to good lyfe & terrifyinge from evill." His work will simply show the reader how to employ all his powers to serve God.[46]

PUBLISHING THE TEXTS

By 1624, John Gee was pointing with disgust to "the swarmes of [recusant] bookes, which you may heare humming up and downe in every corner both of City and Countrey . . . [Catholics] have *Printing-presses* and *Book-sellers* almost in every corner."[47] According to the Allison and Rogers's "Catalogue," nearly two hundred editions of recusant texts published between 1580 and 1603 are still in existence. H. S. Bennett assumes that about half of all works produced in any year were religious, also suggesting that licensed presses were producing just under two hundred editions a year.[48] The magnitude of the Catholic secret press production—about a tenth of the thriving licit market for devotional texts—indicates the energy recusants put into maintaining it.

There were two ways in which the Church could publish such texts: through a secret press in Britain, or by using a Continental press and then importing the books. The latter method was less expensive than the former, where capital costs were incurred more frequently than under normal trade conditions. These included the replacement of confiscated presses (done with Thackwell's press), removal and resetting (as in the perambulations of the Greenhouse Street press), and the training of new staff (necessary in the renovation of the Arundel press). Revenue costs would also be higher. Paper could only be bought cautiously in small lots, not in bulk. Persons writes that "everthing had to be brought from London . . . there were rumours, too . . . that owing to an incautious purchase of paper we should certainly be taken."[49] Printers and assistants had to be housed and fed.

Allen described the costs of publishing for the English mission to Agazzari, the Rector of the English College in Rome. In the year 1581, the mission spent sixteen hundred crowns on printing English texts. Earlier in the letter, he had calculated that he could maintain a student at the college at Rheims for one crown a month.[50] In other words, one year's printing costs could have supported 135 students for an entire year. This high cost may account for what Gee observed, that retail prices of secret-press works were up to four times higher than equivalent publications from the licensed presses.[51] William

Fulke made a similar gibe in criticizing the Rheims New Testament, though he linked the cost of Catholic books to censorship, not avarice:

> who so seeth what unnecessary charge you have put your selves unto, in printing this your translation in so large a volume: may easily perceive you set it not foorth for poore mens profite.[52]

Persons laments that the texts he has ready cannot be printed until sufficient money has been collected. For instance, while the Rheims New Testament was printed in 1582, publication of the Old Testament translation was deferred until 1609 for reasons of expense.[53] Persons's letters to Aquaviva are full of the need for funds to pursue this aspect of the mission. This may be why, between 1580 and 1603, devotional texts amounted to only about a third of all those produced by the British Catholic secret presses. Works on prayer were needed to win souls, but writing talent and cash were absorbed in the struggle to win political sympathy; a more quantifiable and immediate target. Polemical texts required quick, up-to-date production, while it was possible to reprint meditation and catechetical texts of an earlier period or of foreign production without worrying about their currency.

A minor advantage of using a British secret press was that it let the author oversee the production of his text. Many continentally printed editions end by requesting the pious reader to overlook errors caused by printing in a language unfamiliar to the compositor. However, the major advantage was speed, the assurance that "the heretics should not be able to publish anything without its being almost immediately attacked most vigorously."[54] For instance, in 1581 the pursuivant William Fleetwood was amazed to find on his doorstep a printed copy of Robert Persons's *Breefe Censure* against two books written about Campion's "Bragge," only ten days after one of them had been published![55] Effective import of texts, on the other hand, took longer as consignments had to be kept small.

Distribution of the printed work was hazardous and had to be piecemeal. Persons describes the system to Agazzari:

> all the books are brought together to London without any being issued, and, after being distributed into the hands of the priests in parcels of a hundred or fifty, are issued at exactly the same time to all parts of the kingdom . . . there are plenty of young men of birth ready to introduce these books by night into the dwellings of the heretics, into workshops as well as palaces.[56]

This was no idle boast. Campion's *Rationes decem,* giving reasons to members of the universities of why one should become a Catholic, was distributed by placing copies on the seats of St. Mary the Virgin in Oxford at Commencement.[57]

Not that the Church was the only publisher of recusant writing. George Wither's description of the "meere stationer" explains why this is:

> for, what sect or profession soever his customer is of, he will furnish him with Bookes tending to his opinions . . . a Tolleration he would hold well with all, soe he might have but the sole printing of the *Massebooke* or *our Ladyes Psalter.*[58]

As F. S. Siebert has shown, printers "were forced from economic necessity to work on prohibited books in which there was always a large profit."[59] Although the Stationers' Company was intended by the government to act as a mechanism for the suppression of politically "disorderly books," there was some tension between this responsibility and the company's trade privilege of granting exclusive license to print particular copy text. As W. W. Greg said,

> permission to print a certain work may mean either of two quite different things . . . permission, on the part of the author or of some person in possession or control of the copy, to put that copy into print. Or . . . a guarantee, on the part of a censor . . . that the publication of the copy is not contrary to public policy.[60]

There was a trade-off between the government view of the Stationers' Company as a means of censorship, and the trade's self-definition of the Company's powers as upholding a closed-shop agreement. Certain printers had no qualms about printing Catholic material which, because of its illicit status, could be sold for a high price and without question about ownership.

For the purpose of introducing recusant texts published between 1580 and 1603, my pedestrian review makes the divide between polemical and devotional material seem absolute. The texts appear to confirm this impression: the *Manual of Prayers* states that "particular works of devotion . . . are presently more necessary, than farther to treate of any controversie."[61] This echoes Persons's:

> albeit in these our troblesome and quarelous times, [books of controversy] be necessary for defence of our faith against so manie seditious innou-ations, as now daily ar attempted: yet help they litle oftentimes to good life, but rather doe fil the heades and hartes of men with a spirit of contradiction and contention, which for the most part doe hinder deuotion.[62]

Printed English hagiographies on present-day martyrs are scarce, the writers preferring to praise early Church saints. There are a great number of manuscript hagiographies of the contemporary saints, but the Church did not use these for the public image it wished to present. Catechisms would concern themselves only with regulations of the faith, but even those catechisms which approach the realm of casuistry ("rules for life") do not comment on the political situation.

C. S. Lewis links this divide between political and devotional concerns to sanctity: "the saintly and heroic Jesuit Robert Southwell . . . modestly but firmly refused to take any notice, as a poet, of the period in which he was living."[63] Yet this is precisely the attitude against which Ignatius fought—mental claustration was of no use to the mission! I would suggest that the publication of devotional books had as much to do with reproving opposing faiths as saving souls. The translator's epistle at the start of Luis's *Memoriall of a Christian Life* touches on the ill-living caused by the "newe Heretical licentious doctrine of iustification by onelie faith"; his translation is designed to correct this.[64] This statement is repeated by Richard Hopkins in the translator's dedicatory epistle to Luis's *Of Prayer*. Hopkins sees a progression in sin, people becoming "first dissolute in their lives, and after dowtefull in their faithe."[65] Thomas Harding persuaded him to produce the translation as a way of reclaiming schismatics, since

we have nowe verie greate neede of extraordinarie spirituall helpes to strengthen our weake mindes, to withstand so manie deceitfull temptations of the enemie of mankinde, in this so corrupte and daungerous age.[66]

By linking a "good life" and a strong Catholic faith, the devotional texts complemented overt polemic.

3
Meditation as Deliberative Rhetoric

Prayer and meditation books appearing in English between 1580 and 1603 were strongly influenced by translations of Continental meditations by Granada, Loarte, Scupoli, and Estella. This chapter examines how these translations provide a theory of meditation based on controlled reason, before it distinguishes the English works from them, since the latter admit the passions in prayer. While the reader's cogitation is limited by recusant authors who fear interpretative liberty, they are also uneasy about the deceit involved in employing rhetoric to arouse the affections. The chapter following this will look at the meditations' use of deliberative *inventio* and *memoria*, to see if such worry is justified.

MEDITATION THEORY IN CONTINENTAL TEXTS

Luis de Granada conceives of prayer as

> a petition we make unto almightie God, for such thinges as are apperteining to our salvation. Howbeit praier is also taken in an other more large sence; to wit: for everie lifting up of our hart unto god.[1]

Meditation is part of prayer in this larger sense, distinguished by consideration, without which faith is like a

> letter closed up, and sealed: in which althowgh there come notable important newes of verie great sorowe, or ioye: yet it moveth us not at all, neither to the one, nor to the other, no more than if we had receyved no letter at all.[2]

Consideration centers on what Scupoli calls "a continuall exercise of a profound consideration of things as they are in themselves, and not as they appear to be."[3] Scupoli is suspicious of the human will, seeing consideration as a method of cleansing the motives directing it. Eventually, this "profound consideration" turns into an exercise in geometry, recognizing the different perspectives existing between human and divine concerns. Persons remarks in exasperation that

> truelie, nothing in reason can be lesse tollerable in the presence of Gods Maiestie, then wheras he hath published a law unto us with so greate charge to beare it in mynde, to ponder in hart, to studdie and meditate upon it both day & night, at home and abrode, at our uprysinge and at our downe lyinge; to make it our cogitation, our discourse, our talke, our exercise, our rumination, and our delight: that we should not withstanding so contemne the same, as to make it, no part of our thought, but rather to flee the knowlegde [*sic*] thereof.[4]

A "true knowlege of the bountie, and greatnes of God, and of our owne littlenesse" is exemplified by the texts' treatment of the two principal subjects in recusant meditation: the Incarnation, with its tension between Christ's manhood and Godhead, and the Four Last Things.[5] The Nativity and the Passion in particular are seen as points in Christ's life which show the dramatic contrast of the hypostasis. For instance, Loarte's woodcut and verses on the Nativity are prominent in the introduction to the *Exercise of a Christian Life:*

> Behould, O thanklesse wretch, behould,
> Howe, to repaire thy fall,
> The God, that rules the rouling [s]kies,
> Lieth borne in brutish Stall.[6]

Estella's prefatory verses on the Nativity contrast the magnificence of Christ's kingdom with the manger in a similar vein.[7] *The Contempte of the World* urges wisdom in discerning wordly and eternal prospects. Moving from meditations on the Passion to those on the faith, these meditations strongly contrast the mysteries dwelt on and man's comprehension of them. Granada's erotesis, addressed to the dying man, demands if he could "finde in his harte to make a God of his belly, that woulde consider that he shall become there wormes meate?"[8]

The meditations believe that not to act on this "true knowledge" would be unreasonable, indecorous. Appealing to a sense of proportion, Estella declares primly that "it is a monstrous thinge for a man to have his tongue larger then his hande."[9] This is justified by reference to Scripture. In the first Catholic translation for the laity of the New Testament, Martin expounds at length the "Catholic Epistle" of St. James: St. Paul's solafidianism included works as an integral part of faith. Martin includes fervor in devotion as *work*, not limiting this term to acts of social justice.

However, the question of what means will transform this reperception to deeds is not answered by the Continental texts. Granada says airily that "almightie God wil move him that moveth himselfe, and helpe him that helpeth him selfe," and compares consideration to an appetite of the flesh, drawing the soul to good as naturally as an appetite does the body to food.[10] It must be lack of this consideration, which can cause

> manie Christians, which are verie whole and sownd in matters of faith, [to] be yet in there lives verie licentious and dissolute [for they] . . . beleve generallie, and as it were in a fardel or grosse somme, all such thinges as the Catholike Church beleveth.[11]

The only mechanism in these texts for moving from reflection to deeds is that consideration aids understanding and thus, the operation of other virtues. It allows the reader attacked by sin to call to mind the tenets of faith; it illuminates the sources of hope in the Gospels; it indicates that God is the proper recipient of love or charity since "each good thinge is amiable in it selfe, and . . . everie thinge doth naturallie love his owne proper weale." Not least, consideration aids the four cardinal virtues as it cleans the soul, governs the passions, seeks the truth, and ignores the present for things to come.[12] For the continental texts, meditation gives clarity to see virtue and sin in proportion, not excitement to see them with feeling. The reader is not wheedled into action by this technique.

This inspecificity about how to incite repentance can make Catholic meditation sound like the Protestant "conversion experience." Lewalski characterizes this as a movement from election and justification through to glorification. It is

> wholly of God's causation; the Christian will be aware of the effects within himself, and some theologians assign him duties in preparing his heart to receive the call, but neither the preparation of the heart nor the effectual calling is achieved by his own efforts.[13]

Although the Continental Catholic meditations are purposive, not reflecting on a divine other's action on the meditator, the two ideas sound similar because these authors do not examine the problems caused by the corruption of the will. They ignore the effort available to man in acting on his knowledge of the good. The second section of this chapter shows that the English texts have appreciated this omission, relying on the passions to provide a mechanism for acting on consideration.

In two of the four Continental authors a reliance on the understanding to rouse the will turns into a positive distrust of the affections. Estella employs Pauline imagery in describing the manly way to pray, disparaging the use of the natural senses in prayer.

> It is the propertie of litle children when they looke in their bookes, to marke which be the goodliest gay letters in all their bookes, and nothing to regard further the matter that is written in them.

He concludes that consideration is "the worke of our understanding."[14] Scupoli's eponymous conflict is between the "two Wills which are in man": the superior, reason, and the inferior, the senses. Reason is poised between the divine will and this inferior will, each calling it into service. This model of the soul puts the senses and the divine outside the boundary "man," leaving reason as the defining element within. Coming from outside, the passions are likely to be evil, so the individual must resist their sudden motions. Scupoli and Estella see the senses as sinks for the impressions of the world, inhibiting the true perception of God.

> There is nothing in thyne understanding, but that was before in thy senses: and when thyne understandinge cometh to drinke at the cesterne of thy senses, the worlde playeth Iacobs part, and sticketh there downe certayne whyte populer tree wandes, of faire pleasant delightes to beguyle thee withal, and to infecte thereby thyne understanding.[15]

In chapter 6, the suspicion of the visible will be contrasted with English meditations and hagiographies, celebrating a palpable display of the faith.

These two works, both focusing on contempt for the world, are extreme in distrusting the parentage of the affections but not alone in discussing one of the manifestations of the meditations, "spiritual refreshment," as irrelevant. God alone decides whether readers exult in this, in experiencing

> in them selves the trueth of those wordes of the profett, where he saith: *They that trust in our lord, shall change their strength: they shall take winges, as it were, of an Eagle.*[16]

Against a search for spiritual refreshment, Estella warns solemnly that

> many commit spirituall adulterie, in appointing with them selves to make sensible devotion, the uttermost end. . . . Thou must not desire thyne owne consolation, although it be spirituall, but onlie the service of God.[17]

The understanding, Scupoli suggests, should vet the fruits of devotional exercises since "sensible devotion" does not always come from grace.

> If there folow not in thee amendment of life, thou art to doubt lest it be of the divell, or els of nature and so much the more, by how much it shalbe accompanied with greater taste of sweetnesse.[18]

Scupoli fears that, even in meditation, many turn to spiritual exercises which please them rather than to those which tame their affections. They turn to gratifying the passions rather than to obeying the reason.[19] Other Continental manuals do not go so far as to suspect this "sweetnesse" of devilry, but they warn against a faint will when encountering dryness in prayer. Aridity tempts one to stop the exercise and should be resisted. It is either a mark of God's favor, being allowed to exercise devotion in suffering aridity, or (more austerely) the result of a lack of faith or preparation.[20]

Against this inspecificity in Continental texts, lie the passions which are the means the English texts use to move readers to action, discussed in the second part of this chapter. However, the question of "how" to meditate elicits an emphasis on external form rather than feeling, in both English and Continental texts. In the detailed recipe for meditation given by Loarte in *Meditations, of the Life and Passion of our Lord*, it is an exercise of the will recommended by the Church. As Garnet says, it urges formal devotion, "those meanes, by which God determined to gyve thee that thing which thou desirest."[21] No doubt the popularity of Loarte's text lay partly in the sense it gives a reader that meditation is not a contemplative gift but a craft to be worked on.

On starting, the meditator is to shut out external distractions conscientiously, not ignoring but settling them.[22] For the majority of authors the attitude of standing or kneeling to pray affects devotion and cannot be left to the whim of a reader. *A Breefe Collection Concerning the Love of God towards Mankinde* is in typically military mode, urging the meditator to pray "reverently standing upright, with your handes ioyned before your breste, & lifted upp."[23] The *Manual of Prayers* gives precise instructions on how to get up in the mornings: rising, making the sign of the Cross, kneeling.[24] Such behavior physically reinforces an apprehension of the suitor-type relationship with God. At times the model meditator sounds like an orator at work persuading a recalcitrant audience, altering his delivery to suit the divine auditor!

Heere then I present mieself as a poore, and hungrie little whelp before thy riche table; heere I stand beholding thee in the face. . . . Heere I stand changing a thowsand formes, and figures in my hart, and this to bend downe thy hart, that thou take compassion of me.[25]

When the reader has composed himself, Loarte suggests that he expunges worldly thoughts and examines his conscience. Then follows a short period of slow, attentive reading from the meditation manual. Loarte emphasizes that this reading, which is his first manner of meditation, that is, the "historicall or literall," is the basis for all others, "knowing wel the letter and historie of that mysterie which thou purposest to have in minde."[26] By giving the scriptural facts themselves, the manuals control the reading matter. They may be scrupulously directing the reader to outside authorities, but they still prefer such reading to be limited in scope. In the *Manual of Prayers*, during a colloquy between God and St. Catherine of Siena a rule of perfection is set down to render unnecessary "wholle volumes of scriptures and manifold exhortations."[27] Clear instructions are given on reading:

it must not be donne in hast, nor (as the fashion is) for curiositie onlie, to reade three or fower leaves in one place, & so in an other: but it mnst [sic] be donne wich such serious attention, as appertaineth to so great a busynes, which (in trueth) is the weightiest that possiblie under heaven may be taken in hand.[28]

The reader is to go through the historical points of the scene a few at a time, pausing where he finds sweetness; he can always return and finish off the points another time; their efficacy will not seep away.[29]

In reflection following the reading, the question of what a reader should do or experience is never confronted. Certainly, he should explore certain dispositions, looking at Scriptural events with compassion, compunction, a desire to imitate Christ, gratitude, admiration, joy, hope, and love.[30] He could expect results from this exercise: merit, common to all works done in charity; the spiritual good requested; and a refection of the soul.[31] However, the period of consideration itself is described as creating empty time, when what has been read revolves in the mind. Thus, advice turns on what the reader must not do to violate this space, not fixing

his imagination overmuch upon the thinges whereupon he meditateth. For besides that it wearieth the head, a man maye also falle into some deceite by reason of this vehemente apprehension, in perswadinge him selfe that he seeth the thinges reallie in verie deede.[32]

Nor is he to strain his will, wresting out tears in an access of sensibility.

As pride of the flesh, of the senses, is to be avoided in meditation, so also is

> the pride of the understanding being more dangerous then that of the will; for hee that is prowd of wil, wil somtimes obay be cause he houldeth an other mans opinion to be better: But he that doth assuredlie beleeve his owne opinion to be best, by whom can he be cured?[33]

While reflecting, the meditator must not speculate on the mysteries presented, raising arguments and comparisons. He should "eschewe . . . the superfluous speculation of the understandinge, and endevour to use this matter rather with affections, and feelinges of the will, than with discources, and speculations of the understandinge."[34] The creature may not argue with his maker, "no more then the chamber pot may chalenge the Potter why he was not made a drinking pot."[35] Queries do not indicate interest, but spread heresy, says the preface to the *Manual of Prayers*. Both British and Continental texts are encouraging a managed passivity, where the reader stands silently before the scene as though present and his reason scrupulously monitors its own actions, to preempt curiosity. Inevitably, part of the subject of the meditation becomes the reader's mind itself.

Such passivity—watching scenes in the meditation, rather than questioning them—can be compared to the involvement of the exercitant in Protestant meditations, exemplified by John Donne's *Devotions Upon Emergent Occasions* of 1624. Donne's meditations start with himself and reach outward to God; the meditation scene is used as a figure for the meditator's own spiritual history. Lewalski suggests that such antityping underlies all Protestant meditation. They are solitary meditations: there are no other human figures in the scene apart from Donne and an all but inaccessible God. Nor is his concept of God dramatic; Donne listens to nothing, not even to such gruff and monosyllabic asides as are characteristic of Herbert's Creator.

Disallowing conscious activity, recusant manuals become timebased. Loarte suggests a minimum period, of up to two hours at a time, to be spent in meditation; a "rain" rather than a "dew". The soul is simply exposed to God so that he can deal with his creature directly, like dough exposed to heat. Chapter 4 shows how rhetorical amplification impedes the progress of meditation, to prolong the reader's consideration of events.

Why is questioning seen by the recusant texts as insolent? It is partly because of concern for the reader. Annotating a Pauline epistle,

Martin says that "praiers are not made to teache, make learned, or increase knowledge." If correctly recited, the Catholic has done his duty "whether he understand the wordes of his praier or not."[36] What he does not mean is that the laity's comprehension of the faith is irrelevant; he commends the use of intermediary explanations, by preachers. However, Martin denies that the formal parts of faith—the mass, set prayers—need be understood. The informal is subordinated to the formal in the *Manual of Prayers,* which declares that private devotions should never take the place of ordained public prayer.[37] In the same way, the congregation's verbal responses to the mass, in the 1599 *Primer, or Office of the Blessed Virgin Marie,* are not translated from Latin. Only their actions are outlined in English to ensure that they do and say the right thing. The responses to "Our Ladies Litanies" in Garnet's *Societie of the Rosary* are "worthy to be said even of those which understand them not: in the honour of the Blessed Virgin."[38] The struggle over translation became a *topos* of the hagiographies, where priests on the scaffold refused to pray in English rather than Latin. Alphonso de Madrid's *Breefe Methode or Way Teachinge all sortes of Christian People* is highly unusual in demanding that the understanding be integral to worship. It is "beastly" for a man to serve God "without regardinge by his understandinge & reason, whether there be any other manner, wherby he may be able, to serve God more excellently."[39]

Questioning is disallowed partly because of concern for the text also. When it comes to retaining the Vulgate, Martin says that each word from God is of such value that it must be left as he gave it. Such words should not be translated into the decaying language of the present: keeping the same words means keeping the same faith. This is the fear of inkhornism warping prized texts from the past. As Abraham Fraunce remarks, words are as temporary and fragile as leaves so one must keep to "that phrase whiche is most usuall."[40] For Martin, it may be regrettable if the laity have an inadequate grasp of Latin to let them ponder on God's word without help, but it is wrong to risk misrepresenting this word in translating it. Martin leaves certain words untranslated in the Rheims New Testament, lest he misrepresent the *"mira profunditas"* over which Augustine exclaims.[41] The anonymous translator of Campion's *Rationes decem* says he has translated freely and with "pathos". However, he must follow Augustine in not doing this "where the Subiect of the Translation is the *sacred Writt* of God, in the translating whereof a literal playnesse is the best Eloquence; since this Subiect cannot brooke, either adding to, or taking from."[42] Catholic translators concentrated on subject rather than reader. By not translating them, the texts are protected. If they remained in Latin there was some check on the quality of people reading them, and on the production of new interpretations.

There was also physical control over texts. At this point, whatever its view of "the art of propaganda," the Church was aware of the danger of easy lay access to printed matter. Session four of Trent insisted that no one was to oppose their own interpretation of Scriptures, against the Church's. In 1557, the *Index librorum prohibitorum* was set up, and the Congregation of the Faith enlisted in 1571 to oversee the workings of the *Index*. In two surviving casuist manuals from recusant college classes of the last decade of the century, there is detailed thought about when it could be right to read a heretical work.[43] They show a constant tension between the need to use texts in the mission, and the distrust of freedoms the laity may take with the faith; they struggle with interpretative liberty.

There may have been some reason for their anxiety. The first Jesuits on the mission were instructed to converse primarily with gentlemen.[44] Anthony Copley insinuated that such personal targeting of the powerful, leaving the poor untended, was prompted by covetousness.[45] In fact, the trickle-down technique was used by the Jesuits with great success in other mission fields. Thus, many of the texts produced are addressed to the unlearned, and they frequently refer to the cost of books and how the size of each volume has been pared down to suit the reader's pocket.[46] Given this audience, full translation could let an ignorant and presumptuous member of the laity become "teacher, controller and judge of the Doctors, Church and Scripture," as Martin fulminates.

David Crane has compared translations of the *Imitatio Christi* by the Protestant Thomas Rogers in 1580, and by the Catholic Anthony Hoskins in 1613. He concludes that the latter shows a greater fidelity to the words of the original text, treasured as a Catholic work.[47] In many catechisms, common Latin prayers are given with paraphrase rather than translation. In Jacobus Ledisma's catechism of 1597, *The Christian Doctrine, in manner of a Dialogue betweene the Master and the Disciple,* the *Salve regina* is recited in Latin. After it, the Master asks the Disciple what they have said, and the Disciple simply replies "other praises of the same Virgin, demaunding withall her holy favour and helpe."[48] Although the text is too precious to be given in English, a temporary sense can be transmitted which can be revised.

The subjugation of the understanding is demonstrated on the very title page of the Rheims New Testament: "a man must show himself meekminded, lest by stubborn contentions he become incapable and unapt to be taught." For T.H.D., the seventh rock on which the ship of grace founders is that of immoderate study and questioning for the sake of curiosity alone.[49] Silent, passive figures of meditations are models of such meekness; they are quiet and do not presume to form opinions. Martin praises the Virgin

> though litle be spoken of her concerning such matters in the Scriptures, because she was a woman, and not admitted to teach or dispute in publike of high mysteries: yet she knew al these mysteries, and wisely noted and contemplated of al those things . . . about Christ.[50]

One of the articles of Jewel's Challenge contended that the Catholic Church supported ignorance as "the mother and cause of true devotion and obedience." Thomas Harding counters this:

> of the Service in the vulgare tonge, the people will frame lewde and perverse meanings of their owne lewde senses: So of the Latine Service, they will make no constructions either of false doctrine, or of evill life.[51]

Another literary device to control the reader was annotation. The Rheims New Testatment is heavily annotated, to reduce the danger of individual exegesis:

> we have also set forth reasonable large ANNOTATIONS, thereby to shew the studious reader in most places perteining to the controversies of this time, both the heretical corruptions and false deductions, & also the Apostolike tradition.[52]

The Protestant William Fulke, in a *Defense of the sincere and true Translations of the holie Scriptures . . . against . . . Gregorie Martin*, of 1583, gloats that the Catholics have had to translate the New Testament. He notes that their text is

> pestred with so many annotations, both false and unduetifull, by which, under colour of the authoritie of holie Scriptures, they seeke to infecte the mindes of the credulous readers.[53]

This suggests that Martin reverses the ethos of the Bible, so that the annotations become the real text, and the Scriptures a set of authorities to decorate them. Persons's attack on Sir Francis Hastings, in *A Temperate Ward-word, to the Turbulent and Seditious Wach-word of Sir Francis Hastinges* of 1599, denies Fulke's accusation. He loftily pities the reader who is not receiving guidance from the Church: "if the same reader by ignorance did take out of the true woords a fals sence; then sucked he poyson in steed of wholesom doctrine," and he cites

William Hackett's case with barely concealed triumph—the perfect example of bad reading habits![54]

Inhibiting translation to protect both text and reader, the recusant writers could be contrasted with the vigorous way in which Elizabethan secular translators believed they enriched the nation with the knowledge and literature of other countries. The two traditions are summed up in Martin's complaint that "some wilful people do mutter, that the Scriptures are made for all men, and that it is of envie that the Priestes do keepe the holy booke from them," immediately denied: "no, no, the church doth it to keepe them from blind ignorant presumption, and . . . *falsi nominis scientiam* [or] *knowledge falsely so called:* and not to embarre them from the true knowledge."[55]

No matter how tender of the text, the recusant translators appear to have a scrupulous care for the subject rather than the audience, do not see that Scriptures teach through the understanding. Is it a failure of charity to fear to translate a text, as the Protestant Peter Martyr believes: "was this Christs & his Apostles maner of teaching?"[56] Certainly, the ownership of Scripture is handed to those who are verbally competent. This is a sort of reverse censorship: rather than the reader censoring the text, the text censors the reader. William Allen's report of Lawrence Caddy's recantation congratulates Aristotle for using

> hard and difficult termes in Philosophie to drive awaie from the reading of his bookes those that were simple and unlearned . . . lest they should diminish and abase the reverend maiestie of philosophie by their foolish and doting expositions.[57]

I have suggested that there may be a distinction made between the understanding necessary for the ritual and the informal parts of devotion. Martin's preface to the New Testament gives reasons for the use of a Latin rite, most of which are political and founded on the unifying effect of having a single language for the litany and Scripture. One reason refers to the effect of participating in a rite which is unintelligible, stating that the efficacy of any sacrament cannot be dependent on the recipient's understanding. "Sacrament" is extended by Martin to include public prayers, whose words have a "sacramental" value, and he follows Jerome in seeing in the start of the Apocalypse, "as many sacraments or mysteries as wordes." Shugar has concluded that Tridentine rhetorics

> pursue a . . . deep-seated relationship between theology and language relevant to the demands of popular preaching. Their sacramental orienta-

tion, which perceives sensible signs as reflections of invisible realities, separates them from most of their Protestant contemporaries, for whom artistic language masked rather than revealed the power of the Spirit.[58]

Hence, communication does not need to be participative, since the circumstance, the form, of being at prayer is of itself meritous and sufficient.

This could be justified when speaking of ritual prayer, but at the core of meditation must lie interpretative liberty in tasting the scenes. Meditation sketches are filled in by the reader's understanding and imagination. The material used is traditional and traditionally explained, yet the reader attends to the points which mean most to him. Granada remarks comfortably that it is not necessary

> everie tyme we go to meditation, to consider all the principall poyntes, that are there particularlie noted: but it shall suffise to take two, or three of them, moe, or lesse, according as the devotion, and tyme, that everie one hath, shall require.[59]

Ignatius's second annotation tells the spiritual director not to describe everything for the meditator, but to let him sketch the scenes himself. Tension between the writers' inclination to control the meditator's response, and the freedom implicit in this method of prayer, is epitomized by Loarte's *Meditations*. This has terse meditations—barely more than a recital of the facts of each event in the Passion—and long, autocratic prayers, dictating what the reader pulls out from each scene. These prayers act in the same way as the annotations to the New Testament.

Only in the prayer which follows reflection on the scene, do recusant follow Protestant meditations in applying the meditation to the reader's life. Most prayers which do this in the manuals, are long, highly patterned, and for reading rather than for memorizing, or for using as ejaculations, so that a reader's response during his prayer can be supervised. The *Manuall, or Meditation* believes reading is so necessary to meditation that without godly books people cannot pursue godly exercises.[60] Not that prayer is confined to the meditation. The meditator determines to keep throughout the day the devotional feelings engendered in the exercise.[61] Ejaculatory prayer will ensure that the heat of devotion will not be lost (see the arrow about to pierce the heart of the Paraclete, in the illustration on p. 78).

Devotional reading about the events of the meditation must always be subordinated to such prayer.

> As S. Augustine saieth: It is very good both to read, and to praie, if we can doe both the one, and the other: but in case we cannot performe them

both, then praier is better then readinge: But because in praier there is
some times labour, and in readinge a facilitie, therefore our miserable
harte doth oftentimes refuse the labour of praier, and runneth to the
delighte of readinge.[62]

The *Methode, to meditate on the . . . Rosarie* sees a reluctance to pray
as the result of the origin of prayer. In reading, God speaks and the
reader is receptive. The *Manual of Prayers* lists invocations which
must be read because given not by men but by the "holy spirit of
God, the Author and delyverer of all trueth."[63] In prayer, however,
man speaks to God. The effort to communicate comes from the meditator; lapsing into silence is lazy.[64] This contrasts with the Protestant
tradition of giving the Lord a place in which to speak, within the
soul. When George Herbert's verse trails away into groans it fails as
poetry but succeeds as prayer: the Paraclete becomes the Advocate.
Scripture is used in Protestant prayers of the period as "the fruit of
a tradition so pervasive as to constitute almost a language rather than
a source;" a language which replaces sinful human utterance.[65]
   However, when the Catholic meditator lapses into silence he is
refusing to wrestle with his will to do something which is tiring or
dull. These texts have arrogated to themselves mastery over the
Word. Language is not seen by recusant texts as a postlapsarian necessity, a reduction in the purity of prelinguistic communication. No
Catholic writer, Continental or English, denies that one can be so
enraptured by devotion that language is irrelevant, a human invention
distracting from God's Word. However, they see most high points
of religious sensation as capable of expression. This is Augustine's
declaration, in the prologue to *De doctrina Christiana*, that God ac-
cepts the tribute of the human voice even when praising the ineffable.
"Human nature would have been lowered in dignity if God had
seemed unwilling to transmit His word to men through human
means."[66] Catholic texts do not suggest they can even begin to encompass God's praise, so are far from the immodesty of declaring they
cannot try—a suggestion implying that one has. In *The Rosarie of our
Ladie*, Worthington justifies the verbal praise of Mary as necessary,
however inadequate it is to capture the subject. Human utterance
cannot match divine but it still has a place:

shal we therfore be silent and say nothing at al therof? . . . No, in no
wise can we be so excused; but so much the more we are bound to reioice,
and as we can (seing we can not as we would) utter forth the praises of
the mother of mercie.[67]

Loarte does allow "sighes and grones," but only when the meditator cannot think of words. Mutterings are not a sign God is talking![68] The texts will only fade into silence as a sort of *occupatio*, calling attention to the godly magnificence beyond human description. Cheerfully splitting up the Trinity, Chambers's *Palestina* says that it can praise the Son of God but not God himself: the Emperor of Heaven is "ineffable" and "incomparable." As Granada says,

> it is the propertie of devoute sentences (beinge saiede with an earnest minde and attention) to wounde the harte, and to lifte it up unto almightie God: the which devout sentences are so much the more behovefull and necessarie for us, by how much we finde our spirite to be more colde, and distracted.[69]

Thus, at the height of a meditation the *Manual of Prayers* is able to breathe out its devotion in words:

> O derely-beloved, derely-beloved, derely-beloved: O the most derely-beloved of all derely-beloved: O my onely beloved. O my freshe and flourishinge spouse: O my mellifluous and hony-sweete spouse: O the swetenesse of my harte. . . .[70]

During the very moment of conversion within I.C.'s *Marie Magdalen* there is a whole "parlament" of senses discussing Mary's fate: Memory brings forward others who have been saved, Contrition will beg for her, Strong Opinion believes she will be helped, Free Will entertains the idea.[71] The sole fulmination against noise (and that in a Continental text) is directed against communication with the outside world, not against the inner voice speaking out.

> As the pot that is covered will sooner be hoat, & cause the liquor that is in it the sooner to boyle, then that which is uncovered, by reason of keepinge in the vapors, so if thou doest keepe thy mouth shut up close by silence, thou shalt the sooner wax warme and fervent in devotion and gods service.[72]

To summarize this section: sixteenth-century Catholic meditation centers on consideration, a reasoned apprehension of the majesty of God and the insignificance of man. The process of meditation is of formal steps, reading about the Incarnation and the faith, standing passively before a scene from Scripture or doctrine, assenting to it in reason. A final act of prayer completes the exercise, by relating scene and meditator's life. The meditation should issue in good works. Throughout the process, the free use of the understanding in devotional texts is controlled by the authors for pious reasons. In addition, the heights of human devotion are seen as amenable to expression. The following section distinguishes English texts as being more aware of their audience. They add, to this reasoned process, passions aroused by free meditation on the texts and, to some extent, uphold interpretative liberty.

RHETORICAL ASPECTS OF THE ENGLISH MEDITATIONS

Most Continental authors speak to a knowledgeable audience, predisposed to listen. Estella's translator presents meditations in a "kendall coate" rather than a "purple Roabe" to the sisters of St. Bridget's, since he has no need to persuade them to meditate.[73] Loarte writes meditations for his fraternity's use, even though he says there are many such works available.[74] Granada acknowledges that although the laity will use his text, it will be the religious who will spend time with it.[75]

However, the English texts address the layman. In the absence of a priest, meditation will probably not be practised as a supererogatory act by motivated, devoted people. It will be performed as a duty, instead of those religious duties which demand a priest. Texts rarely follow Martin in admitting that the reader's response must be taken into account:

> upon special consideration of the present time, state, and condition of our countrie, unto which, divers thinges are either necessarie, or profitable and medicinable now, that otherwise in the peace of the Church were neither much requisite, nor perchance wholy tolerable,

but English authors tacitly admit it by recognizing that most meditation will be done amid the distractions of a working day.[76] They try hard to gain the interest of their readers. Bucke, for example, obligingly arranges his work to this end:

> and of what good trade, occupacion or qualiiie [sic] so ever you are, whiles you goe about your necessarie businesse in your vocation, or whiles you are travaling by the waye: or in tillinge or plowinge the grownd that hit may bring great increase, you may not withstanding, some-tyme among . . . repeat or thinke upon the Pater noster and Aue Mary . . . and of the verses, or of some of them set downe in the table folowinge.[77]

This corresponds to John Bossy's "domestication of the mass," the necessary move by the recusant community to move devotional practices away from public into private areas.

Other means of persuasion to read are used. The readers of the *Directorie* are flattered with the assumption that they can choose, they have control now, at this instant, in making an election to good or evil. While Persons must include conciliatory chapters on the magnificent rewards waiting for the virtuous, Granada's translator merely regrets that the descriptions of hell will make some sinful laymen uncomfortable! Some texts rely on an ostentatious modesty to coax to them the reader's favor: *Breefe Collection* coyly calls itself "a widow's mite" of prayers; Loarte's translator refers to his work as a red rose to nestle in his friends' bosoms.[78]

Meditation texts could not rely on the majesty of their subject to grasp the readers' attention. As the *Rhetorica ad Herennium* warns, even if "the matter is true, all [persuasive conventions] must none the less be observed . . . for often the truth cannot gain credence otherwise."[79] If a sceptic like Augustine could be tempted to join the Church by Ambrosial rhetoric, why not the church-papist and the Protestant? The meditations heed Ascham's astute comment, that "more papists be made by your merry books of Italy than by your earnest books of Louvain," and have provided the persuasion of pleasure.[80] In rhetorical terms, they follow Cicero in that "the prudent and cautious speaker is controlled by the reception given by his audience—what it rejects has to be modified."[81]

The meditation texts function rhetorically as deliberative orations, persuading the reader to decide to seek virtue. The idea that instruction is not enough urges Persons to compose the *Directorie*.

> A breefe Cathechisme instructeth a man sufficiently in his faith; but al the bookes and sermons that we can read and heare, can not persuade the least part of men to performe so much in life, as by their vocation is required.[82]

As Granada notes, "men do sinne, not so much for want of understanding, as for wante of will," so the texts use the erected wit of rhetorical persuasiveness to correct the infected will.[83] Sidney used this argument to justify the pleasure of poetry, based on rhetoric:

> that moving is of a higher degree than teaching, it may by this appear, that it is well nigh both the cause and effect of teaching. For who will be taught, if he be not moved with desire to be taught? And what so much good doth that teaching bring forth . . . as that it moveth one to do that which it doth teach?[84]

Movere, the third element of the orator's duties to teach, to delight, and to move, is defined by the meditations as Sidney has done, being not just emotion which is aroused but movement also, issuing both in prayer and good works. Like the Continental texts, British authors praise the ability to move us to "welldoing and not wellknowing only," so the *Manual of Prayer* is based on Tb 12: "Prayer, is good, [but] with Fastyng and Almes."[85] As the 1585 translation of Thomas a Kempis sagely remarks, "at the daye of iudgement it shall not be asked of us, what we have read, but what we have done."[86]

Since, in Quintilian's words, "when our audience find it a pleasure to listen, their attention and their readiness to believe what they hear are both alike increased," the English texts make their matter carry by logic and also by pleasure in the style.[87] They are prepared to involve the affections in a positive way, using rhetorical techniques to sway the will through the emotions. Senses are no longer sinks for impressions; the *Manual of Prayers* suggests that a reader devoutly rejoices in their use by remembering who bestowed them.[88] The increasing emphasis on the passions in devotional texts parallels the extension of the word *devotion* in English from a purely religious use to one of intense secular love, in this period. *Meditation* on the other hand, in the sense of thinking deeply, had been in use in both secular and religious contexts since the fourteenth century.

In the preface to *Marie Magdalens Funerall Teares*, Robert Southwell examines the use of the passions. They are the "sequels of our nature" and given us for good; "there is no passion but hath a serviceable use either in the pursuite of good, or avoydance of evill."[89] He urges the reader to use them to sway a rebellious will, to use deliberative rhetoric on himself. Southwell lists the affections as the genesis of virtue: love is "the infancie of true charitie," hatred and anger are necessary to give warmth and a cutting edge against faults; audacity is the armour of strength, "breaking the ice to the hardest exploites." For Southwell, well used means discreetly used, since "excesse in vertue [is] vice." The exception to this is in prayer. The holy saints had perfect passions because they were "commaunded by such a love as could never exceede, because the thing loved was of infinite perfection."[90] Puttenham says the same: "we cannot exhibit overmuch praise, nor belye [God] any wayes, unlesse it be . . . by scarsitie of praise."[91] Texts describing the Passion or Nativity were free to invoke in the reader as much feeling as they could.

In their concentration on the passions, the English texts return to Ignatius Loyola's *Spiritual Exercises*, published in their final form only in 1599. That the *Exercises* had reached English recusants is evident by their inclusion in Canisius's condensed version as a "selling point" in the *Manuall, or Meditation*, although they were not published in English until 1736.[92] The first annotation of the *Exercises* explains that the aim is a sense of proportion, aquired by making "the soul ready and able to rid itself of all irregular attachments, so that, once rid of them, it may look for and discover how God wills it to regulate its life to secure its salvation." The exercitant is given details of the event from Scripture, to expand on. "Any discovery he makes which sheds light on the story, or brings it home to him more, will give him greater delight and more benefit of soul," and, at this stage, "first place is given to the interiorization of the subjects that have been meditated upon."[93] Ignatius looks for spiritual passions: comfort and distress; the meditation is not performed properly if these are not felt. These interior motions are described by the *Exercises*, and the spiritual director must assess their origin, deciding whether they lead the soul away from or toward its creator throughout the whole train of thought.

It is not just style which is amended to suit the reader. Factual accuracy is disregarded. A frequently used and profitable topos is what "probably" happened, even though the Scriptures do not state it. For example, many texts describe Christ meeting the Virgin before he met the Magdalen, after the Resurrection. The commonplace claim to be sweetening sour truths by amending them for ignorant minds, "excusing" John Harington's translation of *Orlando Furioso*, is used sincerely by the English meditations, not as a topos to deflect moral criticism.[94]

In the *Arte or Crafte of Rhethoryke* of 1530, Leonard Cox points out that in deliberative orations there is no need to repeat the facts; everyone knows them, and is waiting to see how they are manipulated to support the interpretation offered by the speaker.[95] Meditations are based on Catholic commonplaces from Scripture and dogma. This material is so well-known through Catholic catechisms and annotations that the prefabricated blocks can be built into a reader's private imaginative construction. Written meditations act as "copia" books for devotion rather than instruction books about the events.

On the surface, the reader has been elevated by the English writers, from pupil to judge. Is this emancipation genuine? Influential Protestant critics of the period thought not. Samuel Harsnet accused papists of actively appealing to fools and women, not to the mature men of a community. John Gee said sardonically of the mass that "as it is in Latin to the *Vulgar*, so it is Greek to the Priest . . . Saint Paul . . . surely intended, that in the Church there should be at least one who should be of an higher forme than an idiote."[96] I would have to agree with these critics. The writers assume a paternal tone when discussing translation and interpretion:

heretikes and ill men that follow their owne spirit and know nothing, but their private fantasie, and not the sense of the holy Church and Doctors, must needes abuse them [selves] to their damnation.[97]

The same assumption that it holds a monopoly on truth over the audience appears in rhetoric, a theory of composition which declares that it makes

use of vices to serve its ends, since it speaks the thing that is not and excites the passions. . . . For judges are not always enlightened and often have to be tricked to prevent them falling into error.[98]

Rhetoric does not inspire this superior attitude, but it does provide a convenient mode of expression. Any such use of rhetoric can be seen as withholding or biasing the truth, since it aims to move the will through pleasure aroused by expression.

Obviously, recusant writers cannot endorse deceit, no matter how pragmatic secular handbooks can be about it. This is made clear by Cyprian Soarez, the sixteenth-century Catholic lecturer on rhetoric, who was selected as a standard author for study by the *Ratio studiorum* of 1599. His *De arte rhetorica* was first published in 1562, and since the late 1570s had been widely in use in Jesuit schools and colleges. It is a compendium of the rules of rhetoric, mainly drawn from Cicero and Quintilian, with some reference to Horace, Aristotle, and Virgil. Soarez fulminates against the pragmatism of Cicero and Quintilian.

Eloquence will recover its marvelous beauty, if there is a pruning of the vanity of errors into which it has fallen through the fault of men ignorant of God's laws. . . .

Let it be understood that it is wicked to envelop an audience in darkness so that they do not perceive the truth, or by speaking, to corrupt their decisions and their way of thinking, which was done time and again by Greek and Roman orators.[99]

Soarez does not condemn rhetoric itself; indeed, it is of a "divine and heavenly beauty" which can be used to help inadequate language express something of the glory of God. However, in company with the other Catholic texts, he neglects to deal with whether a deliberate decoration of the truth which the writer is trying to convey obscures the vision of the audience and weights this truth. Decisions by an audience persuaded by the use of rhetoric have been made corruptly, in Soarez's terms, although they may be right themselves.

Soarez's eccentric initial annexation of the definition of rhetoric, taking the "art of speaking well" to mean clothing virtuous thoughts in carefully chosen words does not wholly satisfy him. He warns that "if we were to teach the ability to speak to people who lack . . . virtues, we would certainly not be training orators but would be providing mad-men with weapons."[100] Quintilian also tries to buttress rhetoric against the latter criticism. He starts by denying the title to the evil man:

> I affirm that no man can be an orator unless he is a good man. For it is impossible to regard those men as gifted with intelligence who on being offered the choice between the two paths of virtue and of vice choose the latter.

Quintilian adds further reasons why evil men cannot excel at oratory. Without peace of mind from virtue, there is insufficient time to study oratory in depth. None but a good man is able to speak of the praiseworthy and honorable, since the wicked man cannot understand what they are. In praising virtue his tongue falters, since it means speaking against his real thoughts.[101] But Soarez and Quintilian plead too much to seem at ease on this point. At heart, they acknowledge that rhetoric is an art that can deceive and that, like the passions, its moral value depends on its usage. Quintilian starts and ends his work with an ineffectual protest: "no one can be a true orator unless he is also a good man and, even if he could be, I would not have it so."[102]

Both Cicero and Quintilian suggest that in "every free nation . . . this one art [of rhetoric] has always flourished above the rest . . . what achievement so mighty and glorious as that the impulses of the crowd, the consciences of the judges, the austerity of the Senate, should suffer transformation through the eloquence of one man?" The statement seems to contradict itself. How can a nation be said to be free, if advantage is taken of the uneloquent by the oratorically self-conscious? Again, there is "no more excellent thing than the power, by means of oratory, to get a hold on assemblies of men, win their good will, direct their inclinations wherever the speaker wishes".[103] This power denies free decision to the audience and it is this denial of free will which can be laid at the door of the recusant meditations, rather than the more theatrical charge of deceit. The Church characterizes man as a creature of free will, voluntarily able to choose or not to choose some good. Meditation concentrates on moulding that will; it is written from a superior attitude. It suggests that the meditator is able to choose freely and then denies him the opportunity to do so.

He does not drop into prayer but vigorously prepares for it, using method to communicate with God. The title page of *Breefe Collection* declares that it is "a devote Meditation to procure Contrition, and excite Devotion." Since procuring meant obtaining a good by self-conscious action and also by gratifying a lust and suborning a witness, such self-management of emotions in devotion is not disguised under an affectation of innocence or spontaneity.

There is no sign that these authors thought their readers felt queasy over being met with such designs on their religious sensibilities. Recusant writers are only uneasy about how effective this sort of persuasion can be. Southwell knows that "none can expresse a passion that he feeleth not, neither dooth the pen deliver but what it coppieth out of the mind"—a religious "Look in thy heart and write."[104] Hyperius, too, insists that "before all thinges it is very necessary that hee which speaketh, doe conceyve such lyke affections in his mynde, and rayse them upp in himselfe."[105] So the deceit becomes internalized. It becomes a matter of persuading oneself, in order to persuade others—a sort of barristers' ethics.

Or does it? Some writers believe that action actually produces sincerity. In rhetorical terms, Cicero states that the power of

> those reflections and commonplaces, discussed and handled in a speech, is great enough to dispense with all make-believe and trickery: for the very quality of the diction, employed to stir the feelings of others, stirs the speaker himself even more deeply than any of the hearers.[106]

Though Ascham would object to being linked to papists, this is what he says in the *Schoolmaster* of 1570: "of corrupted manners spring perverted judgments."[107] Granada avers that "vehement actes of charitie do increase charitie,"

> for like as by writinge well, and with an earnest care and diligence, a man atteineth to be a good writer; by paintinge, a painter: and by the exercise of singinge, a musition: euen so likewise by lovinge, he maie become a lover.[108]

Or, as Estella says,

> as love doth transforme the lover into the thinge that is beloved, so as that lover is brought thereby into the possession of an other thing, and is not maister of hym selfe.[109]

Even Soarez maintains that there can be no pretense in the orator coming under the same emotions as those he has used to stir his audience, for the very quality of style he uses to influence others will necessarily operate on himself.[110]

In Southwell's *Short Rule* the acknowledgment that action operates on feeling promotes an effort to control the demeanor. One should be free

> from all shew of inward disquietnes or unordred passion; which thoughe I cannot choose but sometime feele, yet it is good as much as I may to conceale it; because outward signes do feed the inward distemper.[111]

Natural relationships between the mind's faculties are employed rather than suppressed.

Sincerity during the meditation is not in question. Only before it starts could the reader, as meditator or writer of his own self-persuasive scenes, be said to deceive himself for pious purposes, imagining how he should feel about scenes and projecting himself to that pitch of emotion. Such activity cannot be deceitful because this particular action has been sanctioned by the Church. Advice in the meditations not to wrest out tears is given in a spirit of prudence rather than in of strict honesty, since intemperate emotions wear out quickly and are muddy. As Granada says briskly, "the ioyce of an orange . . . commeth not out so pure, when it is squised with over much mayne force."[112] Of course, this is a rhetorical pose. The reader performs, before the highly critical audience of his own conscience, a private liturgy suitable for each hour of the day or each spiritual complexion. This point will be taken up when catechisms are considered as manuals for fashioning a Christian.

Prayer, then, is a rhetorical assault on self, but the manuals also see it as rhetoric with designs on God. The heresy of persuading God is implied by the care for form manifested by the recusant writers. Prayer appears as a calculated disposal of the reader, in a manner most likely to get God's ear. Meditations address an attentive heavenly audience, elbows reclining on bouffant pillows of cloud, which listens and nods appreciatively at any particularly telling points. Anxious to engage a reader in meditation, writers urge him to use a vocabulary of patron and client, for instance as Garnet does, when speaking of Mary.[113] Vaux explains why the Ave Maria is said, and suggests flattering the Virgin so that she looks favorably on the petitioner:

> who so ever hath anye suite, or request that he would gladly obtaine of a Prince, Magistrate, or his Superiour: he will use often wordes that will please and delighte the minde of him that his suite is to, that thereby his mind may be moved with affection, and made attentive to heare the Suiter, and graunte all his requeste . . . [and] what can more move the blessed virgin to pray to God for us, then the Angelical salutation?[114]

Advice about persuasion against the reader's own will is sensible; trying to use it on the wrong audience, on the Deity, is not. Prayer cannot sway the will of God: it enlightens the supplicant of God's intentions. Such advice is dangerously powerful, however, because a prayerful mood corrects the vision by exchanging an aggressive promotion of the reader's own points for an eager reception of others. It involves humility and a sense of reverence. A suggestion of "ought" will be taken up quickly, even if that suggestion is wrong. The cost of seeing prayer as rhetoric now becomes apparent. A division is opened up between the creature and the creator, where the meditator seems to be in a position of authority, as he persuades his God to listen.

Soarez's unease about rhetoric is ignored by Catholic meditations, which concentrate on the practical good of persuasion. There is a Pauline willingness, on the part of the British authors at least, to be all things to all men, if these poses have the right effect on the reader's motivation. As Fraunce puts it, such orators may

> as referring all to perswasion and victory, omit orderly distributions; obscure thinges purposely; amplifie; digresse; flatter; insinuate; alter; chaunge; and turne all upside downe . . . that with forcible thinges in the beginning, the auditors may bee woonne.[115]

While Herbert demurs over whether he may use the "quaint words, and trim invention" of poetry, for a Southwell or a Verstegan the issue is far simpler.[116] They will cheerily reuse to good purpose, arts dedicated to secular things.

> The vaine conceits of loves delight
> I leave to *Ovids* arte,
> Of warres and bloody broyles to wryte
> Is fit for *Virgils* parte.

Still using "verse and voyce," the subject changes:

> But unto our eternal king
> My verse and voyce I frame
> And of his saintes I meane to sing
> In them to praise his name.[117]

Not that the reader is allowed to lust after the garlic and onions of secular art. Verstegan says primly that it is unseemly to write about things unconnected with God. This is blackmail, infering that it is unseemly for a reader not to prefer religious texts over texts on "warres" and "loves delight"!

The latter half of the chapter has noted a move by the British texts to rhetorize meditation. This gives them the problem of whether they will let the reader control the text, since they must write for his pleasure before they can write for his good. They overcome this dilemma by using one part of *inventio*, amplification on the page and in the mind, which both reinforces the affective elements of the text, and also keeps the reader's view confined to the interpretation they endorse.

4

Inventio and Memoria in English Meditations

Louis Martz suggested that rhetorical invention was fundamental to the composition of places or loci, in meditations.[1] Perhaps it would be more useful to say that these recusant meditations are based on *amplificatio*, or copious invention, rather than on *inventio* itself. This chapter sketches modes of rhetorical invention, and suggests that amplification grew out of their conflation under the *status* system. It then examines meditations where amplification occurs in the memory rather than on the pages of recusant texts.

RHETORICAL INVENTION

Invention is divided by classical manuals into three methods. The first set of techniques deals with proofs which would normally be offered in particular types of cases, and the way in which certainty is acquired, through induction or deduction. The sorts of facts to be considered in these cases are listed by the manuals. The second class of techniques involves looking at areas of knowledge from which topics can be drawn. These topics can be special, depending on the speaker knowing the area concerned—effectively, the same type of proof as that just described. They can also be common, that is, questions which can be asked of every item, such as inquiries about its species, genus, causes, and effects. Finally, the third group of methods used to invent matter rely on commonplaces. These are not questions but statements, ready-made arguments, or descriptions which a speaker could memorize for possible future use. Thus, matter is drawn from facts, from questions, and from ready-prepared statements: has he been murdered? Is murder a sin? Murder is wrong! The speaker can apply all these methods to the same situation, and any topic found in this way can, in its turn, be formally interrogated to produce further matter.

It is the last two groups of methods, invention by logical query and by commonplace, which have an impact on the way in which

meditations are composed; Walter Ong examines the relationship between the techniques. He suggests that the concept of places to be
visited in the mind for arguments was extended to what was regularly
contained in these loci. On one side, he sees a clear, tightly organized
but unsuggestive invention related to logic and to the properties of
terms. On the other he sees a "loose collection" of commonsense
topics. Such topics or headings acted as a "register of the live front
of ideas or motions which at a given era served as effective suggesting-
apparatuses."[2] They were reified into eloquent expressions of received
wisdom, in notebooks as frivolous as the *Palladis tamia*, or as weighty
as the *Common Places of . . . Peter Martyr*, and were standard pedagogical aids. The Jesuit *Constitutions* (governing the Society of Jesus
and composed by Ignatius himself) contain detailed descriptions of
how to use a commonplace notebook.[3] Ignatius recommends that they
are compiled at the time of each lecture, and later indexed and given
"search headings" by the side of each topic.

In confining his analysis to a spatial epistemology, Ong does not
take account of the rhetoric manuals' recognition that both logic and
past experience of successful elements in a speech are necessary to
stir an audience. These two methods of *inventio*—*topics* for argument
and commonplaces within these places—were already combined by
the intrusion of *status* into *inventio*, in the classical textbooks. The
following description of *status* and *inventio* uses central rhetoric manuals: the *ad Herennium*, Cicero's works on the theory of rhetoric, and
those of Quintilian and Soarez.

Compiled as a textbook, the *Rhetorica ad Herennium* contains a
clear description of invention. After sorting the aims of speech into
wanting an audience to admire, decide, or judge, it analyzes the provi-
sion of material. For each, the question of *status* must be considered,
that is, the recognition of "that point which the orator sees to be the
most important for him to make and on which the judge sees that
he must fix all his attention."[4] It answers three questions: whether
something is, how is it described, and what it is; that is to say, questions of reality (conjectural points), definition (legal points), and quality or morality (juridical points). Although *status* is officially confined
to producing material for judicial cases, the *ad Herennium* gives a list
of topics to be considered for conjectural, legal, and juridical questions, under each *genus causa*. These lists do not rigorously interrogate
each case as cover all its aspects. They are loose collections of what
it would be sensible to think about.

To take one *status* question in detail, in conjectural issues in a
judicial case, the following would be discussed: the probability that
the accused committed the crime, given his motive and manner of

life; anyone else who could have committed the deed; the circumstances; why one would think the accused did it; whether his life altered after the event. The list ends with confirmatory proof, both appeals to the judges' pity and hard evidence, such as "decisions of previous courts, rumours, evidence extracted by torture, documents, oaths, and witnesses."[5] The *ad Herennium* only deals with invention under the *status* questions.

There are three different descriptions of invention in another elementary textbook, Cicero's *De partitione oratoria*, relating to the orator, the structure of a speech, and its matter. When summarizing the functions of the orator it draws plausible matter from outside and inside the case, paralleling its distinction between inartificial and artificial proof. Extrinsic matter is collected "without a system" by appeal to confirmatory proof (a process which the *ad Herennium* confined to being a subsection of the conjectural question under the *status* system). Intrinsic evidence, "inherent in the actual facts of the case," is hunted by considering all aspects of the case. In the latter system, Cicero uses the logical processes of the *Topica*. He concedes that not all matter produced by this will be relevant to the case, unlike the commonsense creation of extrinsic or *ad Herennium* research.[6] Although the *Topica*'s translator, H. M. Hubbell, feels that while the text professes to be a recomposition from memory of Aristotle's *Topics,* most of the arguments by Cicero are from Aristotle's *Rhetoric,* Cicero's aim is to get matter for speech in an orderly fashion.[7] Going through species, similarities, differences, corollaries, and antecedents does just that.

When *De partitione* turns from the orator's functions to the structure of a speech, invention is considered by *status* in a similar way to the *ad Herennium*.[8] Conjectural cases, for instance, look at the probable and essential characteristics of the persons, places, actions, times, and occurrences involved in the case. Its advice on this does not refer to the first definition of invention, using confirmatory proof, but rather to listing topics which it would be sensible to think about.

Finally, Cicero deals with the question at issue, producing further lists of points for each *causa*, demonstrative, deliberative, and judicial. He remarks that the latter can be divided into fact, definition, and quality, that is, by *status* (though the points he lists to be queried are those on the structure of the speech).[9] Thus, *De partitione* presents three procedures to invent matter, with no indication of which is to be subsumed under which. *De oratore* does not help, merely mentioning in passing that the orator should gather connected terms, and general heads with their subdivisions, and resemblances and differences, and opposites, and corresponding and concurrent circumstances, and so-called antecedents, and contradictories, and . . . track down the causes of things, and the effects proceeding from causes, and investigate things of relatively greater, equal or lesser significance.[10]

Coming to the *Institutio oratoria*, it is just as hard to see Quintilian's invention. Is it the taxonomic, thorough system of the *Topica*, which may exhume irrelevant matter but which gives confidence in a full coverage of all angles to an issue? Or the commonsense, loose collection of ideas which are likely to bear on the case, since they are recollected from past experience? True to his catholic quality it turns out to be both. For Quintilian, the discussion of *status* turns on conjecture, definition, and quality.[11] Invention, on the other hand, searches for artificial and inartificial proof.[12] He gives some of the characteristics of *status:* it is always about things or persons; can always be inferred from opposites or consequents; and can be aligned in a ladder of credibility as necessary, credible, or merely not impossible.[13] However, unlike the *ad Herennium* and *De partitione*, Quintilian lists topics under *inventio* rather than *status*. These topics are entered as methods of handling artificial proof; of indications, arguments, and examples.[14] For instance, arguments can be drawn from things and persons. For the latter, one would answer questions on birth, race, age, and career. In other words, a commonsense collection of ideas is being put together. Under "actions" (a subsection of "things") Quintilian looks at the three *status* questions, but says it is more practical to go through topics like Cicero's in covering all aspects: definition by genus and species, difference and property, and so on.[15] This should replace the necessity of learning special places for each type of case. Quintilian keeps repeating wearily that one cannot learn all the special places for each case. So only in the case of argument about "things" is any system applied, and even then, the *status* questions are rejected as impractical, leaving only the *Topica* queries.

Soarez's *De arte rhetorica* defines invention as finding arguments, argumentation as unfolding them. Arguments are held in six extrinsic places (the inartificial proofs) and sixteen intrinsic places (from the *Topica*). He sees *status* as the point at issue to which these intrinsic and extrinsic arguments can be applied, in order to exhaust each of the three *status* questions. The clarity of Soarez's work, designed as a basic teaching handbook for beginners to rhetoric, is a result of its attempt to summarize the teaching of the classical manuals. However, in ignoring the looser collections of queries or of obvious things to say which had been accumulated under *status* in *De partitione*, the *ad Herennium*, and the *Institutio oratoria*, the *De arte rhetorica* repudiates the value of the orator's experience in dealing with past cases.

The way in which arguments are demanded from the circumstances being examined has an effect on what facts are elicited. It might not be certain that the looser topics treat the peculiar force and nature of the subject itself, by definition and partition, nor help to link the topic to something unthought of, foreign to it. However, they are emotionally able; they are commonplaces visited for material which the writers know has affected past readers. Stirring the reader to belief is the primary duty of the orator, and rhetorical treatises agree that invention involves more than analyzing the truth of debatable propositions. It creates conviction in the audience, over such doubtful matter.[16] It is no surprise to find that while both methods of invention are used by the recusant meditations, they are used as though all material found was drawn from emotive commonplaces. *Inventio*, then, is concerned with providing just a sufficient number of statements about each topic to be plausible, that is, amplification.

Quintilian describes amplification as "wealth of thought or luxuriance of language," by adding to *inventio* the methods of *tractatio* or the clear handling of arguments. There are four of these: augmentation or *gradatio*, comparison, reasoning, and accumulation. These may appear to be schemes of thought as well as word, but all are confined by Quintilian under the general heading of style: amplification is to concentrate on the effect on the audience, adding nothing to logic or new information. Indeed, the *ad Herennium* specifically links amplification with "the principle of using Commonplaces to stir the hearers."[17] Soarez concurs: amplification is a "weightier kind of assertion which gains credence in the course of speaking by arousing the emotions," not the reason, by using a variety of topics considered important by nature or custom.[18] Soarez links it to the Ciceronian topics he has recommended; logic is not abandoned. It is used as a bonestructure for the impressive flesh of amplification, though too much explanation and open logic is avoided as it distracts from the effect. Topics, whether garnered through a logical process or from an associational node, are to be used discreetly, hidden from the reader.[19] For Soarez, then, part of amplification's effect depends on verbal *sprezzatura*, the author pouring out words and ideas with unsought-for fecundity. Variety and an impression of fecundity join the use of common notions as key elements in amplification. Quality and quantity are maximized: style is impressive and weighty, arguments are many.

Formal recognition of amplification marks off the sixteenth-century rhetorical handbook from its classical predecessor. As Shugar noted, the Tridentine rhetorics include sections on amplification as well as the traditional five parts of rhetoric. Soarez, indeed, sees amplification of words and matter as the principal part of rhetoric. Walter Ong has suggested that Elizabethan rhetoricians encouraged copia by oversight, when rhetoric modulated from an art of public speech to writing, leaving stranded oral tags and repetitions. This, however, ignores a Renaissance confidence in the emotional efficacy of amplification, and debits a meticulously self-conscious art with considerable naivete![20]

Instead, I would suggest that the Renaissance rhetorics noted the inclusion in invention, through the *status* system, of logical exposition of topic and informal association of places and systematized this as copia. When there is no perceived need to cover a subject fully, the extent to which it is explored will depend on the degree to which the audience has been persuaded. In *De duplici copia verborum ac rerum commentarii duo* of 1512, as merely one of eleven methods of amplifying matter, digression, epithet, metaphor, and so on, Erasmus includes Cicero's doctrines on "proofs and arguments"— amplification has swallowed invention. The eleven methods are merely mechanisms to keep on creating credible material. In other words, amplification and invention of matter depend on presentation. The fivefold division of rhetoric seems redundant. Like *elocutio, inventio* depends not on discovery of new material, but on presentation of matter already before the orator. Invention entails referring to loci which have accumulated other men's perceptions, before re-presenting the topics there. Amplification is repeated presentations of the same matter in varying ways for emotional weight. As Peacham reminds us,

> amplification is a certaine affirmation very great and weighty, which by large and plentifule speech moveth the mindes of the hearers, and causeth them to beleeve that which is said.[21]

It is a truly rhetorical scheme, since the *res* is given while *verba* depends wholly on the will of the orator. The degree to which he concertinas a topic in and out has its origin in the emotions it provokes in the audience, not in any need to explain or demonstrate.

This method of dealing with a subject accords with past knowledge, exemplifying things already known. Take the daunting reading plan which Erasmus advocates:

> having made up your mind to cover the whole field of literature in your reading (and anyone who wishes to be thought educated must do this at least once in his life), first provide yourself with a full list of subjects.

> This will consist partly of the main types and subdivisions of vice and virtue, partly of the things of most prominence in human affairs.[22]

This is replete with a lofty confidence that the truth will be fixed in value and position, ready to be dwelt on when the reader has time. W. S. Howell has remarked on the confidence in the stability and depth of man's knowledge which this type of invention denotes. He sees a society at home with its wisdom, stressing organization rather than examination of the truth.[23] The notion of places gives a fixed value to wisdom, discovered through procedures. Like Walter Shandy's Auxiliary Verbs—the who, what, whys—they set

> the soul a going by herself upon the materials as they are brought her; and by the versability of this great engine, round which they are twisted, to open new tracks of enquiry, and make every idea engender millions. . . . The force of this engine, added my father, is incredible, in opening a child's head.[24]

Ascham takes this to its logical conclusion. Commonplaces are "necessary to induce a man into an orderly general knowledge, how to refer orderly all that he readeth *ad certa rerum capita* and not wander in study." For him, they are not even valuable prompts to knowledge but mere aids to *dispositio*.[25]

It is amplification, a multiplication of statements, which is the most appropriate rhetorical device for gaining matter for devotional prose. In his life of Waller, Samuel Johnson declares that

> the essence of poetry is invention; such invention as, by producing something unexpected, surprises and delights. The topicks of devotion are few, and being few are universally known. . . . All that pious verse can do is to help the memory and delight the ear . . . it supplies nothing to the mind.[26]

Lewalski believes that Protestant preaching handbooks saw invention as interpreting rather than creating matter, in a subject which cannot be added to.[27] In the same way, meditations must split fact and meaning; while the *res* is fixed, amplification by quantity and quality of response can take place. Gregory Martin, quoting Augustine, even gives amplification biblical approval.

> [Revelations] tuso repeateth the same things in divers sortes, that seeming to speake of sundry matters, in deede is found but to utter the same things divers waies.[28]

Moreover, religious prose is the ideal environment for amplification. There is no possibility that it could become hypocritical inflation—the Keynesian trap of too much attention chasing too little meaning—because of the nature of the Deity: "we cannot exhibit overmuch praise, nor belye him any wayes."

Significantly, Erasmus uses the same metaphor for amplification as Granada does for consideration. Erasmus suggests that

> the first way of enriching what one has to say on any subject is to take something that can be expressed in brief and general terms, and expand it and separate it into its constituent parts. This is just like displaying some object for sale first of all through a grill or inside a wrapping, and then unwrapping it and opening it out and displaying it fully to the gaze.[29]

Granada says that

> it is consideration that openeth that which is locked, and unfoldeth that which is folded together, and maketh that cleare unto us, which is otherwise darke, and obscure.[30]

In the meditations, authors take a single gesture or a few words from the Scriptures or Church writings and expand on them. With matter already established as part of the faith, amplification gives the charm of variety and emphasis.

This section has examined how two methods of invention, the logical and the associational, are exploited to present rather than examine facts, through the conflation of invention and amplification. Amplification has seemed to be the most appropriate technique to use in writing meditations. The next section describes this amplification, in meditations based on scriptural events, and in those pondering on aspects of the faith.

AMPLIFICATION IN THE MEDITATIONS

Continental and English meditations use both methods of amplification, the loose collection of topics, and the tight, logical exposition of a subject. As the previous chapter noted, they divide devotional material into two: the Passion and incidents of Christ's life as types of passional events, and aspects of the Faith, especially the sacraments of Penance and Communion, and the Four Last Things. In *Of Prayer*, Granada links the two methods of invention to the two types of subject:

this meditation is sometimes upon thinges that maie be figured with the imagination: as are all the pointes of the lyfe and passion of our Saviour Christ. And some times againe this meditation is upon thinges that doe rather appertaine to the understandinge, than to the imagination: as when we think upon the benefites of almightie God, or upon his goodnes, and mercie.[31]

Most texts have elements of scriptural and dogmatic matter.

In associational meditation, the Church's commonplaces of faith are key notions used to accumulate knowledge and description. These meditations give an emotional association of topics rather than a reasoned exposition of each. What are these devotional nodes? In a popular Protestant preaching manual, the *Pathway to the Pulpet* translated in 1577, Hyperius goes through the "divine places" specific to preaching. These are the theological virtues and vices: to "the order of *Love* perteine these places: of the amendement of lyfe, of the integritie of maners, of chastitie, of modestie, of avoyding of offences, of kyndnes and lyberalytie."[32] Hyperius illuminates such places from the Scriptures.

However, recusant authors reverse this process. While in the Protestant texts the places of divinity are the cohering principle; scriptural events are used as examples. In the recusant meditations the scriptures organize the text and commonplaces expand on it. For example, in Southwell's *Marie Magdalen* most paragraphs begin or end with a single Scriptural quotation which is amplified in the body of the paragraph. The tag provides the seed of the paragraph. While the complete scriptural event becomes the organizing principal of the meditation, these tags at the start of each paragraph are the element of *dispositio*, amplification is the "meat." Two loci are prominent in recusant texts: the image of Christ as lover, and the use of a silent, passive figure in the scene to draw in the reader.

The Christ of C.N.'s *Our Ladie*

longed so much to enioy the pleasure of [the Virgin's breasts], that being a most mighty King, hee became in manner a begger, and having given to every thing their beeing, made him selfe almost nothing, feeling neyther want of wine, nor of any thing else, when hee founde himselfe sucking at them.[33]

C.N. is not alone in seeing Christ's sexuality as an important place to search for affecting matter. Helen Gardner suggests that divine poetry absorbs secular forms, including the medieval figure of Christ as chivalric lover. Persecuted recusants, says Southwell, should imagine what they would suffer for a temporal paramour, then think of

Christ, languishing for love as he offers them his "corporall seem-lynesse," "white and ruddie a choise peece out of thousands," "the glorye, maiestye, and beautye of his Godhed."[34]

In meditations, Christ appears to change gender. In a romantic allegory of the Incarnation, Robert Chambers describes a young Prince who loves his Father's adopted daughter enough to give up his life to save the Lady from the spell of the evil Enchanter. The Prince is infinitely desirable for he is infinitely like his Father, in whose presence "both the rarest maiestie seemeth base; and the richest Monarch a beggar."[35] Echoing Marlowe's lyric, Verstegan's "Our Blessed Ladies Lullaby" puts Christ into the feminine role, as he receives the Virgin's entreaties: "Live stil with mee, and bee my love,/ And death wil mee refraine."[36] Before the Resurrection Christ is feminine, a sweet Savior, tender and white against the brutal black figures of his tormentors. After, he is filled with virile power, bursting out of the tomb:

> call to minde how gently thy Saviour (when they butcherly hurled him on the Crosse) stretched foorth his armes which they afterwarde nayled on the Crosse, with huge great nailes, and how mildly he looked on those that put him to so vile and cruell a death.[37]

Since the presentation of the figure of Christ shifts from female to male, it would seem that it is the theological roles themselves which are gendered. Elaine Beilin picks out the way "conventional hierarchical distinctions between male and female aptly reflect traditional theological distinctions between God and the sinning mortal" in Elizabethan women's writing, and this happens in recusant texts.[38] For instance, in a secret-press poem lamenting the loss of Britain to Catholicism, the *Holy Churches Complaint, for her childrens disobedience* of 1598–1601, Christ is the bridegroom to the Church and the heretic Church a female disrupter of traditional family relationships: the "stepdame Heresie," "harlot Heresie," producing a "bastards broode."[39] What Beilin sees as virtues which texts of the period looked for in a woman—humility, mildness, patience, obedience—are those which are credited to Christ in the meditations, for the reader to emulate.[40]

Most recusant texts center on a silent woman, as mediator in the rosary texts, or protagonist in the Magdalen and Nativity texts (occasionally, there will be a quiescent male figure such as Peter or John). The figures are passive, weeping or pondering at the foot of the Cross. Unlike those in recusant texts, women in the Scriptures do not often have major roles, and the choice of a patient, silent female to focus our attention on seems deliberate. These characters' lack of word and gesture makes them profoundly antirhetorical figures.

These women do not move; the meditations continually refocus on them instead. This method is especially useful in nonrosary texts, excusing a review of a scene many times over from different perspectives. C.N.'s participants are as frozen as in an emblem, waiting his touch to bring them to life. The author nudges everyone, even Christ.

> Oh *John!* what did you when you invited Christ unto your mariage and his mother? you promised them a feast, & were not able to give them to drinke. . . . But (O most loving LORD) who is able to feaste thee without thee?[41]

C.N. rushes straight on to answer the questions in his own person. In Southwell's *Mary Magdalen,* Mary's questions about Christ are firmly answered by the author, without her being allowed to speak or act on them. The effect of providing her with no interlocutor other than the narrator, since even the angel's replies to her are mediated through Southwell, is to deny her dramatic individuality. Her passions are created by Southwell to be soothed by Southwell.

> Thou [Mary] wilt say that though hee forbad thee to weepe for him, yet hee left thee free, to weepe for thy selfe. . . . But I answere thee again, that because he is one with thee. . . . Yea but (sayst thou). . . .[42]

This effect is, typically, amplified by Thomas Nashe in *Christs Teares Over Ierusalem* of 1593, where Christ's words to the daughters of Jerusalem are extended by Nashe ("the more to penetrate and inforce, let us suppose Christ in a continued Oration thus pleading with them") for forty pages, before Nashe breaks off the oration: "heere doe I confine our Saviours collachrimate Oration, and putting off his borrowed person, restore him to the tryumphancie of his Passion."[43] Similarly, in *Palestina* Chambers lyrically questions the infant Jesus.

> Tell us sweete babe, who arte an eternall worde, although nowe *too young to speake,* tell us what caused thee to descende from thine unspeakeable dignitie.

It is Chambers himself who confronts the reader with the catechism-style answer. Christ gets no chance to return an answer.

> For the sinne which slew mankind being infinit, in respect that the partie offended was infinitelie more excellent then the offender, it required a

satisfaction infinitely good, which man was not able to make . . . wherefore it was necessarye either that God, who is onely infinite. . . .[44]

This is precisely what Ignatius warned against, why he urged the
spiritual director to withdraw himself and to allow the meditator to
speak to God directly. In I.C.'s *Marie Magdalen*, Christ transforms
Mary's life without appearing in the text.[45] When Christ actually dies,
it seems quite irrelevant to the reader because Mary is busy with her
own thoughts.

> By that time this her sad complaint was done,
> He that gives life had vanquish'de death by dying,
> And *Ioseph* comes t'interr this Holy one,
> Which in this weeper breedes newe cause of crying.[46]

A scene which should have had at least one actor— Christ, if not Mary
also—has none, since Mary's weeping is controlled by the author, and
Christ is certainty not the center of attention. Chambers's Mary lets
"neither word nor deede slippe her without a deepe meditation, con-
ferring every thing together which she heard him speake or see him
do."[47] She doesn't act, only reacts. Metaphors for Mary Magdalen
and the Virgin in *Palestina, Our Ladie,* and the *Magdalens* of Southwell and I.C. are drawn from long-enduring, natural, and insensate
features: fountains, rocks, slabs. Authors refuse their characters the
sins of Eve: loquacity and curiosity.

They intend this passivity should spread to the reader, so that
the spiritual director guides his gaze, as another way of controlling
interpretative liberty. In *A Breefe Collection,* the writer intrusively
tells the reader exactly where to turn his head.

> Behoulde here with the ghostlie Eye of thy Soule Christs pitious paynful
> Passion. . . . Behould then that good Lord . . . aboute him standing
> wicked men voyde of al reason, sore scourging his moste blessed bo-
> die. . . . Looke then aside, upon his blessed Mother, see what sorowe she
> maketh. . . . Turne then again to thy Lord and see how rudelie they
> unbynde him.[48]

Philip Howard emphasizes this in the deathbed scene of the *Foure-
Fould Meditation, of the foure last things* published 1606, where we
draw the very last breath with the sufferer before journeying on with
his soul:

> The houre is come, thy debt thou now must pay,
> And yeeld to death, when life thou most doest need:

> Thy breath is stopt, in twinkling of an eye,
> Thy body dead, in ugly forme doth lye.[49]

Using the *topos* of a passive spectator, authors can answer a reader's misgivings, and at the same time reprove such lack of faith. Each figure provides a role-model of someone meditating deeply, as they stand before the scene without impertinent inquiry. They enact Loarte's advice on meditation.[50]

C.N.'s *Our Ladie* exemplifies both loci. Christ's words from the Cross, establishing the parent/child relationship of Mary and John, also start a comparison of Rachel whose name means "sheep," and Mary, who bore a "Lamb." C.N. explains that both sons were more virtuous than their family, both sold to their enemies by a Judas, both had younger brothers who were difficult to deliver. C.N. has created a younger brother for Christ on the strength of this comparison: John the Beloved. A new son demands a conception and a marriage, so C.N. provides the marriage feast of Cana and explains how it would be fitting (and therefore, probable) that this is John's wedding feast. A powerful, loving Christ is at the feast to validate the state of matrimony. It is the bridegroom who is put into the static, virginal position, as C.N. explains how John gives up his wife at this feast so he can follow Christ!

In C.N.'s Passion, Mary and John mourn at the foot of the Cross, addressed by the author, but never allowed to answer. Why doesn't John die for Christ, especially as Peter has failed to? Why is he mourning the Crucifixion, when it is the only way he can be saved? Does he think he offends Christ by protesting against his death? The questions are in the present tense, immobilizing the figures still further, as the narrator goes around each one, and presents different aspects of their positions. So in C.N.'s meditation, the original slight connection between John and Mary has been amplified to allow other notions to be hung from it, allowing the author to circle the events of Cana and Calvary and arouse devotion.

Henry Garnet's *Treatise of Christian Renunciation* of 1593, appeals directly to the commonplace tradition. Its title page says it is "compiled of ex[act s]entences & as it were diverse homelies of Ancient Fathers: wherin is shewed how farre it is lawfull or necessary for the love of Christ to forsake Father, Mother, wife and children, and all other worldly creatures." Each chapter provides arguments by the fathers in favor of this Christian renunciation, against those of spouses, parents, and others. Rather than digesting these to produce sentences of his own, Garnet has compiled a commonplace book which, although both ye searching and translating of these places have cost me no lesse labour, than if I had undertaken a wholl worke of my owne: yet this treatise shall be reade with exceeding more fruite than if it had proceded from my owne invention.[51]

This is because the sentences are genuine Catholic pronouncements. After all,

in no parte of this Treatise except onely in this preface in the conclusion and in some parte of the third chapter thou must thinke that I speake (gentle Reader) but imagin that the Saintes of God do speake unto thee.[52]

Garnet's book is as much a quarry for material as Richard Bristow's *Demaundes to bee Proposed of Catholickes to the Heretickes* of 1576, republished in 1596–97. This lists questions about the faith which the fervent (and, under the circumstances, heroic) Catholic should propose to heretics and unbelievers.

Typical in the meditations is the use of indices to guide the reader to the right devotional topics for his spiritual need. The *Directorie* gives a "Breefe Methode How to Use the Former treatises, chapters, & considerations to divers purposes, according to the divers qualitie of the person, time, state, place, or neede when they ar to be used." If the reader feels "heavie, lumpish, & [s]louthful" he is to read the first meditation of chapter 1, on inconsideration and the last chapter of part 2, on negligence.[53] If he is a youth procrastinating over electing good, he should read the sections on the danger of delays and on the sudden nature of death (see illustration). This is spiritual home-medicine, a cure-all for each evil mood. Persons's list of sinful occasions are spiritual; the *Manual of Prayers* lists physical occasions to respond to with prayer: "accommodated & prescibed to certayne houres or times bothe for the day and night." There are prayers before rest, then as the reader sits on the bed, then as he throws back the blankets, and finally as he settles himself to sleep.[54] These indices give the impression that all areas of life have been covered by the manuals: the reader has no need to consult further authorities. The meditator is a gourmet of mood and perception. Meditations tend to turn the mind from the subject of faith to a self-scrutiny, and this happens with these indices. Whether of place or mood, there is a certain connoisseur quality to suiting the behavior to the occasion.

Moving from commonplace to logical meditations, the examination of the subject of the meditation is guided by proportion, God's majesty against unregenerate nature. The logical meditations ask formal questions. They prompt the reader to make the comparison for himself, and acknowledge the folly of offending God. Dismissing the

"Finall Impenitence." G6 v in Robert Bellarmine, *A Shorte Catechisme . . . with the Images,* translated 1614. (Reproduced with the permission of the Bodleian Library, Oxford.)

organic associational methods of invention, prefaces to the logical meditations ask you, before you start, to "consider with your selfe wherefore you come, wheraboute you goe, and what busines, you now take in hande."[55] Again, once inside a meditation: "a man [should] consider who he was that suffered: what he suffered: by whom he suffered: and for whom he suffered. . . ."[56] In fact, in Bucke's hands the word *meditation* loses its emotional connotation. Describing seven short matters of meditation, *meditation* is used in the sense of "think often" rather than "take to heart", and later used as "following Christ."[57] Jesuit superiors encouraged the use of diagrams to chart the elimination of sin. In studying Southwell's unpublished meditations, Janelle links the martial character of the Ignatian *Exercises* with the logic which Southwell uses to argue his own contumacious spirit into submission, with "lists of *incentiva,* tabulated arguments, in numbered paragraphs."[58]

The meditation subjects are not processed through the predicaments in the way in which, say, Joseph Hall's *Arte of Divine Meditation* of 1606, encourages us to think. Hall insists that we are all born logicians and therefore capable of meditation. His divine places include an orderly consideration of the material and formal causes of each topic. Another fervent Protestant, Abraham Fraunce, flowcharts this sense of proportion, when discussing logic:

God Created man.	so the	Cause procreant with the effect.
Preserveth man.	affection	Cause conservant with the effect.
Is not man.	is of	Disparats among themselves.
Is not like man.	the	Unlikes among themselves.[59]

After the associational methods of dealing with the theological places of faith, hope, and love, the *Pathway to the Pulpet* briefly considers "philosophical" places, recommending we learn them from books of logic:

for by them we easely learne, what every thinge is, howe many partes or formes be therof, what the causes, what the effectes or duties, what thinges bee of alyaunce, what *Contrary* thereunto, as those that playnly appere to be destinate to the explication of these questions.[60]

No Catholic meditation is so formally precise. However, the logical habit of mind is used to search for matter when producing doctrinal meditations. They fix an event within coordinates, contextualize it. As Granada suggested, Catholic meditations concentrate in this way on doctrinal rather than scriptural topics. The rosary meditations neatly illustrate this. The Joyful and Sorrowful mysteries are about scriptural events, whereas the Glorious mysteries revolve about theological points on the status of the Virgin. In the *Methode*'s standard ten points for each decade, the physical scenes of the Glorious mysteries, for example, the Assumption, are ignored in favor of tabulating their doctrinal import. In contrast, half of the ten points for the other mysteries are given over to describing the people and places. The difficulty of depicting doctrinal points is exemplified when Bucke illustrates every decade of the rosary, except the last four Glorious mysteries.

In the Continental texts, these two methods of invention correspond to a shift in the authors' point of view. In associational scenes, anticipated arguments of the reader are anonymously solved through authorial replies to a figure. However, the logical meditations bring a "me and you" division to their explanations. The writers are emotionally disengaged from the devotion, instructing the reader from a superior, distant position. Granada describes the Passion as though he is looking on with the reader, but the Day of Judgment as though he was exempt; the tone becomes exhortatory. Sunday morning's meditation on the Resurrection describes events as author and reader; Monday evening's meditation, over the page, urges the reader out there to "attende to the knowledge of thy selfe."[61] English authors do not separate themselves from their audience in this way; one more instance, perhaps, of their desire to please.

The two types of meditation are also paralleled by a divided readership noted by certain rhetorics, where the distinction between emotional and logical appeal is seen as one of audience, not material. Hyperius attributes two audiences to the preacher.

> There bee two maner of wayes of interpreting the scriptures used of skilfull divines . . . one is apt for the assembles of learned men. . . . This other is altogether applied to instruct the confused multitude.

The former manner, according to Hyperius, sticks fast to the text being interpreted "as one shut up in a streight prison, pinfolde & enclosure"; the latter suits matter to the time, place, and persons.[62] Howell concurs with this view, while Renaissance logic founded

> itself upon scholarly and scientific discourse and was in fact the theory of communication in the world of learning. . . . Rhetoric was . . . regarded as the theory behind the statements intended for the populace.[63]

This suggests that, for Protestant divines, emotive devotional texts are less strenuous and more immediately attractive than logical ones.

Joseph Hall agrees that the most strenuous part of a meditation is that involving the understanding. Where the imagination and affections are concerned, the meditation will be sweet and easy.[64]

Reversing this, however, recusant authors regard the logical method as an easier devotion to practice than imaginative prayer, recommending the former for religious novices and beginners to meditation.[65] These meditations can be used when the mind "is either weary, or not willing to be pricked forward by the other [types] that are more vehement in exhortation."[66] In such logical meditations, the points are so clearly structured that the reader is reassured about the path to follow. Such reassurance is taxonomic, giving a feeling that all parts of the subject have been named, described, captured.

This chapter does not recognize any effects of Ramus's reform of rhetoric. In describing William Alabaster's poetry, R. V. Caro thought that "invention and memory—the very parts of rhetoric which had contributed to the development of meditation techniques— were excised by Ramus from rhetorical training in the interest of methodizing the arts of discourse."[67] While Caro, like Martz, does not substantiate his historical claim about the origins of meditation, it is true that these two *officia oratoris* are the principal parts of rhetoric used in the sixteenth-century English meditations. Nonetheless, Ramus's division of logic and rhetoric was for educational reasons: he did not support the idea of two separate types of discourse. Rather than the brave attempt to "rerhetorize the passions" with which Caro credits recusant work of the period, the texts are simply combining into one operation, what may have been taught in two. The effects of Ramus's reforms on the British meditations of the period appear to be negligible.

Emotional weight is increased in the devotions by the use of amplification. Rhetorical memory techniques are used to replicate the effects of copia, in those texts where amplification is in the mind rather than on the page. It appears in particular in the rosary texts, where repetition becomes a sort of mental *amplificatio*.

Memory

Classical rhetorics are unanimous in describing a twofold process of memory, based on an imaginative organization of space. Initially, striking images are created and linked to facts or situations to be remembered. Their creation is purely associational. They need not express anything to other people, nor even be displayed to them. They come from a private library of pictures, built up by the reminiscencer. After their creation, they are projected onto imaginary or real places, around which he can walk in memory. This prompts the recall, in order, of the images and their associated facts. The process corresponds to that of rhetorical invention and disposition, using places to order matter and inventing images to refer to it. Umberto Eco calls the system semiotic, where an image signifies a fact to be remembered, held in a syntax of loci.[68]

In meditation, the memory arts keep in mind the elements of devotion to be dwelt on. Meditations are based on internal pictures, created by words or a physical image. Loarte recommends setting before you

> the figure or the Image . . . of the misterye which you are to meditate, the which, when you have first beholden, it shal helpe to keepe you more collected and attentive, For the memory of the Picture shall remayne as it were imprinted in your minde.[69]

As the image becomes imprinted in one's memory, the physical text's usefulness decays, and it can be put away. These mental or paper pictures become richer in associations over time, with each reuse. Thomas Wilson's *Arte of Rhetorique* of 1553, wistfully sees saints' pictures in this way, though hurriedly says that however useful to the memory, such use of images is forbidden by God.[70]

The four texts printed between 1580 and 1603, on how to say the rosary, conform with Loarte's recommendations about using pictures in meditation. In three of the rosary texts—Bucke's *Instructions for the use of the beades*, the anonymous *Methode, to meditate on the . . . Rosarie*, and Worthington's *Rosarie of our Ladie*—the layout of the page makes it clear that the reader is to read the instructions on the recto of the page, before turning to gaze at the picture on the verso of the preceding page, while reciting the rosary. For instance, the *Methode* has on C5 v, two verses and a picture of the Annunciation and on C6 r, the preparation and instructions for reading about this mystery. C9 r is left blank, since the previous mystery finished on C8 v and to have printed on C9 r would have made it impossible to glance at the picture when directed to do so by the text.

Worthington recomends that the rosary is said after reading the verses. The instructions given are to prepare by ejaculatory prayer, often repeated; read the verses over the picture as verbal aids to recollection, then "meditate." The author does not mean the reader to dwell on the text. He gives three or four crisp doctrinal points, leaving recitation of facts to the verses over the picture. The reader is then instructed to give thanks and make a request for some gift of grace. Only then is he told to "begin [his] beades." At this point, he turns back to the picture to endow it with ideas received in the reading. Should he need reminding of them, the verses are there. At each future repetition of the decade, the need to refer to the text will lessen, and the affective nature of the meditation grow. The minimum time-limit imposed by reciting the entire decade means that a meditator cannot quickly "tick off" in his mind the points of the picture. Instead, the image becomes increasingly sodden with feeling, moving him away from the terse style of the actual meditation points made.

In Bucke's work, the same thing happens. Each of the mysteries is given a picture, with instructions to recite the Pater Noster beneath it. Then follows a small piece of connecting narrative or doctrinal explanation. Finally come ten facts to be remembered about the event. The number of facts mirrors the number of Aves to be said. Bucke claims that the pictures help concentration in the initial reading, rather than as aids to recall. Yet the verses he appends to each picture in the "table" at the back of the book are allusive only. It seems unlikely that the pictures did not help the person praying to remember the fuller explanations and descriptions within the main text.

The architectural metaphor of "places" in the memory manuals is retained by the rosary texts. Worthington shows events occurring simultaneously to the same person, in different architectural niches of a picture. For instance, the second Sorrowful mystery shows Christ tied to a pillar in the foreground and scourged. The pillar itself supports two rooms behind the scene; in one, Christ is condemned by Caiaphas, in the other, Peter listens to a cock crow. Bucke's "table" should be circled, rather than looked at as one coherent picture. The eyes stop at each small roundel (see also the illustration on p. 105). This is a romance method, starting stories and cutting them off midway with the next tale. It denies the reader an overall picture, but allows the memory of the last story or scene to comment on the one being gazed at.

Physically extending the mnemotechnic of building, English seminaries employed pictures as stations on which to meditate. Persons describes how students at Valladolid set up emblems around the hall to welcome Philip II when he visited the college.[71] This practice, to promote academic competition among students, was demanded on special feast days by the *Ratio studiorum*. In a mnemonic context, the places— college or church walls—have words to be remembered on real rather than imaginary walls.

Apart from pictures, whether pasted in the book or created in the mind, the other mnemonic used by the rosary texts is verse. All use four-line stanzas for each mystery to point out a fact or an application.

The *Methode* also gives summary poems, on the Passion and the Four Last Things, stating that the meditations for the week are "contained shortly in verse, for the better remembring of them."[72] These have biblical references in the margins to allow readers to expand on the facts for themselves, but the summary poems are merely aide-mémoire.

There is one use of the memnotechnic image which is a-metaphoric. This is when the body of Christ becomes a memory place for the meditations. Ideas to be recollected are placed on each of Christ's members. Loarte points out every limb and wound of Christ on the Cross, linking each to a particular type of sin.[73] Rather than the suggestive conflation of sign and signified of the memory image, there are direct links, one-to-one, between a virtue and a scene, a vice and a tortured limb. Christ himself has become a collection of memorable relics. The *Primer*'s section on meditation starts with a picture of nothing but the Sacred Wounds ascending to Heaven—without the body around them! Bucke's title page woodcut depicts a rosary where the Pater Noster beads are the Sacred Heart, hands, and feet. Prayers on each of the wounds see them as extraordinary relics, efficacious in synecdoche when prayed to and not just through, as with saints' relics. As in Thomas Elyot's description of swearing, Christ is chopped into "numbles."[74] The hypostasis falls apart in such texts: the Son becomes inanimate and we address the Father over his head.

Francis Yates speculates that there was a revival of interest in the art of memory in the Catholic Low Countries at this point, on the basis of an oration made in Louvain in favor of Simonides's art in 1560, published the following year in Brussels.[75] Also, and unusually for sixteenth-century manuals, Soarez gives a full-length description of the art. There may be a moral point to this interest. Yates describes how the virtue of prudence is divided into three parts in Cicero's *De inventione:* memory recalls what has happened, intelligence ascertains what a thing is, and foresight sees that something will occur before it happens.[76] Although Quintilian deals with memory purely as an art of speech, not a virtue, the *ad Herennium* distinguishes it as necessary for the right rather than the merely praiseworthy, since wisdom depends on distingushing good from bad, which in turn depends on a well-stocked memory. The value of memory therefore, seems to lie in the sense of proportion between different circumstances, some past, some present. Sixteenth-century rhetoricians concurred:

> there is nothing in man of all the potential parts of his mind (reason and will except) more noble or more necessary to the *active* life then memory; because it maketh most to a sound iudgement and perfect worldly wised-

ome, examining and comparing the times past with the present, and, by them both considering the time to come, concludeth with a stedfast resolution what is the best course to be taken in all his actions and advices in this world.[77]

This sense of proportion between the divine and human perspectives is gained through remembering past scriptural scenes.

Absorbing the meditation depends on the repetition of prayers. The fourth text, Garnet's *Societie of the Rosary*, deals clumsily with the effect of reiteration, merely noting that it stirs "affections," and is not a superstitious practice—one can never have too much of a good thing.[78] This analysis is not much more perceptive than the *Methode*'s numerological analysis of patterns of prayers in the rosary, refering to the number of persons in the Trinity, the five wounds, and so on. The *Methode* ends by scoring smug linguistic points: "we cannot pray but with number, except wee will pray but once in our lives," since we have to use the same words over and again.[79] Worthington glides over the problem, repeating that it is a custom sanctioned by the primitive Church and used in the Bible.

Although the texts do not effectively defend it from being seen as idle (for repetition could suggest an efficacy in the words themselves, rather than in a change in a reader's understanding), they recognize a weariness in prayer which lies not in ennui but in exhaustion, the sense of having done too much of the same thing rather than being unfulfilled or bored.[80] Martin in the *Roma Sancta* praises the students who can meditate for up to two hours a day, or even more if strong enough to bear it,

> bycause this Meditation or mental prayer (which is nothing els but occupyng of the minde and al the wittes wholy in silence and inward contemplation of the [bliss of heaven and contempt of the world]) is very painful, as al great and deepe studie is.[81]

Against the childish fear of a wearisome Paradise, Chambers insists that the angels have perpetually refreshed appetites for praise.[82] Texts use time profitably, reclaiming it for God by saying the rosary. The themes of maximization and references to an "accompt" run through theme. Bucke says we are "lent, not given to life: And for that we must render an accompt . . . of each moment of time spent here. . . ." Verstegan's St. Peter sues for grace:

> Love is my debt, for love and mercy due,
> And gratitude the intrest thereon rising,
> The obligation standes in heavens view,

And was set downe by equities devising,
The date it beares is endlesse to avail,
My soule the pawne to forfait yf I fail.[83]

Persons spends the first of the three volumes projected for the *Christian Directorie* in explaining why meditative prayer is so "profitable."

In turning to texts not based on the rosary, the benefit of repetition is lost. The time that the reader spends on an exercise will now depend on the length of the text. The author himself will have to go through the images which he wants the reader to dwell on, in great detail. Most of these meditations are deliberately lengthy, so the reader has to spend as much time on them as the author does. One example of this impeding technique is the number of questions addressed to the silent figures in each meditation scene, such as Southwell's constant requests for self-analysis from his silent Magdalen. It is interesting that Patricia Parker sees partition, the denial of any closure, as fundamental to amplification. She suggests that the dilation of a text is paralleled by commentators on rhetoric with the inability of woman to keep silent and formally chaste. In the context of the meditations, a degree of amplification around the silent female figures kept the text open until it had affected the meditator, and the silence of recollection could fall.

In other words, the rosary texts can provide meditations with images and without words, so that the majority of the meditation takes place within the reader's mind. However, the nonrosary texts must make the pictures for the reader, since they are based on word pictures and the invention comes from within rather than from outside the text. Thus, the nonrosary texts' use of *memoria* is less marked than that of the rosary texts. They have to depend more on invention to keep the reader's attention, until the text has been absorbed.

To sum up: meditation texts urge the reader to use deliberative rhetoric against himself. They keep the texts open with amplification or memory techniques, until the loci have been absorbed. The two types of amplification, logical and associational, are married to the two subjects of the meditations, the faith and the Incarnation. The next three chapters move on to examine English hagiographies and catechisms published between 1580 and 1603. Rather than acting as simple demonstrative orations, these texts join meditations in using deliberative techniques to sway the will of the reader. The saints' images presented are to be emulated, while the catechisms re-create these images within the reader.

5

Hagiography and Catechism: Producing a Saint

De partitione oratoria celebrates epideictic rhetoric: "there is no class of oratory capable of producing more copious rhetoric or of doing more service to the state, nor any in which the speaker is more occupied in recognizing the virtues and vices." In *De oratore*, however, this exalted role dwindles to supporting the deliberative and judicial *causae*, as one of the many techniques which an orator uses to illuminate his subject.[1] Evidently, the display of exempla was not sufficient to move a listener to serve the state. Recusant hagiographies follow *De oratore;* they praise their subject deliberatively, with action in mind. Thus Robert Persons, in *A Treatise of Three Conversions of England* of 1603–4, does not indulge in naive praise of recusant martyrs, but remarks grimly that

> my end & scope in writing this treatise . . . is not indeed so much (if I shall confess the truth) to delight, as to moove and proffit thee (good reader. . . .).[2]

These saints' lives have more in common with the proofs and rules of catechisms than with the wonder-tale panegyrics of the *Golden Legend*. Saints' lives are manipulated as rhetorical examples, proving the faith's truth and illuminating its expression. Recusant catechisms and books of rules for virtuous living provide a sound basis of faith and then clarify its expression in the reader's life. Catechisms will be examined to see how their rules create the saints modeled by the hagiographies. Encouraging such imitation is a positive concept of rules and roles, a rhetorical self. The texts do not see a parallel between the display of simple demonstrative rhetoric and that of hagiography.

Examples as Inartificial Proof of the Faith

It is difficult to give a coherent rhetorical description of what an example does. It is a figure of embellishment, clarifying points already proved. It appears in a structural role, as part of inartificial proof in suborning authorities to the orator's cause (a play on ethos) and as an element of induction. Hagiographies rely on the latter, inartificial proof; saints are witnesses to the truth at the time of their death and after.

Inartificial proofs are produced outside the art of speaking, and adapted by the orator. Quintilian splits them into two: "indications" are simply physical, necessary signs of a fact: smoke must come from a fire; a pregnant woman cannot be a virgin. The second class are all statements made by men, within a legal framework: decisions of previous courts, oaths, the statements of a witness, rumors, and evidence extracted by torture. Quintilian does not analyze their differences, eagerly hurrying on to how to use such evidence.

To our ears, there is a scientific, dependable sound to inartificial proof, and especially to indications. This, however, is not its value to the rhetoric manuals. For them, it merely provides topics to support a preexistent argument. Quintilian does warn that "though in themselves [these proofs] involve no art, all the powers of eloquence are as a rule required to disparage or refute them," because of their powerful impression of impartiality.[3] However, his section on inartificial proof goes on to point out the rhetorical nature of those inartificial proofs not indications, depending on speech and hence on ethos. The manuals put examples into this category of inartificial proof. Reference to precedents or witnesses is an appeal to examples with a direct bearing on the case.

Like all categories in rhetoric, that of witness can be subdivided further, into those of witness and authority. These are distinct in application, not quality: both are forms of inartificial proof, gained from outside the case; both depend for their effect on ethos. Aristotle distinguishes them by time.

> Witnesses are of two kinds, ancient and recent; of the latter some share the risk of the trial, others are outside it. By ancient I mean the poets and men of repute whose judgements are known to all.[4]

Those who "share some risk" are those who give evidence directly related to the trial, and who run the risk of being thought perjurous. The others, both modern and ancient, are those whose comments and decisions were made on issues unrelated to the trial, but which can be applied as *obiter dicta* or precedent.

Recusant texts depend on authorities. Martin starts his defense of pilgrimage, *A Treatyse of Christian Peregrination* of 1583, by flattering the reader into agreeing with the fathers and bishops of the ancient Church:

doubtest thou Reader, whether ever anye such thinge hath bene done or no? . . . But thou art a reasonable man, thou wilte beleeve those that in thyne own iudgemente are, worthye of credit, if they tell it thee. To omit *S. Ambrose, Chrisostome, Hierome,* and others . . . let *S. Austen* suffice.[5]

The magnificent dispassionate ethos is given by stressing the antiquity of these reverend witnesses, especially when relating traditions of the Church. As Quintilian says, these types of witnesses

form a sort of testimony, which is rendered all the more impressive by the fact that it was not given to suit special cases, but was the utterance or action of minds swayed neither by prejudice or influence, simply because it seemed the most honourable or honest thing to say or do.[6]

It lies behind Garnet's compiling of "exact sentences and as it were, diverse homilies of Ancient Fathers" in *A Treatise of Christian Renunciation* of 1593. Debate with present-day divines is renounced in *Demaundes to bee Proponed of Catholickes to the Heretickes.* Instead, Bristow tells us to ask the heretic debators "whether they will be contente to trie this controversie of Religion, which is betwene us by the Religion of those ancient Martyrs, and others then in persecution."[7] Triumphantly, Persons points out that after Jewel's challenge, at Paul's Cross in 1560, offering to convert to Catholicism if any commonplaces of the fathers could be shown to support Rome, Louvain writers showered him with "Fathers, Doctors, Councells and historyes."[8]

The ethos of authorities is more important than accurate reporting of their speech. All witnesses must convince the audience of the truth of the character they present, before the probability of their evidence is weighed. Aristotle says goodwill, good sense, and virtue are necessary to persuade by ethos. This trinity deals in miniature with the three elements of a speech: the audience's attitude to the speaker, the method of unfolding the subject, and the orator's self, yet all as part of dealing with "self" (that is, within the proof of the ethos)—a potentially endless regression. Good sense and virtue encompass active virtues of courage, self-control, magnificence, liberality, gentleness, and passive virtues of practical and speculative wisdom. Aristotle describes the elements within good sense and virtue, when dealing with deliberative rhetoric, displaying a speaker concerned solely with his topic, wise and impartial. However, his description of goodwill is reserved for the second book of the *Rhetoric*, which dissects the passions. Goodwill is concerned with points outside the speaker, engaging the audience by manipulating their affections, not offering the topic or the speaker's qualities for the reasoned approbation of the audience.

Quintilian agrees with Aristotle that both pathos and ethos are more effective in persuading the listener than using rational arguments.[9] Ethos makes an emotional appeal in the guise of sober truth. The speaker stresses the good ethos of his witnesses and authorities, because the value of such testimony lies in the audience believing them to be men of good sense and virtue, giving directly applicable advice which is coming from outside the case. They are guest speakers, introduced by the main orator.

Quintilian splits such an appeal to the audience in terms of affections raised. One sort of appeal

> is called *pathos* by the Greeks and is rightly and correctly expressed in Latin by *adfectus* [emotion]: the other is called *ethos* . . . rendered by *mores* [morals].[10]

Quintilian uses this distinction to develop Aristotle's ethos, of good sense, goodwill, and virtue, in terms of violence of emotion. Pathos, for Quintilian, means the faculty of arousing disturbing and violent emotions in the audience, and ethos the production of calming and gentle sensations in them. In other words, what Aristotle sees as a personal appeal to the audience through the gentle, reasonable qualities of good sense and moral virtue (that is, subject and self), Quintilian labels ethos. What Aristotle sees as a personal appeal concentrating on the passions of the audience, Quintilian calls pathos. The difference lies in the site of this appeal. For Aristotle, pathos is aroused in the audience by the ethos of the speaker; for Quintilian, both lie in the audience. There is a coalescence of speaker and audience, and the persuader becomes the persuaded.

Both sides were alert to the possibilities of manipulating quotation, where the ethos of another authority or work was kidnapped. Martin claims that "heretikes alleage scriptures, as here the Devil doeth, in the false sense: the Churche useth them, as Christ doeth, in the true sense."[11] Peter Martyr's quotation of the fathers is described by an indignant Persons in *Conversions:*

> eyther the wordes next going before, or immediatly following, or both (making wholly against them) are purposely left out, and others put in or mistranslated.[12]

While *Conversions* purports to trace the dramatic history of the ancient Church to the present, it merely lists Church divines who supported or opposed similar concepts, but never actually examines the doctrines in detail. In other words, Persons uses the ethos of the doctors, not their reasoning. For instance, cataloging the heresies of Patrick Hamilton, *"that a man hath no freewill at all . . . that the holy Patriarcks were in heaven before Christs passion . . . that no Pope after Saint Peter had power to loose or bynd synnes,"* Persons does not pause to comment on the fearful consequences of these opinions. He simply says that Hamilton says nothing "either against the reall presence or the masse, that might tend to *Zwinglianisme* or *Calvinisme* . . . so as *Maister Patricke* could not be of Fox his religion, whatsoever religion he was of."[13] In the same way, the secular priest Thomas Wright stuffs his margins with authorities, without dealing with their ideas. He assures the reader that though he was unable to consult these authorities in writing *A Treatise, Shewing the possibilitie . . . of the reall presence* of 1596, "a little reading would quickly have filled the margines."[14]

This reliance on ethos means that while examples are logical mechanisms, they are at least able to promote belief, in a chain of proof running from syllogism through to enthymeme and induction down to example. Soarez sees them as "incomplete induction, or, what comes to the same thing, rhetorical induction."[15] These methods are a sort of *gradatio* in validity, moving downward in the credibility conferred on an argument from syllogism to example, but moving in the opposite direction in terms of emotional effect—as with *inventio*.

What sort of witness do the recusant authors claim? There are the persons of great "descent, education, wealth, kinds of power, titles to fame, citizenship, friendships, and the like," lauded for good ethos in the *ad Herennium*.[16] Puttenham reasons why this is:

> for who passeth to follow the steps and maner of life of a craftes man, shepheard or sailer, though he were his father or dearest friend? yea how almost is it possible that such maner of men should be of any vertue other then their profession requireth?[17]

Higher estates are not merely more striking, but the virtue each practises is greater. Luis de Granada's translator, Richard Hopkins, believes those who have temporal power because they have the virtue to use it properly.[18] Either this (or snobbery) causes a complacent Persons to recommend Catholicism to the reader,

> when he shall have seene and pondered with some attention, how many great and wealthy grounds, both of Scriptures, Fathers, Councells, Antiquity, Continuance, Consent of Nations, Miracles, Sanctity, Wisdome,

Learning and other such motives, which these articles have for arguments of their infallible truth: and on the other side shall see a company of ignorant and unlearned people, artificers, craftesmen, spinsters, and other poore weomen.[19]

In his *True Sincere and Modest Defence of English Catholiques* of 1584, William Allen gives a shopping list of quality Catholic martyrs ranged against the pretended saints: "fourtene noble and most worthie Bishops . . . two worthie English Prelates . . . a doosen of famous learned Deanes . . . fourtene Archdeacons," all the way down to the *"laici inferioris ordinis plurimi"* of the *Concertatio.*[20]

Allen continues by gloating about

how exceding few you gayne or get from us; whilest we in the meane space (through Gods great grace) receive hundrethes of your Ministers, a nomber of your best wits, manie delicate yong gentlemen, and divers heires of al ages, voluntarily fleeing from your damnable condition.[21]

He is echoed sourly in a 1581 letter from the Privy Council to the Vice-Chancellor of Oxford: "most of the seminary priests which at this time disturb the Church have been heretofore scholars of [your] university."[22] This is true. As appendix 1 shows, nearly two-thirds of the writers studied here were at either Oxford or Cambridge, and Bossy calculates that more than one hundred fellows and senior members left Oxford in the first decade of Elizabeth's reign. Moreover, about half of those who did go over to the Catholic colleges were sons of the gentry, natural, when the costs of travelling and maintainance there are remembered.[23] Allen has the last word, however. In *XII. Reverend Priests* he reverses the topos of witnessing for God:

we therfor for their cleering and our owne in that case, and al the Catholikes in the realme, *cal God and his holy Angels to witnes,* that these men of God were most iniuriously, and wilfully murdered.[24]

The idea of status gave impetus to the image of Catholic priests, and Jesuits in particular, as high-living, well-dressed, attractive, and monied individuals. Persons wryly tells Agazzari that "there is tremendous talk here of Jesuits, and more fables perhaps are told about them than were told of old about monsters."[25] As Gee says,

if, about *Bloomesbury* or *Holborne,* thou meet a good smug Fellow in a gold-laced suit, a cloke lined thorow with velvet, one that hath good store of coin in his purse, Rings on his fingers, a Watch in his pocket . . . a Stiletto by his side . . . then take heed of a Iesuite. . . . This man has vowed *poverty*. Feare not to trust him with thy wife: he hath vowed also *chastity*.[26]

This picture is confirmed by the Jesuit characters drawn by Thomas Overbury, John Earle, and William Vaughan: ladies' men, powerful, treacherous, military, Machiavellian. This is far from the monkish fusty ignorance of the typical Catholic, "in our forefathers" time, when papistry as a standing pool covered and overflowed all England, [and] few books were read in our tongue," described by Ascham.[27] The *topos* of good breeding was sufficiently established in debate for the 1591 Proclamation to go out of its way to suggest that seminarians, led by traitors "base of birth," were "a multitude of dissolute yong men, who have partly for lacke of living, partly for crimes committed, become Fugitives, Rebelles, and Traitors."[28] There was acrimonious crossfire over the "base birth" of both Persons and Cecil, when Persons answered the Proclamation.

Recusant martyrs are shown as noble and powerful, but also as meek and gentle. The authors take advantage of Quintilian's advice that willing witnesses should seem reluctant to oppose others, upheld solely by the justice of their cause.[29] Southwell's poem "I dye without desert" piles up this impression of his martyr (possibly Philip Howard): "Men pitty may, but helpe me god alone," an "orphane Childe enwrapt in swathing bands," "relinquisht Lamb in solitarye wood / With dying bleat."[30] Neither seditious or bold purveyors of liberation theology, the martyrs are seen to conform politically. Allen's *XII. Reverend Priests* and Worthington's *Relation of Sixtene Martyrs* carefully state that on the scaffold the martyrs pray for the Queen.

Conversely, when dealing with Protestant martyrs in *Conversions*, Persons cites Augustine on arrogance in choosing doctrines, and damns the pertinacity of heretic pseudo-martyrs in holding to them. These martyrs, especially the women, are characterized as "wilful," full of "intollerable pryde, presumption, and obstinacy in heresie."[31] Their unity comes solely through aggression against the Catholic Church. Against this is recusant approval of the silent, meek women of the meditations, prefiguring the conformable, innocent figures of the hagiography.

The concept of "ethos" is fundamental to recusant catechisms. Pity the Protestant reading his catechism; its very form runs counter to that of his faith. The deductive nature of catechism is antithetical to Scripture's direct revelation. The concept of inner spiritual knowledge in each man, espoused by the free churches, does not reconcile to the public and communal knowledge offered by catechetical forms. Alexander Nowell's popular *Catechisme or First Instruction and Learn-*

ing of Christian Religion, translated from Latin in 1570, attempts to mitigate the strain of using a form which moves away from the Scriptures. He ties each statement to biblical texts, deflecting development from biblical literalism. He appeals to reasons beyond the "bare and naked affirmations" of the catechism, so that the reader understands, not recites the answers. Nowell's preface proudly notes that the catechism does not teach the scholar, already able to answer on all questions of faith. Instead,

> the maister opposeth the scholar to see how he hath profited, & the scholar rendereth to the maister to geve accompt of his memory and diligence.[32]

The truth is uncovered within, not revealed without. Thus, the *Catechisme* shifts uneasily between the roles of schoolbook to learn Latin, courtesy manual, and aid to realizing the grounds for a faith which is already possessed.

Compare this to the confidence in its rules and subject, breathing through every Catholic catechism. The form of the recusant catechism does not war with its belief that revelation comes from outside the soul and that it can be learned by man. The reader interprets rather than perceives or invents. Richard Broughton reuses Persons's title and aspirations, in the *First Part of the Resolution of Religion* of 1603, claiming to resolve everything into "that first and infallible veritie," though Broughton shifts Persons's concept of resolution away from self-determination, and toward the idea of reducing issues to first principles. Following the *Directorie,* Southwell's *Short Rule* marshalls "foundations" and rules. Bristow's *Briefe Treatise of Divers Plaine and sure waies to finde out the truth* of 1574 boasts that

> by reading this treatise, yea or any part almost thereof, [he shall] learne all truth, and that not only that is in this day in question, but also that eyther hath bin, or may be in question betweene the Christians.[33]

The anxiety about subject and author with which modern critical theory endows texts does not touch recusant catechisms. Of the three variables in a persuasive piece of writing—presentation of the speaker, subject itself, and attitude of the listener—only the latter can be modified in a Catholic text. Not that this firm subject is the Scriptures; these are accepted as texts, diachronically compiled and in need of interpretation. The subject of recusant catechisms, the faith, is founded on a two-tier approach to knowledge which is ordered by God's ethos. "Faith is grounded upon a more certaine foundation, then is humaine science, to wit upon the credit and authority of God himself"; one must constantly consider "the Maiestie of allmightie God, who will be beleeved at his woord, without being asked for proofe or reason for the same," says *Conversions*.[34] So Catholics have the confidence to write catechisms which retail facts of the faith, solely because their subject is rhetorically based.

The writers can dignify readers by a degree of ratiocination, without actually examining the faith. Since he considers that these will be consulted frequently, Granada separates out rules for behavior in his *Memoriall*, but thinks the first volume of reasoning on the faith will be discarded after the first reading.[35] Persons sees the proofs offered his *Directorie* as a concession to the laity, not required in a well-regulated church. The *Directorie* sports a spurious air of "getting down to basics" and "knowing where we stand on an issue." Thus, the first book digests theology, listing means to prove the nature and existence of God by using moral and natural philosophy and appealing to history to show how others have been persuaded of the truth. Persons addresses all markets, referring to proofs from the three philosophies, to cabbalism, Hermes Trismegistus, and comparative religion. The very style of the Bible is proof of its veracity: the facts of the Nativity must be true, because humble shepherds could not make up such a story. The preface puts the work in the context of "bookes of controversies" of these "troblesome and quarelous times." Calling philosophers the patriarchs of heretics, initially he flatters with a show of reason, but ends by asking the reader to "captivate his understanding to the obedience of Christ, which is to beleeve such things as Christ by his Church proposeth unto him."[36] The second edition of 1585, published to correct Protestant amendments by Edmund Bunny, has new chapters against schism and heresy in the Church. These were intended to defeat the relativism which Persons saw as a consequence of religious debate. He repeatedly links these with a developing degree of scepticism. People "hearing such contrariety, contention and fight of words . . . come at length to beleeve little or nothing."[37]

Worries about the form of disputation are often expressed, even in Persons's overtly polemical works. The *Temperate Warn-word to . . . Sir Francis Hastinges* rebuts the idea, promulgated by Hastings's *Wastword* and *Wardword*, that Catholics incite folly and treason. Answering the charge that the Church relies on faith alone, refusing to let people make up their own minds, Persons says that

all men have not always such variety of books, as to see all controverses discussed therin, & yf they had, yet have not all such leasure or learning to read or discuss all, nor capacity or understanding to discerne or iudge:

so as if their everlasting understanding must depend of reading over all controversyes, and making resolution upon the same, it must needs be impossible to many thousands both men and women in our countrey at this day to be saved.[38]

Models for disputation offered are those where truth is demonstrated, taught, not researched. Much of Persons's work persuades readers by reason, but he explains in *Conversions* how although matters of importance are matters of faith, God does not go against reason. It is

an obedience founded in all reason of probability, inducement and credibility . . . [which] (together with the help of our pious affection, and assistance of Gods grace) be much more sure firme and ummoveable, than that, which is gotten by humaine knowledge.

This is Augustine's distinction in *De civitate Dei:* the human mind is so darkened by sin that it can no longer perceive reason in divine truth, except through faith.[39] The Catholic Church does allow a degree of rational debate, Persons protests. Both sides are represented in a disputation on a question before the Church finally determines it. "Disputation is a good meanes and profitable instrument, to examine and try out truth"; he gives many examples of how the Fathers used it.

Yet despite all this, Persons concludes of disputation that

as it is a fitt meanes to styrre up mans understandinge to attend the truth, by layinge forth the difficultyes on both sides; so is yt not always sufficient to resolve his iudgement, for that yt moveth more doubts then he can aunswere or dissolve.[40]

He drew up (though never published himself) a manifesto of how the country would be run under a Catholic adminstration. This *Memorial* planned disputations with recalcitrant Protestants, so that the one truth would eventually appear. T. H. Clancy has concluded by this that Persons

did not think that this government-sponsored religious unity would be a source of suffering for any man of good will. All those who really desired to know the truth would be amenable to reason. That left only "wilfull Apostates or malicious persecutors",

and those, of course, you burned.[41]

Eventually, Persons concludes that disputation is a dangerous technique, since it is better to believe something which is wrong than nothing at all. The sectaries do depend only upon probability, and persuasibility of speach, or wryting one against another, *by which* (as *Tully* saith) *nothinge is so incredible, that may not be made probable.*

Thus, Persons sees academic scepticism as one of the most unsafe opinions which Augustine held. Heretics can say what they do not believe in, but not what they do:

hereticall doctrine is negative for the most part, & their instruction to the simple people is to jest, scoffe, doubt or deny. Which are points that are easily learned, & pleasing to the corrupted humour of mans sinfull state and condition.[42]

Establishing a general agreement on faith which is not shattered by schism or heresy moves hagiographies to expand on the uniformity of their martyrs' faith. In *XII. Reverend Priests*, for example, Allen conflates the answers of eleven Catholics condemned in November 1581 in a circular argument—one which Luis de Granada recommends in repudiating the devil when tempted to despair—"what do you believe?" "I believe what the Catholic Church believes." "What does the Catholic Church believe?" "What I believe." One of Persons's major concerns in *Conversions* is to show that there can be no martyrs in the Established Church, because of its upholders' fissiparous doctrines. The first book of *Conversions* traces nine sects among Protestant martyrs who cannot be martyrs since they have no community of belief. Their deaths are redundant, proving nothing, for "yt is not the punishment, but the cause that maketh a martyr" and "heretiks . . . dyinge for defence of their particular opinions, dy not for Christ, but for the founders of their Sects."[43] The Rheims New Testament insists that

heretikes and other malefactours sometime suffer willingly and stoutly: but they are not blessed, because they suffer not for iustice. For (sayth S. Aug.) they can not suffer for iustice, that have devided the Churche.[44]

Since this is unchallenged by William Fulke's parallel Bible, pejoratively comparing Catholic translation with Protestant, it can be taken as the recognized position for both sides.
  Quintilian argues that

since an argument is a process of reasoning which provides proof and enables one thing to be inferred from another and confirms facts which are uncertain by reference to facts which are certain, there must needs be something in every case which requires no proof.[45]

Examples should be drawn from commonly accepted notions when used for argument by analogy, depending on gross numbers of people believing them.

This uniformity of belief is held by sheer numbers of martyrs. Henry Garnet, translating Canisius's catechism, adds a list of all doctors cited, so the reader is impressed not only with the quality but also with the "multitude of witnesses of [the Church's] sincerity."[46] The number of Catholic saints and martyrs in heaven is Campion's tenth reason for remaining in the Church, says *Campian Englished*.[47] *Conversions* proudly analyzes statistical comparisons between the 3,704 Catholics who died for their "faith," and Foxe's mere 456 Protestants dying for their "opinions." Saints are heaped up in Verstegan's "Triumphe of feminyne Saintes," in the *Odes*. Initially, each woman is dignified by a brief stanza about her station in life, before being decorously martyred. Several pages on, stanzas gallop into couplets:

> With tearing hookes and iron combes,
> Was Tatiana torn.
> Cointha trayled along the streetes,
> Her flesh from bones was worne.

By the end of the poem there are reckless job lots of martyrdoms: "Six that were called Candida," "Seven of the name of Julia"![48]

This pseudo-reasoning is only apparent in the "rules for life" texts, as distinguished from those basic catechisms produced for beginners in the faith. The latter tell, to the same audience, tales of saints, miracles, images, and relics, and suggest that learning is unimportant to develop faith. Bellarmine, Vaux, and Martin piously murmur "the books of the unlearned" about these aids. Vaux and Bellarmine group young children learning the words of prayers and gestures of the mass with "unlearned people," making no concessions to the maturity and curiosity of the latter. While Persons, Granada, and Southwell provide tables of contents and indices for the reader to organize his own programme of research, Bellarmine and Vaux do not. Their readers can only approach the text in the order they give.

It would seem that reason is irrelevant to catechisms and hagiographies. The catechisms point out that the efficacy of the sacraments, the Church's central conduit of grace, does not depend on the understanding, "the infant, innocent, idiote and unlearned, taking no lesse fruite of Baptisme and al other divine offices . . . then the learnedst Clerke in the Realme."[49] As Persons says,

> faith is grounded upon a more certaine foundation, then is humaine science, to wit upon the credit and authority of God himselfe.[50]

Proof is not seen by them as necessary, but weighed up for the advantageous impression of factual honesty—that is, its effect on ethos.

Thus, the hagiographies work hard to give the appearance of veracity to their statements. In *A true report of the death & martyrdome of M. Campion,* Alfield uses *martyria,* confirmation by one's own testimony, in repeating an idle conversation between some gentlemen standing in front of him at Campion's execution about the sun's motion from east to west. Alfield asks them to agree that this was what they said, so people will know he was really there to hear it.[51] The ingenuity of this technique provokes conviction, even in those who did not hear them. *Martyria,* however, is a dangerous figure to use, if a good ethos is not assumed. Persons mocks Francis Hastings for using the scheme: if Hastings has said something, it is that much more likely to be false.

> Who are yow (Sir) that we should yeld unto yow this Pythagoricall authoritie of *ipse dixit?* graunting all things upon your owne assertion without further proofes.[52]

When no direct-speech reporting is possible, the proceedings of trial and execution are set out in letters. However, printed letters in recusant texts are an appeal to documentary evidence (like the ethos of the witness, a portion of inartificial proof), authentic statements from both Catholic and Protestant. The epistolary form was encouraged by the Jesuit *Constitutions* as a way of solving the problem of the isolation of missioners and of promoting interest in mission work. At least one letter from each mission station was expected by the provincial each month. Allen prints letters written in expectation of death by almost all the martyrs, and works to make us aware that these are genuine. For instance, he gives an incomplete last letter by Sherwin to his friend, which Allen says wants "iii or iiii of the latter lines" as though he had the travel-stained document before him, but would not edit it, in scrupulous fear of misrepresenting the martyr's own words. Allen uses the method with great success in *The Late Apprehension and Imprisonnement of Iohn Nicols, Minister, at Roan* of 1583, in the controversy over why Nicols was imprisoned by the Catholics. "In setting it downe, no one title is altered, not the very incongruities of his speach amended."[53] Allen briefly explains where such and such a person was, while writing each document, but most of the text is of letters and reports by others. After many of them, Allen reprints the seal of the notary who copied them, representing each document as a true copy; an endless circle of documentary evidence!

An effect of using this form is to create the impression of an interested circle of addressees who are already in discussion before the new reader overhears what is said. This world is stable, not predicated on the reader's attention. The letter form alienates the writer from his own text, making it easier for the reader to believe in the latter's objectivity. In *Conversions* before the French King, the Bishop of Evreux and Lord Duplessis-Mornay debate what constitutes fair quotation or extrapolation from texts, as the Bishop strives to prove that Duplessis-Mornay has misquoted the fathers in his description of the true Church. Persons reports much of this trial of loci through letters exchanged between the two, giving the debate reality and immediacy. Henry himself notes the advantage of publishing letters, in turning a private, scholarly dispute into a public issue, and so into a means of converting people outside the debate. Of course, Henry's remarks are in a letter themselves, reported by Persons in a text on conversion![54]

This technique is not confined to letters. Writers often refer to other recusant texts, suggesting a circle of other speakers to confirm what is said in the present work. The *Short Rule* praises the *Christian Directorie*, which, in its turn, praises Loarte's *Exercise*. *Conversions* suggests that one should read Bristow's *Motives* and the *Directorie*. *Campian Englished* mentions Martin, and so on.

Allen's texts are distinguished by their gnomic printing, separating direct and reported speech by different characters, and pointing up sententiae. In *A True Report Of . . . Iohn* Nicols of 1583, he prints documents in bold or light roman type, varying the point size of each, while his own commentary is in bold or light italic. These letters and reports appear as from a miscellany of pens, not as a single document written or heavily edited by Allen. This printing technique is picked up by Persons in the debates in *Conversions* and in his *De persecutione Anglicana libellus*, printing martyrs' letters as holy relics of their spirits.

There are several layers of conviction being manipulated here. Does the reader believe that the facts of the execution are reported correctly? This is the impression which Alfield's *martyria* and Allen's printing techniques intend to convey. Does the reader believe that the martyr was sincere? This is dependent on the previous impression of an actual execution; martyrdoms of the will are useless for this. If the martyr lied, deliberately, at the point of death and beyond the possibility of absolution, he would damn himself eternally. Lies would be unlikely, given that he was dying because he believed in salvation and damnation. Finally, but most importantly, given the purpose of the works, does the reader believe what the martyr is saying?

With this question, we move back into the realm of definition, of martyr or suicide, that is, the realm of text. Single events in the hagiographies become *topoi*, around which different interpretations of their significance are marshalled, by both Catholic and Protestant. While Cecil says Alexander Briant was not starved but wilfully refused to write for food, Persons says Briant was forced to lap condensation from the walls. Campion was humiliatingly silenced in the disputes in the Tower, *pace* Anthony Munday, or so thoroughly quashed the Protestant disputants that the arguments could not be published, according to Allen. Mirror-images to the hagiographic poems in Alfield appear in Munday's *breefe aunswer made unto two seditious Pamphlets* of 1582. Alfield's Campion, whose

> lowly minde possest a learned place,
> and sugred speach a rare and vertuous wil

is answered by one with

> climing minde, reiecting wisedomes call,
> A sugred tongue, to shrowde a vicious will.[55]

Conversions inverts John Foxe's *Acts and Monuments*: Persons produces a mirror-image text of this book, reprinting the calendars of both churches and sardonically commenting on the testimony of each Anglican martyr.

Thus, the most bitter denunciations of Elizabeth's actions by recusant authors come not in response to the executions, but in response to their definitions as rewards for treason. Cecil made the government's stance clear in his first, defensive, pamphlet, *The Execution of Iustice* of 1583. Against this description, Alfield says martydoms are "misconstred, how truth is made treason, religion rebellion."[56] In 1591, Southwell ended the *Humble Supplication to Her Maiestie* by lamenting that this charge of treason added most to Catholic misery.[57] This peristrophe, this redefinition, was described by recusant texts meant for an overseas audience as Machiavellian. Allen, in *A True Sincere and Modest Defence, of English Catholiques*, declares

> how uniustlie the Protestants doe charge Catholiques with treason; how untrulie they deny their persecution for Religion; and how deceitfullie they seeke to abuse strangers about the cause, greatnes, and maner of their sufferinges.[58]

The question of treason was pressed on each martyr by his executioners, immediately before death. Given that the customary acknowledgment of treason would spare their families further harassment, the fact that all martyrs denied plotting against the Queen highlights an appreciation on both sides that while the cause makes the martyr, the definition makes the convert.

Definitions of its own actions proffered by the government did not deny or react to recusant descriptions, they were positive, creating an image. Allen's preface to *XII. Priests* notes the government's need to maintain its self-definition as just and reasonable. Cecil's pamphlet for the home audience, *A Declaration of the favourable dealing of her Maiesties Commissioners* of 1583, deals with the same topics as *The Execution of Iustice,* but finds it necessary to admit that the rack has been used. Even then, Cecil says in a tone of mild reproof of unreasonable cavilers, the warders "whose office and act it is to handle the racke, were ever . . . specially charged, to use it in as charitable maner as such a thing might be."[59]

Thus, the martyrdom itself quickly becomes irrelevant, as texts move away from discussing the saint, and begin to answer and therefore take on the shape and aims of the opposing side's books. The martydoms are quickly textualized. *A Discovery of E. Campion,* Anthony Munday's pamphlet on the deaths of Campion, Sherwin, and Briant, was entered in the Stationers' Register within two days of the execution in 1581, and H. E. Rollins is able to list five hostile ballads produced about Campion, up to 1603. Allen criticizes the government for preprinting a program for the executions for distribution on that day, with details of the three men's examinations, but on the Catholic side also, while Alfield notes the presence of many people to witness the passage of such virtue, he says firmly that he went solely to write about the event.[60] Persons exclaims that

> endless is the number of books, dialogues, discourses, poems, witticisms, that are made and published, sometimes in print, sometimes in manuscript, in praise of these martyrs and in condemnation of their adversaries.[61]

George Birkhead, the Superior of the English secular clergy, equates the importance of books and men on the mission. In 1584 he told Agazzari that the recent increase of fervor in Britain could be put down to three causes:

> the holy deaths last year of so many martyrs . . . the careful and constant zeal for preaching in our priests, and especially the great variety of books . . . which have been written since your fathers first came to England.[62]

This meant that John Gibbons's offer to the mission, of writing the *Concertatio ecclesiae Catholicae in Anglia* rather than going himself, could be gratefully accepted by his superiors.

Not just the events but the martyrs themselves become books which testified to Christ's power. Campion's rhetorical skill is established by Alfield before he begins to say anything about the martyr's devotion or constancy. The emphasis is picked up by the 1632 translator of *Rationes decem,* who spends the first three pages of his introduction in an excited *gradatio,* which lists Campion's success in debate, his decorous words, swelling metaphors, frequencies and diminutives, his interrogations, shortness and sublimity, his transitions, graduations, and vehemency—before remarking, rather flatly, that "besides all this artificiall furniture of Speach, there is found a wonderfull *Christian fervour* in his words"![63] Alfield's concluding verses see the reader's own conscience, and then London itself, as pages on which Campion wrote out his faith:

> his vertues nowe are written in the skyes,
> and often read with holy inward eyes . . .
> the streets, the stones, the steps you haled them by,
> proclaime the cause for which these martirs dy.[64]

Campion is as uncomfortably omnipresent as Nancy's eyes to Sikes. *Campian Englished* says Dr. Case of Oxford, on seeing the martyrs' heads on poles, felt that *"their dead bodies preach to this day."*[65] This view of people as witnesses or texts of God is not confined to hagiographies. In the *Short Rule,* Southwell notes,

> all creatures must be as it were bookes to me to read therein the love, presence, providence and fatherly care, that God hath over me.[66]

William Alabaster takes up the theme, in "The Sponge":

> My tongue shall be my pen, mine eyes shall rain
> Tears for my ink. . . .
> When I have done, do thou, Jesu divine,
> Take up the tart sponge of thy Passion
> And blot it forth; then be thy spirit the quill,
> Thy blood the ink, and with compassion
> Write thus upon my soul: thy Jesu still.[67]

An article by Ronald Corthell, which is unique in applying new historicism to recusant texts, sees loyalty to the Supreme Other being redefined by the state as disloyalty to the absolute authority of government. He suggests that "an estranged or divided subject . . . potentially productive of a discourse of interiority or conscience" is produced by the double allegiance owed by Catholics to Church and

State, since it sets the concept of a transcendent individual against one which is produced historically.[68] Corthell is right to recognize the original loyalties of Catholics, but could take account of the timing of the struggle between the two allegiances. In the writers he cites, this question has been settled before they return to Britain on the mission. They recite the *topos* to show how, with clear affections and a sense of proportion, no such conflict could arise. The hierarchy of loyalties is obvious.

The textualization of martyrs suggests the other type of inartificial proof of the hagiographies: relics and miracles. Using a more modern, forensic concept of proof, the martyrs' relics and images are used as physical evidence, that is, rhetorical "indications" of the truth of faith. The martyrs act up to their immediate conversion after death into relics by the crowd, and literary remains by the authors. When Rigby prepares for execution he deliberately throws his neckerchief into the crowd, "wherupon some said: that wil be taken up for a Relique."[69] This contributes to the clinical presentation of executions and tortures, authors often losing the sense of the person involved (see the diagramatic labeling of the illustration on p. 105). Phrases of the recusant Thomas Pounde rip up martyrs:

> And some by them were lykwyse drawen in twaine
> some picemeell hewen some stripped of their skin
> some boyled, some broylde, & some with bodkines slaine,
> & some hoot oyle, & ledd were dipped in. . . .[70]

Augustine sanctions the possibility of future miracles: "the bodies of the dead are not to be contemned and cast away, [and] chiefly of the righteous and faithful, which the Holy Ghost used as organs and instruments unto all good works."[71] However, sixteenth-century theologians believed that miracles proved God's power and his agreement with the intentions of the intecessor, followed Augustine in also feeling that

> to alleage later myracles was not necessary, because at the beginning they were requisite til faith was planted, [and] afterwarde they were not to be loked for.[72]

Nonetheless, Martin explains that to relate "wicked spirits cast out, the blind to see, the lame to go, the dead to rise agayne" is valuable in two ways. These events indicate where the true faith lies, since such deeds could only be performed by a member of the true Church. Where miracles come from the intercession of martyrs, one miracle

"Persecutions contre les Catholicques, parles protestans Machiavellistes en Angleterre." Note the careful numbering of each torture. Ki r in Richard Verstegan, *Theatre des Cruatez des Hereticques*, 1588. (Reproduced with the permission of the Bodleian Library, Oxford.)

is as useful to prove the supernatural as a million. More prudently, Martin says miracles help to rouse devotion, even if they cannot be proved:

> he honoreth undoutedly the principall it selfe in heaven [ie. the saint who has been invoked], howsoever he be deceaved agaynst his will in mistaking some earthly monumente or remembrance therof.[73]

Samuel Harsnet similarly describes the purpose of "popish impostures" or exorcisms by several priests in 1585–86. Although Harsnet may have exaggerated his descriptions of the exorcisms, the comment he reports by a fellow priest to Anthony Tyrell, when he expressed dissatisfaction about the affair, could have come from Martin himself:

> such Catholiques, as have beene present at such fits, have receaved it for a truth, that the parties are possessed. And although I for my part will not make it an article of my Creede, yet I thinke that godlie credulitie doth much good, for the furthering of the Catholique cause.[74]

Echoing John Harington's comment, that if a romantic tale such as *Orlando Furioso* could bring "an honest and serious consideration" into his mind then it was no "toy," Martin praises those with the grace to reap great devotion from little things like relics.[75] So, although wary of Trent's injunctions against labeling incidents as miracles, Allen describes how Cuthbert Mayne's chamber is mysteriously illuminated, and Worthington, how John Rigby's chains fall from him without aid. Worthington cautiously prompts the reader to recognize the significance of the event:

> most men that saw it, or have heard of it, undoubtedly thinck it to be miraculous. What the Iudges with the rest of the bench, and others in authoritie thinck of it, is hard to iudge.[76]

The relics reported on by the texts can even act without request. They can be involuntarily powerful, though the catechisms of Vaux and Bellarmine warn that *latria* and *dulia* are not to be confused, the relic acting as duct for God's mercies, not as producer of miracles. In the *Roma sancta,* an unpublished eulogy of his stay in Rome in 1581, Martin details Gregory's care in sending out only a little of the dust filed from the chains which bound St. Paul, since to send the whole of Paul's head, as requested, would be far too dangerous. Donne mocks this mechanical aspect in *Ignatius His Conclave* of 1611. The Gregorian calendar has disturbed the heavens so much, Saints Stephen and John can scarcely perform their miracles since they are appealed to on the wrong day.[77]

Relics and texts are both substantial residues of great events, efficacious in recognition or consumption. Such indications of the saints (textual and physical) are meant to be retained in the memory. Martin makes this a material process of absorption. It was right

> to love sacred monuments, to be desirous to see them, to goe farre and neere unto them, to touch, to kisse, to licke them, to weepe in the place, to conceave such a lyvely imagination of thinges done there by Christ or his Saynts, and withall such a sensible feeling of heavenly devotion, that it was a payne to remove from thence.[78]

The *Manual of Prayers* reverses who is absorbed in who; addressing the "moste bountifull harte," the sacred blood, the "venerable woundes," it requires the reader to cry "drowne me in them, hyde me in them: write and prynte them deeply in my harte."[79] In Martin's *Roma sancta,* relics are also startling images as are memory images, to "reneweth our memorie, eftsones fraile and forgetfull."[80] They are furnished with a memorable icon of the saint's particular virtue or suffering; St. Joseph has his carpentry tools, St. Catherine her wheel. When the recusant authors provide detailed scenes of bloody last ends they are not just appealing for pity but providing an enduring, though unmoving, image of the struggle.

The reader can pilgrimage in his imagination, just as the meditation texts enjoin. Martin's eulogy of Rome, "a verie shambles of martyrizing Christians" is satirized by Anthony Munday's description, in *The English Romane Lyfe* of 1582, of how the students at the English college brought home bones they found while walking, "and thus (saving your reverence) increaseth the genealogy of the holy relics in Rome."[81] Munday has not grasped the insubstantial nature of Martin's relics. These bones are symbols of a past glory of Christianity, repeated in the present. Their antique provenance is irrelevant; only their ability to provoke devotion is important.

Extending the "place and image" mnemotechnic, Southwell's *Short Rule* recommends that we bring virtues to mind by creating a "paradise" in each room at home.

> I must in everye roome of the house where I dwell imagin in some decent place therof a throne or chair of estate, and dedicate the same & the whole roome to some Saint, that whensoever I enter into it, I enter as it were into a chappel or church that is devoted to such a Sainte.

Southwell's emphasis, in this "spiritual recreation," is on memory. Saints are not to be switched around rooms or we will get hazy on which saint is where. We can build up the number in each room slowly, "as the roome will minister conveniency to frame their places for the better conceiving and remembring of them." Matching the saint and the virtue needed in each room will help this, putting saints of spare diet in the dining room, for example. Like Campion's appearances, this vision feels claustrophobic: saints "not only in the house, but also in the walkes, gardens and orchardes about the house." Even members of the family represent saints.[82] Aspects of the physical world wither into signs of the virtues of God's elect, as the creator speaks metanomically through creation to us.

So beneath the impartial formality of inartificial proof lie the rhetorical and the pathetic. Even catechisms rely on ethos rather than on reason; the form of disputation is mere show. The factual presentation of martyrs as witnesses dissolves under deliberative pressure, depending on ethos. Not only have these authorities been hieratically moulded, but the least susceptible elements of inartificial proof—physical indications or relics—have been softened into digestible fragments for the memory. The following chapter extends this view of hagiography as an exemplary form, illuminating the faith.

6

Hagiographies as Examples
to Clarify the Faith

Recusant hagiographies show standard forms of action, indicating what a saint was likely to do rather than what he did. Their purpose is to urge the reader to imitation; sharing demonstrative rhetoric's display, not its distaste for action. This chapter discusses how such display is to be read, where the images presented are referents, not sensuous.

SAINTS' LIVES AS CHRIAE

Rhetorics of the period, regarding the general as clearer than the particular, use classification rather than induction. The successful Ramist logic and rhetoric codified this, a matter of display rather than discovery, demonstrating generals before specifics. Sixteenth-century rhetorics treat examples more as clarifying some previously acknowledged general law, than as part of induction, working toward new knowledge. As Puttenham puts it, example "is but the representation of old memories."[1] For the *ad Herennium,* "examples are set forth, not to confirm or bear witness, but to clarify. . . . [By] example we clarify the nature of our statement, while by testimony we establish its truth."[2]

However, Quintilian argues that display in illustrative rhetoric can be enhanced by a semblance of proof, which need not be argued too closely. Display is not inimicable to proof, but it has different concerns. As illustrations of holy lives and deaths, reported martyrdoms were more concerned to be memorable and effective in stirring the audience to emulation, than to be factually accurate. Sidney's "feigned example" had as much force to teach and probably more to move than a true one, since it was adapted to the audience.[3] With Augustine himself having used quotations from the poets in *De civitate Dei,* religious authors could excuse the pious use of fiction.

Recusant authors were thus at liberty to mould their material affectively. They were also trained to do this. Composition of *chriae* on the qualities of the good man, the bad, the old, the young (exemplified by Richard Rainolde's redaction of Aphthonius's progymnasmata, in *The Foundacion of Rhetorike* of 1563) was one of their earliest school exercises. This was training in imagining the probable rather than the observable characteristics of each estate. Sidney called this perception framing "the example to that which is most reasonable" for "an example only informs a conjectured likelihood."[4] Helen White describes such shaping in hagiographies as a logical extension of the probable way a saint would act. Having decided that an execution is a martyrdom, the author decides on how a man imbued with God's grace would behave, and then describes him doing so. White charts an unconscious hagiographical evolution, where a saint's story mutates through official notices by the interrogators, those of eyewitnesses, reports of these reports, historical and then imaginative romances, ending at last in flat forgery.[5] However, recusant authors are neither ignorant of the facts nor dependent on the imagination; on the contrary, they are very close to the real scenes of execution. They choose not to rely on these, communicating a hieratic form; elements of real action are there for display only.

The hagiographies resemble standard forms of service, where the martyr's name is substituted for *N*. In one manuscript of Southwell's "Decease release," the lines "Alive a Queene, now dead I am a Sainte, / Once N: calld, my name nowe Martyr is" have the name "Mary" written over *N*; in another manuscript they have "Anne," the name of James's wife, reputed to have died a Catholic.[6]

This formalism allows Southwell the liberty to depict Margaret Sackville to her half-brother, the Earl of Arundel, in *Triumphs over Death* published in 1596. While extolling her life and character, Southwell admits he has never met her, but also that it was not necessary to have met her to be able to imitate her, in text and in life. Like a grain of dust inside an oyster, the real Margaret left the memory of perfect characteristics which could be written on. Since everyone knows of her example, the woman herself need not be present.[7] When Janelle criticizes the temperate tone of the *Triumphs* for showing too little personal sorrow, as "a preposterous adaptation of the classical mood to religious ends," he misses what is being mourned.[8]

There are two hagiographical *topoi* observable in these texts: the good humor with which the martyrs meet death, and the learning they use to confute the arguments of ministers sent to them. Worthington shows John Rigby teasing members of the Sessions which try him.

What are you that will sweare? . . . I am a man: but what more? . . . At
which his replie (not able to forbeare laughter) I said: Sir what can I be
more then a man?

When gibberish is quoted at him as though a Catholic prayer in Latin,
Rigby is "not able to forbeare laughter," saying "for myn owne part,
though I understand Latin, I do not understand what you said.
Wherat al the bench laghed with me for companie."[9] Alfield and Allen
praise Campion for his gentle ways with his jailers, elaborating on his
"joyfully comming to receive his reward and crown."[10] As examples
of true resolution, Persons choses martyrs who rejoice to be captured:
his Polycarp plays hide-and-seek with his pursuivants before offering
himself to martyrdom (when he has fled long enough to escape the
sin of spiritual pride).[11] Recusant hagiographers say signs of fear in
the martyrs are merely malicious rumors started by the Protestants.
Alfield's printer (possibly Stephen Vallenger) publishes the *true report*
because he fears that, as with reports about Everard Hanse's death,
there would be attempts to "diminish the honour of their resolute
departure & Martirdome, as that M Campion was timerous and fear-
full, & that M Sherwin died a protestant."[12] Allen says Shert instinct-
ively caught hold of the rope as the cart was drawn away, not in fear.
Of the twelve martyrs, the only life Allen gives, apart from Campion,
is Cottam's, who is shown as anxious to be captured and to earn his
martyr's crown. Cottam is also the only one of Allen's martyrs who
appears to hesitate over whether to recant and save his life.

The second major *topos* to describe the martyrs is that the martyrs
are credited with learning. Alfield says proudly that they "fight with
word & not with sword," and notes "M. Elmers" folly in suggesting
that if "a Notebooke or two of [Campion's] felowes [was] taken from
him, he had nothing in him."[13] Thomas Sprot and Thomas Hunt can
so confute Protestant scholars brought in to argue with them that

the Magistrats commanded the Ministers to hold their peace. And in
steed of their babling, prosecuted their owne farre stronger arguments,
of fetters, halters, and butchers knives.[14]

Alfield apologizes that Briant only had a B.A. degree, but insists his
ignorance did not harm his faith.

Of course, Campion receives most of such praise.

From rack in Tower they broght him to dispute,
bookeles, alone, to answere al that came,
yet Christ gave grace, he did them all confute . . .
they thought it best to take his life away,

> because they saw he would their matter marre,
> And leave them shortly nought at al to say.[15]

Allen describes how clergy disputed with Campion three times in the Tower but failed to move him, and Alfield promises to publish these glorious debates when he has the means. Even Anthony Munday

> wyll not denie, but that this good irreligious *Campion,* handled every cause with a smoothe and cullorable countenance, beeing verie present and quick to him selfe, in Sophistical conveyances, and farre set deepe pointes of Logique.[16]

Campion's skill is not apocryphal: two future recusants, Campion and Bristow, were chosen out of all the scholars of Oxford to welcome the Queen to the city in 1566.

These two *topoi* enhance the impression of individuals in control of their own deaths. Laughter shows a degree of disengagement and self-control. These Catholics are not the ignorant, frightened, superstitious mass which Protestant publicity would have them; nor are they bold, seditious, desperate. Instead, the martyrs are strong, debonair, charming individuals, choosing to suffer for the faith. This element of triumph comes out in Guiney's collection of published and unpublished recusant verse. Those writers not on the mission look backward, to before the Reformation, plaintively sighing with William Blundell:

> The time hath beene we had one faith
> and all trode right one antient path. . . .
> The time hath beene preists did accorde
> in exposition of gods worde. . . .
> The time hath beene the sheepe obey'de. . . .
> The time hath beene. . . .

The few writers in Guiney who were missioners (Southwell, Henry Walpole, and the poets in Alfield's *Campion*) sound victoriously active; they are in control. Only two days before his death, Walpole exults in the "River of pleasure sea of Delight," the "princlie palace royall court" to which he will be summoned.[17] At the conclusion of Campion's martyrdom, the Alfield poet cries:

> religion ioyed to see so mild a man,
> men, angels, saints, and al that saw hym dye,
> forgot their grief, his ioyes appeard so nye.[18]

In Southwell's "Decease release" reclines a dignified Mary Stuart:

> My skaffold was the bedd where ease I founde,
> The blocke a pillowe of Eternall reste,
> My hedman cast me in a blisfull swounde,
> His axe cutt off my cares from combred breste.[19]

The predominant opening image of the martyrs is of a glass or a spectacle: "this short relation here exhibitid," "a lively Image of resolute martirs," "lanterns of piety," "a light and lanterne, a paterne and exawple [sic] to youth, to age, to lerned, to unlerned, to religious, and to the laytie of al sort."[20] Christ himself is likened to an image in a looking glass, "begotten by Gods only beholding himselfe," though more substantial than the shadows of saints.[21] Verstegan uses this spectacle metaphor for his "visions of the worlds instabillitie," with a theater before him, hung with black and fit to display some tragedy (the context is far from the gloomy Trumps of Estella and Granada).[22] The metaphor is picked up sardonically by Harsnet:

> every person may appear in his owne proper colours, the devill in his, and the devils charmers in theyrs, that every part may be considered, how well it hath been plaied, and what actor hath best deserved the *plaudite* or *suspendite* . . . come and see it set out, in the sacred robes out of the holy wardrop from Rome. . . .[23]

The faculties of administering the sacraments and spiritual guidance, which the priests could offer as priests, were considered less valuable than this publicity from their deaths. Thus, Persons can remark that if the martyrs' lives "had been prolonged to their hundredth year they could not have benefited their cause as much as has their short life, but glorious death."[24] Henry More approvingly details how Henry Walpole, when captured in the first week of his mission, was offered a means of escape. He asked his superior in Britain, whether he should accept it. Richard Holtby answered that the cause would be better served if Walpole was not seen to be fleeing from martyrdom.[25]

These exemplary scenes are dramatized. Peter Holmes believes the historical trials and executions became showcases for propaganda effort on both sides. They were one of the few times a mission priest could speak openly to a large audience.[26] In the texts, adding to the impression of live drama, authors intervene in court proceedings as though present. The latter months of *Conversions* report many trials through direct speech. Persons, in the undignified though theologically correct position of defending the Marian persecutions, interposes in these scenes to limit admiration for Protestant martyrs. There are three participants in the following interchange: Winchester, Lambert, and an indignant Persons intervening in the last phrase, speaking from under Winchester's elbow:

> the Bishopp of *Winchester* added a place or two in confirmation . . . *where-*
> *unto* (saith Fox) *Lambert answered that he doubted* . . . which is a ridiculous
> answere yf yow marke yt.[27]

Persons is particularly venomous in his interpolations at the trials of Latimer and Ridley; the latter's good humor on these occasions predisposes the audience to like them, and Persons can sense their Catholic interlocutors losing position. He recounts the answers of women at trials exasperatedly:

> for no man of wisdome will imagine (I weene) that *Alice Driver,* though
> she were nevere so prachant & forward in heresie, and bold through the
> pride therof, could make such a conference of her selfe, with such learned
> men as [were against her].[28]

Petulantly aware that the Catholic side has lost the reader's sympathy, he concludes that Foxe has discredited himself, since it is improbable that a woman could make such wise answers. (This reverses John Bale's praise of witty answers by Anne Askew and other Protestant female martyrs: because women could not respond so well, God must have put words into their mouths).[29]

As executions progress, authors observe the reaction of the crowd. Allen weighs up the audience at Campion's trial, attended by many who are not doubtful of the issue but of the way the jury will vote, given Campion's appeal to them. Allen notes that Ralph Sherwin, standing with his eyes closed in the cart, asked if "the people expect that I should speake?" Worthington notes that the "people going away muttered much at the crueltie used in the execution" of Rigby.[30] *De civitate Dei* sets a precedent for regarding the audience as an integral part of a miracle. Augustine chides Innocentia for concealing a miracle cure, and regrets that these "are not so famous, nor so fastened in the memory by often reading, that they might not be forgotten."[31] Audience reaction is necessary inside each text, where miracles such as the martyrs' fortitude need an audience to verify that God is working outside the natural order. The reaction then moves outside the text; the reader is edified just as the audience within the work has been affected. As in the meditations, the reader is simultaneously within the scene as audience with Mary and the Magdalen, and outside the text as the reading audience.

Yet although the works start with some dramatic effect, this often drains away, leaving all the theater of a catechism. Despite the liberal use of stage metaphors and the construction of a dramatic framework, authors of the hagiographies are as reluctant as those of the meditations to free their examples of godliness into independent action. In Bristow's *Demaundes,* a debate is set up between a heretic and a recusant. Bristow heavily orchestrates the speeches: "ask them if they . . . and if they say then you say. . . ." In Persons's *Conference About the Next Succession* of 1594, two lawyers discourse dryly about genealogy tables and the royal prerogative. At each chapter end, Persons gestures toward creating a scene, abruptly and coyly suggesting the lawyers take a walk or have lunch. He is just as heavy-footed when introducing a description of the college at Valladolid, in a letter purporting to reply to an exiled friend, who ignores his own situation to inquire earnestly about the fate of an obscure college in Spain.[32] Such texts gratefully abandon any vestige of drama when plunging into the main theme. Since an impression that they document living scenes has been created, they have no need to further engage the reader.

In their question-and-answer formats, catechisms are attenuated attempts at drama. Most catechisms do not accost the reader in the direct manner of the start of Ledisma's catechism: "Are you a Christian?" "Yea."[33] They are inspecific in their questions: "what is a Christian?" "A Christian is. . . ." Nonetheless, the reader is invited to mimic the knowledge of the disciple answering the master, until he can vie with the disciple. The dramatic shell promotes such close imitation of the pupil that the barrier between the part of reader and disciple breaks down, and the shell becomes redundant. Thus, both writers of hagiographies and catechisms minimize dramatic particularity and action. They are emblematic. Writers of hagiography turn the lessons learned from the martyrs' deaths into memorable epitomes of wisdom. They are not concerned with making the portraits living, but polished and portable. Trial and death scenes are sketched, where the martyrs do only what they are expected to, in an ethical framework shared by reader and author.

Such rhetorical handling of hagiography affects not only its audience, but also its subjects. Authors manipulating saints as examples can be less than respectful. Southwell strikes the right note, advising the reader to use reverent familiarity with his guardian saint. He personalizes them, can see they even have faults but feels these may profit us as a warning.[34] Bellarmine views the saints distantly, a spiritual treasury of grace to resist temptation. It is the socially ill at ease Persons who looses his balance when addressing this august group, trying to stir up a brawl in heaven. In his dedication of the third volume of *Conversions* to the "glorious Company of English Sainctes," he fumbles with the idea of omnipotence, muttering that he does not have to remind them of their "injury" in being thrust from their feast days by Foxe. He is simply reminding himself that they should feel indignant enough to answer the prayers of Catholics in Britian—and to blight the upstarts![35]

There appears to be no link between recusant texts and the sort of romantic hagiography epitomized by the thirteenth-century *Golden Legend* of Jacobus de Voragine, which ran to over one hundred and fifty editions in Latin and English before 1532. This was a collection of the lives of saints, biblical stories, and short treatises about Christian festivals, disposed according to the Church year. White thinks it was popular as a combination of classical encomium and Celtic wonder-tale. However, the recusant texts are certainly not "a religious Arabian Nights Entertainment for every day of the year," which could be enjoyed with a clear conscience.[36] It is true that recusant authors acknowledge a pleasure to be gained in the "gratefull variety both of tymes, men, and affaires" of the liturgy of saints.[37] Moreover, the element of the legendary, as summed up by Auerbach, is present in sixteenth-century hagiographies;

> all cross-currents, all friction, all that is casual, secondary to the main events and themes, everything unresolved, truncated, and uncertain . . . has disappeared.[38]

However, the romance has gone. These are not exciting stories of supernatural victories over the laws of nature or the powers of evil. Everything happens as one would expect. A small group of troublemakers gets hung by a strong, determined government. In Southwell's "I dye without desert," the sense of a fairy tale gone wrong, hangs over the poem as it did over the disciples at Pentecost:

> For right is wrong'd, and vertue wag'd with blood,
> The badd are blissd, god murdred in the good.[39]

The victory is purely moral, without heartwarming concessions to earthly concerns. New iconographic traditions have come into place, for the new saints and the new messages of discipline and rigor which Trent communicated. The reader would not relax of an evening with a book whose possession could make him suffer like the hero. Indeed, there were literary martyrs. William Carter was executed in 1584 for printing Catholic works, Thomas Alfield in 1585 for distributing Allen's *Defence*. Campion's very last speech was primarily concerned with an (unsuccessful) attempt to clear someone who had been caught with one of his books.

To show that romance is deliberately downplayed in recusant texts before 1603, it is useful to contrast them with the thoroughly romantic *Life and Death of Mr. Edmund Geninges Priest*, written by his brother John and published in 1614. John commands his "mournful muse" to sound out the "doleful accident" of Edmund's death. This is not the note of triumph noticeable in most hagiographies. We hear of Edmund's special childhood; born with teeth; fond of gazing of the heavens; the armies which fought in the sky as he watched; his young manhood and conversion; his death and subsequent miracle-working.[40] This work is actually concerned with the martyr at the center of it. Edmund is not passed over for the political and devotional capital which can be made out of his execution, though from the point of view of an Allen or a Persons, there could be little else to be made out of a ministry which ended within a few months of Gennings' landing in Britain. There is little drama or romance in most recusant illustrations of Christian fortitude.

HAGIOGRAPHY AS DEMONSTRATIVE RHETORIC

Should there be a link between hagiography and epideictic rhetoric? Cicero subordinates this *causa* to supporting forensic and deliberative orations, demonstrating goods of fortune, of physical attributes, and of qualities of character. Although they acknowledge demonstrative rhetoric as a separate *genus causa*, the *ad Herennium* and *Institutio oratoria* follow Cicero in also dealing with its features under deliberative rhetoric. They divide the latter between the expedient and the honorable. Under the latter, good fortune and physical advantage are merely touched on, as part of securing an advantage. The honorable is further divided by the *ad Herennium* into the praiseworthy and the right, because "although the praiseworthy has its source in the right . . . if praise accrues, the desire to strive after the right is doubled."[41] It is qualities of character which come under the right, that is, character is described as internal and fundamental (the right), whereas body and fortune are seen as valuable if noticed by others (the praiseworthy), and not as worthy in themselves. For the classical rhetorics, the valued qualities of character are virtues of proportion. They "rest on our judgement and thought: wisdom, justice, courage, temperance, and their contraries." Moreover, Quintilian emphasizes that "praise awarded to external and accidental advantages is given, not to their possession, but to their honourable employment."[42] So virtue has the double meaning of a power or quality, under the right, and the correct use of fortune or physical attributes, under the honorable.

Thus, Soarez splits the four qualities of virtue listed by Quintilian and the *ad Herennium* (wisdom, courage, justice, and temperance) into two types: virtue in learning and virtue in action. The former combines prudence and wisdom. Wisdom is an unfocused virtue, a knowledge of the truth or falsehood of things human and divine, while prudence is a more specific knowledge of things to be sought and avoided. Both are served by dialectic and rhetoric which sort, more or less briefly, the true from the false. Virtue in action, however, is what is aimed at by deliberative rhetoric, comprising the other three qualities of virtue: courage, justice, and temperance.[43] For Soarez, the truly virtuous speech is one that stirs to action, the deliberative speech.

The manuals have discussed the topics of demonstrative rhetoric as a support to deliberative rhetoric, so their hierarchy of presentation puts virtue in action over virtue in learning and both virtues over external goods. Yet Harry Caplan in his translation of the *ad Herennium* feels that

> whereas in both deliberative and judicial causes the speaker seeks to persuade his hearers to a course of action, in epideictic his primary purpose is by means of his art to impress his ideas upon them, *without action as a goal.*[44]

The contradiction between Caplan's view and the actual presentation of the classical rhetorics can be explained by demonstrative rhetoric's refusal to display open intent. As Quintilian says, "wherever the orator displays his art unveiled, the hearer says, 'The truth is not in him,'" and his purpose is frustrated.[45] In demonstrative rhetoric the suspicion of intention which spoils the effect is absent, leaving the *causa* free to extol norms of society which will become valued by an auditor, who will act on them. This purpose for epideictic rhetoric excuses its use for Plato, and his reasoning is repeated by many Renaissance theorists anxious to attribute morality to art.

So do the rhetorics believe that there can be such a thing as pure display, a demonstrative oration? The difference between the *genera* in the manuals does not lie in purpose since all are equally bound on persuasion. As Terry Eagleton says, rhetoric sees

> speaking and writing not merely as textual objects, to be aesthetically contemplated or endlessly deconstructed, but as forms of *activity* inseparable from the wider social relations between writers and readers, orators and audiences.[46]

Nor does it lie in subject, since demonstrative rhetoric is used as a *topos* for deliberative and judicial rhetoric. The difference lies in the style only, in the degree of concealment which the *genera* use. In two the aim is manifest, in the third, latent.

All this suggests why there is no direct alignment between demonstrative rhetoric and the recusant hagiographies. Their subject is not a display of godliness, innocent of intent on the reader's morals. As Loarte says, while they are "grateful" to read because of their variety, more importantly they are "lively paterns of christian perfection" which are to be read actively, "committing some spiritual poynt to memorie, which thy soule may amongst thy other busines, nourishe and comfort her self withal."[47] The texts are not there to praise saints themselves, unless this admiration reflects incidentally on the value of the testimony. This is why Gennings's *Life* looks so out of place.

The display aspect of demonstrative rhetoric is prominent in the hagiographies. As Trent's Session 25 emphasized, thinking with images is natural, not idolatrous. Thus in his appendix to Canisius's *Summe of Christian Doctrine* Garnet notes that

> it is necessarie that evrie one whilest he understandeth in this life: forme him selfe a phantasie or likenesse of that thing which he understandeth in his imagination.

This being so, Garnet affirms that one can use palpable images. Both physical image and thought about the divine are merely shadows of the reality, the latter no more real than the former. For Garnet pictures "help us to doe that which our own imagination must needs doe, though not so perfectly without the Image."[48] This is paralleled by the recusant texts' belief that they can express devotion in words; they are happy to communicate in man-made signs. The hagiographies and meditations realize that they present—and can only present—portraits, not pictures.

Although this lays recusant texts open to Protestant charges of idolatry, there is actually common ground between the way the two sets of authors regard images. For Catholic authors images have a cognitive function: texts do not dwell on their sensuous aspect. Public rather than private meanings are promoted. Trent has an austere view of physical images: "all sensual appeal must be avoided, so that images are not to be painted or adorned with seductive charm." Moreoover, they must not suggest that they can do more than signify, certainly not depict, the divine. The physical is charged with meaning as a system of signs. Trent encourages the consumer of the images to see that their meaning lies in interpretation, since "the honour showed to them is referred to the original which they represent."[49] Relics are handled in this way, where real martyrs are dissolved into a form, or Southwell's friends become mnemonic symbols for virtues. It occurs in the meditations, where Christ's body is dismembered and some pious meaning attached to each limb.

Bellarmine explains that images of spiritual things do not show what a thing is itself, but what properties it has or what effects it works.[50] Granada warns against reading the images incorrectly, not referring them to their purposed meaning but consuming them grossly. This is the idolatry of literal interpretation:

> not that in hell theise thinges are altogether so materially donne, but that by them we might in some manner understande somewhat of the varietie and multitude of the paines.[51]

Caddy's recantation throws the charge of idolatry back onto the Protestant critic. Because they take the Word too literally, the "plaine carnal men and Idolaters" lack proper, referential, reading skills, "writhing the sacred words to their own erronious and damnable sect against the proper nature and plaine sense."[52]

Frequent controversy over the visible Church expresses this. Campion's third reason for remaining a Catholic is that "the name of the Church [Calvin] subtilly retayneth, the thing itself by defining he utterly overthroweth." Calvin does this by withdrawing the Church "from all sensible apprehension (like to *Plato's Idea*) [and exposing] her to the sight of some few men." Campion points out that this contradicts the palpable nature of Salvation through the Incarnation.[53] Garnet fumes that

> Calvin dreameth out a Church invisible, and manifest onely unto the eies of God. Of this Church if you desire to be, you may easely dreame it: but then are you not of the trew Church, but of a dreamed Church . . . as the trew Church of God is visible it selfe: so is the union therwith visible.[54]

These ideas run counter to Foxe's preface, addressed to the "True and Faithful Congregation of Christ's Universal Church," which suggested that

> like as is the nature of truth, so is the proper condition of the true church, that commonly none seeth it, but such only as be the members and partakers thereof.[55]

Conversions challenges Foxe's project to create a Church out of his "Dreaming Imagination . . . about the fall of the Roman Church . . .

as he lay on his bedde upon a Sonday in the morninge." As Persons says innocently, Foxe's 'greatest difficulty seemeth to be about the tyme and causes. To witt, where, or when, or how, or upon what occasion, [the Roman Church] perished or vanished away."[56] Persons stoutly defines the Church as "a society not of Angells, spirits or soules departed; but of men and women in this life." He accuses Foxe of defining his Church in opposition to the Catholic faith only: "one *Collyns* therfore belongeth *to the holy company of saincts, for that he was condemned by the Bishop of Rome.*"[57] The preface to *Campian Englished* turns the argument against the Established Church: since it contains Zwingli the swashbuckler, Luther the dissipated monk, Calvin the stigmatical, it is "no wonder if [the members] be constrayned to vaunt of their Church . . . as lying in a perpetuall obscuritie"![58]

The difference between the two camps is more than the necessity of maintaining that the apostolic succession need not be visible to claim authority (though it is true that the English mission is endlessly defined as reflecting the early Church, because of the stress on maintaining a visible succession). More importantly, the recusant camp believe that communal perception of the truth is possible. A visible Church is a sign of tradition or communal memory, more authoritative than any private interpretation of a text.

Solipsistic reading practices cause Protestant authors to further restrict the usefulness of images. For them, images should not be hung in places whose ethos would cause us to forget the element of fiction in the image and collate it with what we think is real. The two great ducts of lay instruction in the Anglican Church, the *Book of Homilies* and Nowell's catechism, emphasize that while images are not wrong in themselves, the context in which they are placed can make them so. They should not be displayed in churches, for instance. Margaret Aston has suggested that Protestant unease with images made catechism a peculiarly suitable form for Anglican devotion, since it used a schematic form of "self-examination . . . at the bar of the decalogue." She demonstrates how the revelation of the Scriptures, entailing pictures and events, is reduced to diagrams of relationships and laws in Thomas Rogers's Ramist presentation in *The English Creede* of 1585.[59] Protestant critics further note that images should not be used in devotion because their meaning can be exhausted. As Peter Martyr says,

> let the idiot or unlearned return as oft as he will unto a picture, it will alwaies tell one thing: and if any doubt happen unto him, while he beholdeth the same, it will never answer anie thing for resolving thereof.[60]

This Protestant fear is expressed as a suggestion that the emphasis on the visible is a determination to keep the laity ignorant. John Gee, speaking with someone who uses an image to help prayer, remarks that since one can never grasp what Christ was like it is foolish to use an image of him.[61]

Recusant authors have to admit that an overfamiliar image does degenerate into an organizing device for new material provided by the reader, when he dwells on the mysteries of faith. However, confident that they can provide sufficient annotation for the correct reading to take place, the hagiographies and catechisms carry on using images. In the illustration of the tenth commandment on the following page, while hell's goods are sensual representations of a female devil's gold and wine, heaven's goods are represented only by a verbal symbol hovering above. The *Christian Directorie* points out that the Scriptures were preceded by the visual examples of Christ's actions:

> for that his divine wisdome did easily foresee, that deedes have much more force to persuade then wordes, he did set forth this doctrine most exactly in the example of his owne life.[62]

One of the things for which Persons praised his lay helper, George Gilbert, was financing the paintings of the figures of new martyrs, on the walls of the church of the English College at Rome.[63] These were copied in the hagiographes such as the *Theatrum crudelitatum haereticorum nostri temporis* of 1582, and overshadow the texts in a reader's mind, partly accounting for the popularity overseas of these works.

I have suggested that saints' lives act as examples. They "prove" that the faith is true, by being the constituents of inartificial proof, witnesses of good ethos, and physical indications of God's power. Hagiographies act as examples to make an apprehension of the faith clearer and more impressive, in static rather than dramatic fashion. Hagiography has been divided from demonstrative rhetoric in purpose; both have designs on the reader, but recusant hagiography has no need to conceal its relationship to deliberative rhetoric. Finally, the link between image and communication in the texts has been asserted, beyond the sensual aspect.

In the *Directorie* Persons links the two genres of catechism and hagiography by a eulogy on martyrs who have lived out his recommendations, entitled "Examples of True Resolution." The next chapter will look at this fashioning of a saint, by recusant catechisms.

"Thou shalt not covet thy neighbour's goods." D3 r in Robert Bellarmine, *A Shorte Catechisme . . . with the Images,* translated 1614. (Reproduced with the permission of the Bodleian Library, Oxford.)

7

Catechisms: Auditing the Self

Using the example given by recusant hagiographies, the catechisms teach the skill of spiritual self-formation. They provide a dramatic script, which ends by being absorbed through the pressure of repetition; memory is, once again, important in moral formation. An active reading process is entailed by such self-definition, which is characterized by the texts as a female technique, and which is exemplified by the figures of the meditations.

DESCRIBING THE SELF

A Memoriall of a Christian Life echos sixteenth-century courtesy manuals:

> some there have bene, which beinge affectionated unto the bewtie of eloquence have emploied themselves to frame a perfit orator, takinge him from his childehode, and leadinge him through all the steppes and degrees of that facultie, until they have brought him unto the highest perfection of the same. Others have endeavored after the like sorte to forme a perfecte prince, others a capitaine, others a courtier. . . .
>
> Nowe of this are we right well assured, that emonge all the thinges of this world, there is nothing of greater price and estimation, nothinge more excellente & divine, than a perfecte Christian.[1]

In the recusant catechisms, there are no belittling, Romantic ideas about the innate genius of man which cannot be controlled or produced. The authors write as though each reader fashions himself, building up a spiritual body by devotional exercises. Such dealing is within the reach of every member of the laity. The reader is not elected, his desire to pray is sufficient; he does not need special ability, the manuals give him all the technical knowledge needed.

Crisp self-definition enlivens these catechisms—they ask you who is God, who are you, who do you want to be—and then tell you, in

123

a disconcertingly simple way, how to be it (a "Breefe Methode or Way Teaching all sortes of Christian people, how to serve God in a moste perfect manner" or a "Memoriall of a Christian life, wherein are treated all such thinges, as apperteyne unto a Christian to doe, from the beginninge of his conversion, until the ende of his perfection").

Put into the reading situation as a learner, the reader becomes the rules which he learns: the catechisms are a means of processing him as he works through the text. Richard Lanham describes such reshaping by self-description as

> the center of a nominalist view of rhetoric, a new definition of persuasion. One thinks of it as changing the opponent's mind. This is hard to do; this is the philosopher's way. Far easier—here sophist and Madison Avenue are one—to change his self. To redefine him so that he will do what you like, spontaneously, hypnotically, by desire.[2]

The change occurs by the way something is said: the subject of the text becomes an occasion to allow the form to do its work on the real subject, the reader. Quintilian insists that such invention is not dependent on divine afflatus but on human effort:

> so long as we do not lie back with eyes turned up to the ceiling, trying to fire our imagination by muttering to ourselves . . . but turn our thoughts to consider what the circumstances of the case demand, what suits the characters involved, what is the nature of the occasion and the temper of the judge.[3]

Lanham goes on to say that a self created by this rhetorical "taxonomy of impersonation" would not be

> naive and bubbly. Rhetorical man is an actor; his reality public, dramatic. . . . From birth, almost, he has dwelt not in a single value-structure but in several. . . . He makes an unlikely zealot.[4]

This cannot be true for fundamentalist literature, seeking to impose its own reality on the reader. The role of the Catholic created by the catechism is as real and strong as the actor himself, because the part has been divinely appointed. Auerbach defines such religious literature, and in particular, the Scriptures, as

> far from seeking . . . merely to make us forget our own reality for a few hours, it seeks to overcome our reality: we are to fit our own life into its world, feel ourselves to be elements in its structure of universal history.[5]

Paradoxically, by stepping out of his own reality and into one constructed by the Church, the reader receives an access of assurance and stability, not of relativism.

By insisting that people act in a certain way, catechisms force a change of self. As Southwell says, "outward signes do feed the inward distemper." Thus for Southwell, the chief rule in conversation is "alwaies to forsee and provid my selfe against the occasions, that by every company are likely to be offered me." He manufactures a correct demeanour before he enters society: "in countenance, I must avoide an unstayed kind of variety and often change; keeping as neere as I may one setled tenour therof," "my speach ought not to be so much, as to make me be noted for talkative," "I must also take heed of affected speach, and impertinent ceremonies," apparel "must be handsome & cleane, & as much as may be, without singularity."[6]

The concept of a role more dependable and correct than the self may explain why meditations like Estella's *Contempte of the World,* Scupoli's *Spiritual Conflict,* and Garnet's *Christian Renunciation* prepare the reader to become a martyr by urging self-renunciation first. Garnet's "rooted hatred even to [one's] own life and soul" helps fulfil "the necessary obligation to suffer martyrdom when otherwise God might be offended." Scupoli says the reader 'aspiring to the top of so great perfection, must use force with thy selfe, and couragiously overcome thy owne will."[7] The recusant notion of self appears in flight from itself. Exclaiming that "sinnes-selfe I am growne," I.C.'s Magdalen is owlish in her desire for solitude, as she passes through streets where women "monster-like me to their children show." As the *Manual of Prayers* ruminates,

I have lost thee, & also my selfe by inordinate love that I have had to my selfe, and [only] in seking of thee againe, I have found bothe thee & mee.[8]

In many of Southwell's poems, people abuse traditional gendered identities, such as the virtues of male courage or female chastity. The sequence of poems on Peter starts by demanding: "how can I live, that have my life deny'de?" while the longer "Saint Peters Complaint" enjoins Peter to "Flie not from forreine evils, flie from thy hart," since it has yielded not only to fear but also to feminine garrulity, "a maidens easie breath."[9] Similarly, Granada wonders if he has

defaced so much as laie in me al the holie misterie of thy Incarnation? Thou hast made thy selfe man to make me a God: and I (lovinge myne owne vilenes) have made my selfe a beaste, & the sonne of Satan.[10]

Thus, the merit of a good action comes from its degree of strangeness or pain. This, says *Breefe Collection*, is why God takes greater delight in our service than that of the angels:

> because man doth not only serve God of love as the Angels doe: but also with laboure & paine, which they doe not.[11]

Such "labour and paine" completes nature. Authors sketch a virtuous mirror image of the reader's present spiritual state; he is urged to practise those virtues directly contrary to temptations he suffers.[12] Just as the hagiographies use images and deny sensuousness, the catechisms urge introspection and destroy the self.

Stanley Fish finds a similar paradox in Protestant seventeenth-century literature. The artist, producing work centred on self-awareness, is set against the religious personality, which struggles to put God at its center. Fish shows George Herbert's recognition that taking an individual moral stance is presumptuous, as he undoes the self and even its literary products. An endless regression is set up, as the moral self creates itself by fleeing from itself.[13] However, Fish's views are only valid where a desire for virtue is the result, not the cause, of salvation. There is no such thing as the presumption of a moral stance in recusant catechisms. Suspicion of effort and intent would seem reasonable from a Protestant's point of view, but redundant from that of a Catholic. Since cooperation with grace is possible, recusant hagiographies can openly show their subjects' efforts, and be equally unreserved about exhorting the reader to emulate them.

Texts balance the drama of self-creation with a recognition that error occurs in all of man's work. The Catholic catechisms refuse to allow the claim that the conscience was all-powerful. T. H. Clancy has suggested that, in *A Brief Discours contayning certayne Reasons Why Catholiques refuse to goe to Church* of 1580, Persons showed himself to be the first English recusant writer to support the supremacy of the individual conscience. However, this ignores the fact that Persons only talks about a well-regulated conscience, one which obeys the commandments of the Church.[14] His exceedingly mild side-note, that "Actes of religion [are] not to be enforced," is followed by the brisk 'Heretiques maye be enforced."[15]

Categorical thinking affects the meditations, where amplification inventories rather than explores material. In the catechisms, it seems that a conscientious reader has only to learn the given answers and there will be no aspect of faith which will be beyond him. This is reassuring, but problematic. It is graceless to brood on plans for self-perfection; emphasis on the will can mean the subject is closed to outside experience. A false belief that a boundary to every subject is in sight is encouraged. As Augustine found out,

> thinking that absolutely everything that exists is comprehended under the ten categories, I tried to conceive you also, my God, wonderfully simple and immutable, as if you too were a subject of which magnitude and beauty are attributes

—and failed.[16] In the interest of naming all parts of a subject the hierarchical ordering necessary for comprehension can be lost, since all areas of knowledge are given equal value.

Despite such reservations, no recusant text believes it is impractical to try to invent yourself. This is implicit in the confidence of the very first sentence of Loarte's *Exercise:*

> what thing he ought first of al to doe, that purposeth to beginne a newe life, and to spende his time henceforth sincerely in Gods service.[17]

Despite Trent's statement in Session 6, that grace can work without help, Jesuit theologians continued to debate the Molinist belief that human effort was essential, and therefore possible, to render grace efficacious. Discussion between them and Dominicans supporting Trent continued until 1607, when papal decree suspended further writing on the topic (rather than settling the dispute). English catechisms take the hopeful, Jesuit line.

A craft, not an inspiration, is how Alphonso de Madrid's popular *Breefe Methode,* sees the pursuit of salvation. The translator starts briskly: "Sainct *Ambrose* saith, that ignorance of the order & manner how to woorke, greatly troubleth the qualitie of our meritt." He dismisses the fathers and turns to Aristotle for support: "the Philosopher in his Metaphysicks affirmeth, that mankinde livethe by arte: in which place he semeth by this propertie to distinguish man from unreasonable creatures."[18] Eschewing an apocalyptic conversion experience initiated from outside, catechisms use the image of steps to perfection. The *Nine Rockes To Be Avoided, of those which Sayle towards the Port of Perfection* explains that this step arrangement of its material is primarily to aid the memory. The effect of navigating one-by-one past the rocks of vainglory, sensuality, or self-love gives a do-it-yourself aspect to this manual. Martz saw one element of the popularity of meditations in the period being that they cultivate the "basic, the lower levels of the spiritual life . . . not, properly speaking, a mystical activity, but a part of the duties of everyman in daily life."[19] E. Allison Peers also concludes that *Of Prayer* is concerned "with the ordinary, rather than the exceptional Christian, its emphasis on method, and its use of the imagination."[20]

Spontaneous devotion is set aside in favor of a sound business plan and shrewd commercial sense. Estella thinks it profitable to "suffer a little for godssake, and thereby to lyve after in happines for ever."

> He is a foole that passeth many a day in payne, & many a night without rest, throughe the continuall payne of his teeth rather then he will abide a shorte payne in the taking out of the rotten tooth that greeveth him.[21]

Garnet sets up scales: Christ, "for one brittle and transitory life, either despised or lost for his name, will repay an eternall and most happy immortality."[22] J. A. Moore noticed the same trope in Granada's *Of Prayer*:

> scientific principles of measurement caused him to weigh sins and to suggest that their atonement could also be weighed.[23]

Persons believes that the peculiar evil of mortal sin is deliberately weighing God against pleasure.[24] The texts' harsh treatment of martyrdom as plain duty is commercial: to suffer martyrdom is to recompense Christ. Trading metaphors were used by the missioners about their own work. Southwell, for instance, asks Persons if he can unload any of "his wares"—the faith—at Southwell's family home.[25] Bossy characterizes the situation of a missioner as

> a "merchant" doing "business" with "customers", a commercial traveller for an old-established firm offering to the householder, in competition with new and vigorous rivals, a commodity for whose consumption there was a limited demand.[26]

Prayer seems less like rhapsody before the Paraclete, and more like a business meeting with the boss, considering beforehand who the reader is to meet, what he should say, what aim for, what give up. Southwell reminds himself to "always enter upon prayer as being about to treat of some entirely new affair with Almighty God."[27] Indeed, L. B. Wright argues that

> since the attainment of worldly success was closely linked in middle-class thinking with the virtues which also lead to a comfortable assurance of heaven,

such trading ethics permeated every area of behavior literature.[28] This reverses the position which the reader was in when he meditated, now a merchant in control, not a debtor in trouble.

When the catechisms fashion a saint, it is a grand occasion for self-control. Southwell grimly urges the reader to

> perswade him selfe, that when he hath setled his mind seriously to follow this buisnes, hell it selfe and all the enemies of God and mans soule will conspire against him.[29]

Granada gives a sense of gathering forces.

> He then that ernestlie, and with al his hart desireth to take in hand this so greate an enterprise (in comparison of which, al that is under heaven, is to be esteemed as nothing) the summe of al that he ought to doe, consisteth in one onlie thing, to wit, that a man haue in his mind a most stedfast, and determinate purpose, never to commit anie mortal sinne.

He collapses into flabbergasted erotesis over what can be gained or lost.

> Is there any witte or Iudgement in this worlde? Have men their right senses? Doe they understande what theise wordes do importe? Or are they peradventure persuaded that theise are onlie fables of Poetes?[30]

Most hagiographies also agree with Southwell when he exalts the sufferings of the recusants by a comparison with the "intollerable torments" of the early Church martyrs. (Typically, it is only Persons who is less enthusiastic: their torments were "farre exceeding any that [God] layeth upon us in these later times, though we complayne much more then they did"!)[31]

The heroic was encouraged even among missionary students, each living the drama of a potential martyr. Persons describes the English College at Valladolid. The students come over

> with that determinacion, to stand and dy in the Catholique cause, & this in such sorte as they seeme to have nothing in their myndes from the first hower of their vocation and resolution, unto the tyme they retourne home againe for execution of the same, but the Imprisonments, tortures, and martyrdomes of Ingland.[32]

His view is confirmed by Anthony Munday's description of the meals at the English Roman College in 1579, accompanied by readings from Church hagiographies, expanded to include saints martyred in England in the 1570s.[33] English students at the college at Rome were admitted on condition that they swore to promote the mission, and searched their consciences over whether they could withstand torture.

College plays were written about past and present martyrs, and students became accustomed to acting these roles.

Using Stephen Greenblatt's term, how does Catholic *self-fashioning* work? Martz concludes his study of sixteenth-century meditations by discussing imagination and self-discipline in morality. He sees active virtue as theatrical and consciously dramatic, not the passive acceptance of a moral code.[34] The reader of meditations, hagiographies, and catechisms pulls himself into the parts provided by their scripts so that there need be less reliance on the untutored conscience.

In her study of Protestant casuistry, Margaret Slights touches on Continental Catholic casuist manuals of the period. She sees sixteenth-century Protestants criticizing these manuals for concentrating on action rather than on the moral quality of the man acting, and for moving between God and his people. She concurs with this view; the manuals were merely "a complicated system of ratiocination designed to show men how to avoid their clear moral duties."[35] However, her judgment misses the creative aspect of the actions in these rules of life: they recognize a symbiosis between a subject and his actions. Gestures or acts change the nature of the person performing them; they are meaningful and not merely done, as Martz suggested of the morally strenuous culture of Protestantism, to preserve the sanity of the elect. There are no morally neutral moments in the catechisms' scheme of life. Granada emphasizes that it is not enough

> for a penitent sinner to Confesse to his Ghostlie Father in a generall sorte, that he is a sinner: but he must also Confesse unto him all his deadlie sinnes in particular wise.[36]

Southwell convinces himself that

> if there be one single houre in which I neither do nor suffer anything for the love of God, I am not leading the life of a true religious.[37]

His *Spiritual Exercises,* noted by him before joining the mission, make frequent reference to formal, diagramed decisions to become a Jesuit, or continue his novitiate, or offer himself for the mission.

This is why catechisms are rhetorically problematic, deductive, and abstract, moving inflexibly downward from theory to experience. Rules reverse the order of experience, in being expository summaries rather than participatory experiences. Catechisms are the Ramist handbooks of faith, which cannot be adapted to the time or the audience. What more hostile a situation for persuasive rhetoric could there be? And yet, Catholic catechisms do see rules as productive. In them, the analytical element becomes a trellis frame to encourage and organize experience. They contain fossilized situations, little dramas to be played out in real life. They ask the reader to consider what he should do when confronted by a sacrament or a heresy or a temptation.

The essence of understanding the rhetoric of the catechisms lies in seeing that, as rules, they point toward their embodiment: the examples of true resolution, published, as Gennings says, to "stirre us up to imitate them."[38] The subject of demonstrative rhetoric is in the past, but it operates in the present, arousing admiration then emulation. The publisher of Southwell's *Short Rule* advises the reader to

> fashion thy life & manners according to these devout rules which are a most perfecte mirror of his godly life and in so doing thou maist happely attaine thy selfe also to the like crowne of glory.[39]

They are the dynamic examples of Peter Martyr: "we should imitate and use them . . . allow and commend those things which we perceive have beene doone by excellent men."[40] Catechisms' links with hagiography make them creative signs, and not just references to a divine reality. They are instructions on how to imitate the good, more than abstracts on how the good have behaved.

So the genre of catechism is the rhetorical thesis of hagiography's hypothesis. If the life of a saint exemplified divinity in one man, catechisms are useful as external consciences, "case divinity," or eternal principles extrapolated from and then applied to human situations. Thus, the Ignatian *Exercises* reify the conscience in this way, encouraging the exercitant to map out the sins of the day, with rows of dots for each occurrence of sin. As Fraunce says,

> Art, which first was but the scholler of nature, is now become the maystres of nature, and as it were a Glasse wherein she . . . may washe out those spottes and blemishes of naturall imperfection.[41]

As with catechism and hagiography, Renaissance educators split into groups advocating a system of learning by analysis and subsequent synthesis, and those supporting absorption of the classics by imitation. Some, like Ascham, prescribed imitation of the great authors through close reading, tanning by walking in the sunshine of their style. Imitation, "a faculty to express lively and perfectly that example which ye go about to follow," is natural, since "all the works of nature in a manner be examples for art to follow."[42] Ascham uses Aristotlian theory, where imitation is natural to man from childhood.[43] The second group followed Ramus in requiring examination of the general principles exemplified by a text, before a close reading.

Both these groups share aims: both require the learner to analyze passages from the writer to be imitated, before synthesizing the passages' rules of grammar and style by writing himself. Moreover, both feel that

> the imitator ought to study not only his Latinity but his resources of wisdom and factual knowledge, and most of all his virtues of conduct and character.[44]

This view, from Gabriel Harvey's Cambridge lectures commending Ramus, accords perfectly with Ascham's. The reader reproduces not just Cicero's prose but also his abilities, from education and experience. For both Ramist and Aristotelian, imitation can be expounded in treatises on literary education, but is about reproducing the persons of the classical authors, not their works. In such mimesis, the external is made internal, a reversal of the Romantic position. It is a serious miming, which depends on a reader's participation to enact what he reads. It is in this context, as Farrell noted, that Jesuit schools encouraged the emulation of other pupils as a fruitful method of learning by being.[45]

Close imitation actually creates a likeness to the example, since the element of theatricality in imitation dissolves under the pressure of repetition, removing the qualifier from Aristotle's statement "that which has become habitual becomes as it were natural. . . ."[46] The *Confessions* show Augustine wrestling with the idea of habit and self-creation. "The consequence of a distorted will is passion. By servitude to passion, habit is formed, and habit to which there is no resistance becomes necessity."[47] I.C.'s Magdalen exclaims that "from custome we another nature take," accusing herself of being "partner" in her own sin by repeating it.[48] Repetition or habit is as important to the catechisms as the rosary texts.

Habit depends on the memory's ability to absorb examples proposed by the imagination. The physical pictures of the meditations and hagiographies consolidate the intellectual to sensible things, and so strike the memory more poignantly. For instance, the hermit introducing Alphonso's pilgrim knight to the spiritual life sees sin take away the taste, not the ability, to act correctly. We overcome this distaste by mingling God's grace and "good habits of vertues which we may plant in our soules, by diligent exercise of our superior powers," that is, our understanding and will. These are exercised using imagination, suggesting that to will to will something requires a change in one's image of it.[49] The retention of images is not the only important moral feature of memory. Past actions are not just a record of men's actions, but of God's providence, and wisdom or experience "is no more than a masse of memories assembled."[50] In absorbing past experiences as though one's own, character is created. Learning, in this context, is vital.

GOOD READING HABITS

An ability to reuse what has been read distinguishes book from student. This was held to be important for there was a perceived danger that the reading material would overcome the reader. Meeting a text was an occasion; not something slipped into accidentally, as if the written word was all around. In *Palladis tamia* of 1598 Francis Meres anxiously warns that "as they that are wise do not forthwith drinke out of every fountaine . . . so it is not safe to read every booke" and "as it is safe to lie uppon the hearbe *Tryfolie*, because serpentes cannot abide to come neare it: so wee shoulde be conversant in those books, in which no infection is to be feared."[51] Over a quarter of Mere's similies for reading depict books as fearsome linguistic monsters, waiting to pounce on effeminate and unprepared readers.

To fight off these, a cannibalistic reading technique was encouraged by the notebook culture of sixteenth-century schools. As chapter 3 described, commonplace books were used as an integral part of the school day. The reader was to stand outside the text he was consuming, sufficiently distanced from its message to be able to gut it for gobbets to be digested into other texts he would write in the future. Such a process allowed the host text even less integrity than the endless system of intertextual reference sponsored by twentieth-century semiotics. The individual's own conceptual framework was imposed on any text he read.

This technique is demonstrated by the ease with which Catholic texts were cannibalized by Protestants. H. S. Bennett estimates that about half the production of licensed presses during this period was manuals of religious controversy. There were few Protestant meditations, and Bennett believes that recusant texts were recycled.[52] The recusant works may have a wider circulation and so a little more influence than critics have appreciated hitherto.

The truth of the first point is borne out by the triumph with which Catholic writers announce yet another book of meditations or rules for life. For instance, in *A True Report Of . . . John Nicols* Allen animadverts on those who burned the *Imitatio Christi* and Granada's *Of Prayer,* targeted because the Protestant religion had no such works of devotion. They burned books of contemplation, meditation and instruction of Christian life and manners, conteining no dispute of religion at al. . . . Assure your selves that they cannot abide such bookes of al others, knowing that devout praier onely, penaunce and amendement of life, will easily bring men from their pretended Religion. . . . Neither, if you marke well, shall you ever finde that the learned of the Protestants writ or treat of any such argument.

Persons's preface to the *Directorie* makes the same point.[53] Indeed, one of the most famous conversions in literature, Robert Greene, was bruited as due to the *Directorie*. In his *Repentance*, he describes how he took up the book when sick, and realized

the miserable state of the reprobate, what Hell was, what the worme of Conscience was, what tormentes there was appointed for the damned soules . . . that there was nothing but feare, horrour, vexation of mind.[54]

This is exactly, if sensationally, how Persons wanted the *Directorie* to be used; a confessional scene is induced by private reading.

Bennett's view is also corroborated by the anxiety of Protestant authors to repudiate suggestions of devotional poverty. Richard Rogers can only deny what

the Papists cast in our teeth, that we have nothing set out for the certaine and daily direction of a Christian, when yet they have published (they say) many treatises of that argument,

and say that devotional aspects of the Protestant texts exist, though scattered throughout catechisms.[55] Reviewing the state of religion, Edwin Sandys is uneasily aware that the Catholics

conceive to have so surpassed theyr opposites that they forbear not to reproach unto them theyr povertie, weaknesse, and coldnesse in that kind as being forced to take the Catholicks books to supply therein. Which . . . cannot be altogether denied to be true.[56]

Commenting on Rogers's unease, Barbara Lewalski lists a number of seventeenth-century meditation works. However, none of the authors are from Elizabeth's reign, so her assumption that "the polemical assertions of Parsons and others to the effect that contemporary Protestants borrowed Roman works because they could not produce their own be greeted with some scepticism" must itself be considered groundless, for the period before 1600.[57]

Not that this trade was one way: Catholics used licensed press productions, in spite of the danger to their souls which was pointed out in the preface to the Rheims New Testament. The controls over reading devotional texts were doubled by the Church for heretical texts. It was not always done with reprehensible curiosity. The first time Campion's letter to the Lords of the Council could be published was in the Protestant Meredith Hanmer's *Great Bragge and Challenge of M. Champion a Iesuite* in 1581.[58] Catholics must have been particularly grateful for William Fulke's 1589 refutation of the Rheims translation of the New Testament. *The Text of the New Testament . . . by the Papists . . . Whereunto is Added the Translation . . . Used in the Church of England* reprints the entire recusant translation, including annotations, in parallel with the Established Church version. The probate inventory of Stephen Vallenger, prosecuted for helping publish Alfield's *Campion*, shows that the closest Vallenger could get to acquiring works by his English Catholic contemporaries was the Bunny version of the *Directorie* and Fulke's New Testament.[59] Peter Milward describes the complaint of the publisher of the third edition of Thomas Cooper's attack on the mass, of 1562. Cooper was answering an anonymous defense of the institution, and had injudiciously included a copy of the treatise in his own work. Recusants, sniffed the publisher, were buying up the edition, tearing out Cooper's pages, and keeping the Catholic defense of the mass![60]

Such trade between the texts was possible because the new men of the Counter-Reformation, such as Persons, Campion, and Martin, had extensive links with Protestantism before becoming Catholic. As Bossy notes, they shared a frame of reference with their adversaries.[61] Peristrophe, a figure which repeats but changes an opponent's arguments, is the tropical equivalent of the cannibalism of reading matter. Its use ranges from Munday's skit on hagiographical verses at the end of Alfield's *Campion*, to the concordance-style, line-on-line answer which Southwell gives to the 1591 Proclamation in *An Humble Supplication*. Persons tabulates ways fact can be manipulated, analyzing Hastings's replies in the *Warn-word*'s "Third Table of Certaine Notorious Shifts, Slieghtes, Deceits and impostures." Heretics pass over major points in silence, answering only the easy ones. If a point cannot be ignored, a general answer is given, before Hastings passes on as though it was a full answer. When convicted of error, heretics simply accuse Catholics of the same fault. Reasons of state are alleged to explain why no proofs are given. Catholic texts are misquoted, and other authorities are either without exact references or are selectively applied to twist the sense. Irrelevant matters are discussed and internal contradictions in the argument ignored. And finally, of course, Persons accuses heretics of plain lying.[62]

Persons adds two further accusations, when commenting in the preface to the *Directorie* on Bunny's changes. Bunny "maketh many divisions and subdivisions, every thing running therin by couples, wherin he is so fertile and abundant, as by methode he confoundeth al memorie" (possibly a reference to Ramist methods of dividing a subject). Moreover, Bunny adds parentheses to change the meaning of the *Directorie*, giving them credence by stuffing the margin with the names of authors (something Persons does himself in the Catholic side of the calendar of *Conversions*).[63] When the *Directorie* describes the false proof of the heretics, it uses the parts of rhetoric. Protestant doctrine is changeable, for it is "in the invention, iudgment, and memorye of the sectarye himselfe."[64]

The Bunny-Persons controversy has been described by White, Bennett, Southern, and Janelle. Put briefly, in 1582 Persons extended Loarte's *Exercise of a Christian Life* into *The First Booke of the Christian Exercise, appertayning to resolution*, appealing to those who had not yet elected to lead a Christian life. This work was popular, and in 1584, Edmund Bunny, the vicar of Bolton Percy, produced a Protestant version, *Perused, and accompanied now with a Treatise tending to Pacification*. Bunny had "taken the pains, both to purge it of certain points that carried either some manifest error, or else some other inconvenience with them." He compares it to other texts, such as the *Imitatio Christi*, which Protestant divines had purified from traces of Catholicism, "leaving out the corruption of it, and taking onlie that which was sound." Persons responded angrily in his 1585 revision: "he maketh me speake after the phrase of Protestants," and again, "M. Buny maketh me to speake like a good minister of England." Catholic and Protestant versions continued to be produced into the following reign. Bunny confined his reply to a contemptuous pamphlet, the *Briefe Answer, unto those idle and frivolous quarrels of R.P. against the late edition of the Resolution* of 1589, which claimed that he had indeed made the *Directorie* safe for reading.[65]

Bunny explains his three types of alteration: replacing Catholic theological terms with their scriptural equivalents; removing authorities which Persons has quoted, where Bunny thinks they add nothing to the argument, and simply changing points which do not agree with the truth. He uses the term *purged*, which Persons takes up indignantly, as purging the author from the text. The reader, Bunny, claims responsibilty for the meaning, while Persons believes that the meaning lies in the author's intentions. Bunny says he restored a fallen text, finding "the paradise within."[66] They struggle over possession of meaning, a debate paralleled by that over the vernacular translation of the Bible. In relation to the habit of notebook or extrapolatory reading, the irrelevancy of context and author has been cleansed from the text.

Bunny was not alone in recognizing the market potential of Catholic texts. Richard Loomis has analyzed the 1620 Barrett version of Southwell's *Short Rule,* printed by a licensed press, showing how explicitly Catholic elements were removed.[67] There are numerous adaptations, frequently reprinted, made by Francis Meres and Thomas Lodge of Luis de Granada's work: *The flowers of Lodowicke of Granado, Granados devotion, The conversion of a sinner, Of Prayer, The sinners guyde, Granados spirituall and heavenlie exercises.* There is room for study of the symbiosis between these Catholic and Protestant works.

Against such an aggressive reading technique, imposing its own cognitive architecture on texts read, recusant authors commend a quite different active reading habit. A reader must be humbly submissive in approaching devotional texts. He is to be silent and obedient to the text's meaning. Perhaps "she" would be more appropriate, since the listening figure inside each meditation is most often female, and the reader is expected to model his reception on hers. Lyrical writers in Guiney's *Recusant Poets* give female models of reception, like Constable's "let my soule mayd chaste, passe for a Mayde" or "lyke a woman spowse my sowle shalbee . . . betrothed to goddes sonne above."[68]

The chapter on meditations described how authors kept refocusing on the passive characters in the scene; lay members, readers, are expected to watch but not to pray. Like a meek wallflower, readers wait to be picked up by the text's eloquence or subject. The texts' reference points are used by the reader rather than him furnishing his own: the decalogue and the theological virtues. Texts recommend this reading technique for everyone, not just for women. Dedications of the works are obviously rare and do not say much about their intended audience. However, the conventual withdrawal into booklined 'cells' was necessary for all recusants, even though in a secular context these reading circumstances were confined to women. Where the recusant read, just as much as how, parallels the Renaissance female reading experience.

This is exemplified in hagiography, where the martyr constantly brings himself into line with a religious text, composing himself as a devotional work on how a saint acts. Descriptions of martyrdom are careful to show this as the climax of a virtuous life. Hagiographies are arts of holy living, not dying, which, although concentrating on the moment of execution, imply a previous course of self-martyrdom. Thus, Southwell's printer sees martyrs first to have killed their passions, before they be killed by persecutours; first to have bene exercised in a spirituall conflicte of mortification, before they be tried in the fornace of Christian Confession; first to have become their own butchers, before they be delivered to the hangmans shambles.[69]

Since the martyrdom is of self-will, actual death is unnecessary to illuminate the life. C.N. praises John the Beloved for standing at the foot of the Cross to suffer with Christ, "a Martyr in life, in minde, in will, but not in death." Although nothing actually harms Verstegan's Tecla,

> Yet shee a martyr is estem'd,
> That martred was in mynde.[70]

Facts are not given to be judged on by the reader. William Allen is sceptical of private interpretation, quoting what Lawrence Caddy said at his recantation:

> it was the property of al hereticks to abuse, wrest and wring [Scriptures], to whatsoever themselves list, and particularly to the private sence of every secte maistèr, ech one for his owne erronious doctrine and the condemnation of his fellowes.[71]

This was not a peculiarly British concern: the Council of Trent's fourteenth and eighteenth sessions dealt with "petulant spirits" who wrested the canon of Scripture their own way, evidenced by the *Index librorum prohibitorum* of 1557. The first three of Campion's *Rationes decem,* on remaining Catholic, center on the ill-judged reading techniques of sectaries who concentrate on private interpretation. At his trial, Alfield says he is condemned because jurors are refusing to read the words of Allen's *True Sincere and Modest Defence of English Catholiques* in context.[72] The writers trust words, and link signs to their public rather than private exposition.

That recusant authors acknowledge a "common word," communication dependent on another's understanding, is evident when they discuss the position of church-papists. For Garnet, going to an heretical church is amoral in itself but must be regarded as immoral, because Protestants see it as a gesture signifying consent to the Church of England. "That is the meaning of wordes and signes and actions, which either their own nature or the common use of men hath imposed, not that which your selfe would intend."[73] Persons repeats this, in *Reasons Why Catholiques refuse to goe to Church:* "goynge or not goeyng to the Church, is made a signe now in England distinctive, betwyxt . . . a Catholicke, and a Schismatyke." Moreover, "what doth make a thing to be a proper and peculier signel but the iudgment and opinion of men?"[74] Even while defending equivocation at his trial, Southwell accepted Lord Justice Popham's concept of communication: "we are men, and no Gods, and cane iudge but accordinge to theire outward actiones and speeches, and not accordinge to there secrette and inward intentiones."[75]

Against this is a need to justify equivocation, to save a large enough body of Catholics to be a viable Church group. Put bluntly, a greater spiritual gain could come from powerful Catholics or priests being kept alive through equivocation, than in them bearing witness to the faith by their death. The doctrine of equivocation developed "wayes how to conceal a trewth without makinge of a lye," according to Garnet's treatise on it.[76] Mental reservations were not sinful if a "reasonable" man would remain undeceived by them, regardless of what he actually understood. Equivocation splits statements into four types: propositions can be made mentally, vocally, physically, or by a mixture of the three, allowing modification of outright statements. For instance, Southwell told Anne Bellamy, who later betrayed his hiding place to pursuivants, that "yf uppon her othe, shee were asked whether she hade seene a Priste or not, she might lawfully say not, though she had seen one, keepinge this meaning in her mynd, that she did not see any, with intent to bewray him."[77] The conditions imposed before it was necessary to ensure that the other party understood the speaker were onerous. He had to be a lawful superior, with authority over the speaker and in the subject being examined; he had to proceed according to a just law and could only expect an unequivocable answer if the matter was important. The impossibility of an exchange of meaning when equivocation is allowed was emphasized by the nervous reiterations of the 1606 Oath of Alleigance:

> these things I do plainly and sincerely acknowledge and swear, according to these express words by me spoken, and according to the plain and common sense and understanding of the same words, without any equivocation, or . . . secret reservation whatsoever.[78]

This theory of communication parallels that of the Family of Love, to whom Persons gave the same degree of prominence as papists in *A Brief Discours contayning certayne Reasons Why Catholiques refuse to goe to Church*.[79] Enabled by doctrine (not just necessity) to assign their own meanings to church ritual, they transcended not only questions of discipline but also of theology. Janet Halley suggests that "the conditions of meaning are themselves a terrain of political struggle," in the identity of the members of this sect. She sees church-papists as another group who assigned their own meaning to public statements.[80]

There is a contradiction between the way recusant authors talk about equivocation, and their belief that the public aspect of communication outweighs the private, when advising readers not to attend schismatic services. This is resolved by recognizing that the audience which recusant texts have in mind is divine rather than human. "Neyther skylleth it that the partye to whom I speake understandeth not that which I reserve . . . for at the least God understandeth the speech of the mynde," says Garnet.[81] Propositions are completed, and therefore made true or false, by God, so that real-time, actual communication with persons around the speaker, is secondary. What is actually said to them takes second place to why it is said and to whom.

Since, as Martin says of the New Testament,

> all take not the holy Scripture in one and the same sense, because of the deepenes thereof . . . there may almost as many senses be picked out of it, as there be men,

the Church enforces interpretative submission.[82] The chapters on meditation showed how the reader's gaze is controlled, reducing the multivalent text to one. This chapter has also shown how the values of recusant texts are taken on by the reader, who is told how to approach the texts. Granada's *Memoriall* enjoins the reader to avoid "sleightie or negligent careles running over of books, without dewe weyghinge of the same." In fact, for Granada, catechetical reading is exactly like meditation, "except that Meditation doth staie it selfe somewhat more in things."[83] Persons says that "it must not be donne in hast, nor (as the fashion is) for curiositie onlie, to reade three or fower leaves in one place, & so in an other."[84] On holy days, says Southwell,

> in steed of my worke I must bestowe those daies in reading good bookes, hearing sermons, and such like godly exercises, not lightly runing over them, thinking it enough to have red or heard good things, but pawsing upon such thinges as move my affection, & printing them well in my mind & memory.[85]

This is a generous reading, where the reader allows himnself to be absorbed by the subject. Its very generosity may have caused the *Ratio studiorum* to impose stringent safeguards on the use of drama in Jesuit schools. As W. H. McCabe has shown, drama was valued for animating language learning, for providing good publicity for the schools, and for imparting some moral instruction. Yet the Jesuits felt that the latter depended on suitable parts: all plays were to exclude female roles and concentrate wholly on edifying themes.[86] The order credited drama with great power to change the players, who might not be able to separate the text from themselves.

In conclusion, this chapter has followed the fashioning of a saint by using the rules of catechisms. Categories of experience are imposed on, not formed from, the texts read. The reader is not wholly dependent on an outside initiative to change himself: at first, he flies from himself, then on razed foundations he uses actions and rules to outline a desired character. This scaffolding eventually gets built-in permanently, impressing the memory by repetition. Finally, the mode of reading which produces this absorption is described by the texts in terms of female reading techniques and is generous, valuing the text more than the reader.

8

Conclusion

This study started by asking if it was possible to divine a recusant theory of rhetoric, from the practice of Catholic secret-press authors of the late sixteenth century. Could they reconcile the recusant wish to restrain a reader's freedom to interpret a work, and the rhetor's need to see his text from an audience's point of view?

The first chapter on meditations looked at them as self-persuasive orations, where deliberative rhetoric is used by the meditator to sway his own will. Material for meditations is presented for absorption and not for questioning, it is organized in terms of time spent in prayer. The chapter following this explored the way in which texts find such material. Rhetorical amplification and memory techniques are used to allow the meditator's mind to center on the subject for long enough to assimilate it. The chapters on hagiographies pointed out that this deliberative rhetoric is supported by topics from epideictic theory, so that hagiographies provide examples of true resolution for the meditator to aim at. These saints' lives describe what a life should be, not what is, so are dependent on a formal manipulation of ethos. This formalism means that the images of these saints are not presented as sensual but as communicative, needing to be interpreted. The final chapter showed how these images can be created in the reader, using the dramatic scripts of the catechisms. Such self-formation comes by absorbing the texts through a submissive reading technique—and so the argument comes full circle, back to the meditations.

All three genres believe that communication with God and with other men is possible. The effort of prayer must come from man; when he is silent, he is lazy. Meditation authors believe they speak to God without the Protestant worry over presumption, because the human voice was created for praise. Nor do they see problems in speaking to man: church-papists are excoriated partly because they scandalize recusants, but mainly because they give a sign of consent to the Established Church, a sign understood by Protestants. However, this confidence that meaning can be exchanged with man does not suggest that it is. The doctrine of equivocation warns that the main recipient of discourse is God.

The texts see God's communication with man, through themselves, as more valuable than the reader's comprehension of their message. Works like the Rheims New Testament censor the reader, for instance, by not translating crucial scriptural texts, lest they breed error. The text being disseminated is seen as a script for the reader. The reader absorbs this hierarchy of God-over-text-over-reader, to recreate the work in himself. Catechisms give him a dramatic script which he is to use as an exoskeleton, taking on its points of reference for his own. As the meditations showed, this is not difficult to do in prayer. The reader flees from himself, constructing instead a self modeled on the saints and on the rules of the catechisms. Repetition habituates him to his new role, and such actions become less theatrical.

Recusant devotional texts are not confined to those in print; the world is seen as a supplementary preacher. There are many examples of this: images of saints are not tasted but interpreted; martyrs become texts; relics are not just bones but proofs of the constancy of the saints; pilgrimages are made in the mind; people remind one of virtues, small daily household acts of prayers. Far from being idolatrously literal in their interpretation of this world, as their Protestant critics exclaim, Catholic writers constantly urge readers to relate creation to its origin.

As I examined certain techniques of rhetoric—*inventio, memoria, amplificatio,* the use of examples to prove and to clarify—these themes about recusant rhetoric became apparent in each of the three devotional genres. However, perhaps I could reverse this briefly, and ask if rhetoric has helped to create, not just express, these ideas about communication. In other words, is recusant rhetoric merely decorative rhetoric; where recusant authors seem to delight

> in following the rhetorical rules of the Ancients . . . it was always interesting . . . to see how many figures [they] could use in elaborating a single fact,

or is a rhetorical frame of mind fundamental to the texts' aims?[1]

Each devotional practice has centered on the writer knowing his audience, what he spoke about and how he presented himself in speaking. He has considered his speaker, subject and audience as suggested by the *ad Herennium* and the *Institutio oratoria.* However, what the Catholic speaks about is fixed; the materials of his faith are true commonplaces. Moreover, the Church has limited his expository freedom toward these materials. Only one thing is flexible—the reader—so Catholic devotional works aim at altering him. They urge him to use rhetoric on himself, engrossing the text so thoroughly, it becomes the way he lives. The reader persuades himself to the good.

This suggestion moves recusant rhetoric far from the bleats of critics who see it as emasculating strong prose, and even, religious fervor. The rhetoric in recusant texts does not gild the wearisome duties of devotion, it acts like trelliswork to support the growth of a regenerating character. Any reader can provide for his own salvation; he need not wait for election. Believing that the individual can craft his own character, grubbing for souls without principle, on principle, these Catholic texts see rhetoric as irresistibly attractive.

Appendix:
The Rhetorical Education of Recusant Writers

The introduction suggested that the self-conscious use of rhetoric in Catholic texts was to be expected, given the education which the writers received. This appendix shows where the authors were educated, and what rhetorical manuals they were likely to have used. I have confirmed or corrected information in J. Gillow's *Bibliographical . . . Dictionary of the English Catholics* of 1885–1902, by consulting G. Anstruther's dictionary of secular priests, a recent monograph by D. Bellenger giving the place of ecclesiastical training of the missionary priests, and lists of alumni from Oxford and Cambridge.[1] Only place of education up to the point at which it is likely that rhetoric would have been learned has been noted. Included are all writers directly connected with the mission, divided between authors who produced original texts, and compilers or translators.

WRITERS

Thomas Alfield (secular priest): Eton. King's, Cambridge (1568). B.A. (1572), age 20.

William Allen (secular): educated at home. Oriel, Oxford (1547). B.A. (1550), age 18.

Richard Bristow (secular): educated at home. Exeter College, Oxford (1555). B.A. (1559), age 20.

Richard Broughton (secular): Pembroke College, Cambridge (1577–83), age 16–22. No record of degree.

John Bucke: nothing known.

Robert Chambers (secular): English College, Rheims (1582–92), age 11–21.

Henry Garnet (S.J.): Winchester School (1567–73), age 12–18. Did not attend university.

John Gennings (Order of Friars Minor): probably at Lichfield grammar school with his brother Edmund. No university records. At the English College, Rome (1598–1600), age 22–24.

Philip Howard (lay): educated at home (tutored by Gregory Martin). At St. John's, Cambridge (1576) and awarded an honorary M.A., age 19.

Gregory Martin (secular): St. John's, Oxford (1557). B.A. (1560), age unknown.

Robert Persons (S.J.): Stogursey grammar school. St. Mary's Hall, Oxford (1564–66) then Balliol, Oxford (1566–68). B.A. (1568), age 22.

Robert Southwell (S.J.): Douay (1576), age 15, then Paris (probably to the Jesuit College de Clermont) in 1577. At English College, Rome (1578–80), age 17–19.

Lawrence Vaux (secular): possibly Manchester grammar school.[2] Queen's and Corpus Christi, Oxford, before taking orders (1542), age 23. No record of degree.

Richard Verstegan (lay): at Christ Church, Oxford (1565–69), age 15–19. Refused to take the Oath of Supremacy and left without a degree.

Thomas Worthington (secular): Brasenose, Oxford (1566). B.A. (1570), age either 16 or 24.

TRANSLATORS AND COMPILERS

Stephen Brinkley (lay): nothing known.

George Cotton: nothing known.

George Flinton (lay): nothing known.

John Gerard (S.J.): at Douay (1577–80), age 12–15. Jesuit College de Clermont, Paris (1580–81), age 16.

Richard Gibbons (S.J.): when entered Louvain University (1570), age 21, took only philosophy, so must have made his humanities studies in Britain. No university records.

Richard Haydock (secular): no university records. At Douay (1573–77), age 22–26.

Richard Hopkins (lay): St. Alban's Hall, Oxford (1563), age 17. No record of degree.

Most of these writers were instructed in Britain until their late teens, well past the stage when they learned rhetoric. This confirms J. X. Evans's suspicion that such timing was encouraged because the students'

matriculation in England was no small benefit to the colleges abroad, for it reduced the educational and financial burdens of the seminaries at a time when both faculty and funds were hard to obtain.[3]

Only three of those writers reviewed here were educated primarily by Church institutions: Chambers, Southwell, and Gerard. I start by looking at rhetoric in British school curricula, then turn to Catholic colleges.

In looking at the place of dialectic in sixteenth-century universities, Lisa Jardine points out that a third of the trivium, grammar, was studied before the student went up. Facility in mathematics, logic, and rhetoric was the basis for the B.A. course, in preparation for the more strenuous studies of the philosophies.[4] However, some rhetorical theory was also usually prepared in schools, so it is to these that one should turn first for information on rhetorical education. T. W. Baldwin describes the education given in Elizabethan schools from two sources: pedagogical works of advice, and, where they survive, curricula of schools themselves. The latter use the *ad Herennium* and *Institutio oratoria* as guides to rhetorical theory, first when the pupil learns about *inventio* and *elocutio,* and after as a means of analyzing the rhetoric in the poetry, history, and orations making up the syllabus. Thus, these basic rhetoric manuals (sometimes supplemented by the *De partitione*) are initially used as rules for the composition of themes and orations, then as aids to literary criticism. Statutes of schools tend to name the authors read rather than the rhetorical guides, "but in five out of the six cases where oratorical texts are mentioned at all Cicero's rhetoric, or *ad Herennium,* is specified"; three of these five schools also include Quintilian in their curricula. He cites the grammar schools at Bury St. Edmund's, Rivington, and Norwich, and the cathedral school at Durham which use these two authors in this way.[5] Baldwin's evidence is less meager than it looks, since he is able to connect groups of schools together to produce similar probable syllabi for schools like Paul's, Eton, and Winchester.

Baldwin points out that educational theorists also sponsored this use of Quintilian and the real and pseudo-Cicero. Thomas Elyot's *Boke Named The Governour* of 1531 lets the pupil around the age of fifteen reflect on the philosophy of rhetoric, with Quintilian and the *De partitione* as guides.[6] Joannes Sturmius's treatise on education of 1538, *De literarum ludis recte aperiendis liber,* employs the *ad Herennium* to guide the learner through the first stages of *elocutio,* before he uses *De partitione* to analyze literary texts.[7] Quintilian is yielded equal place with Cicero in literary formation, by William Kempe's *Education of Children* of 1588.[8] For Erasmus, composition of the epistle and the theme is learned by consulting Aphthonius and Cicero's *Topica,* and the oration is made with the help of Cicero and Quintilian.[9] Such syllabi were not confined to schools. It seems unlikely that any home tutor would brave the expectations of parents and pedagogues, to produce a curriculum for his pupils which ignored authors regarded as the bedrock of rhetorical studies.

The majority of recusant authors spent some time at one of the universities. When the student passed on to Oxford or Cambridge, rhetoric continued to form a part of his work. Elizabethan statutes of both universities required the undergraduate to spend his first year in rhetoric, based on a study of the practice of Cicero and the theory of Quintilian, Hermogenes, and Aristotle. M. H. Curtis has warned that statutes can only give a partial picture of the studies actually carried out in the universities, since they take no account of the competing system of education offered by the colleges' lecturers and the students' own tutors.[10] Nonetheless, statutes do offer a guide to the sort of standards in rhetoric which a student would be expected to attain, perhaps through the college.

The education of the three students who did not go to British institutions was based on the *Ratio studiorum*. This is a set of rules and methods of teaching to be employed in Jesuit schools, also used by the English College at Rheims and Douay.[11] It was drawn from the Society's experience of their first school at Messina (a success from its inception in 1551), and Ignatius's description of educational practices in the *Constitutions*. The *Ratio* underwent extensive testing and revision by all the Jesuit Provinces between 1586 and its final version in 1599; the latter version became binding on all Jesuit schools from that point. It is possible, therefore, to be definite about the texts which Southwell, Gerard, and Chambers studied. The penultimate, fourth class used Soarez and *De partitione* to lay a foundation for eloquence. The fifth class aimed at a perfect command of language, by studying the philosophy of rhetoric and its use in the classic authors, with Quintilian, Aristotle, and Cicero as guides. The thorough way these texts were assimilated is attested to, in that each Jesuit was expected to be able to teach the humanities (fourth) class himself, at the end of this education.[12]

It would therefore seem reasonable to assume, as I have done, that the recusant writers did know thoroughly the rhetorical theorists cited: Quintilian, Cicero and, for those educated under the Jesuit system, Soarez.

Notes

Chapter 1. Introduction

1. Luis de Granada, *A Memoriall of a Christian Life,* trans. R. Hopkins (Rouen, 1586), 19 (2d signature ser.). A translation of the *Memorial de la vida cristiana.*

2. J. Bossy, *The English Catholic Community 1570–1850* (London, 1975), 279, 191.

3. L. Martz, *The Poetry of Meditation* (1954; New Haven, 1962), 6, 31, 164.

4. B. Lewalski, *Protestant Poetics and the Seventeenth-Century Religious Lyric* (Princeton, 1979), ix, 13.

5. Lewalski, Ibid., 149; R. Rogers, *Seven Treatises, Containing Such Direction as is Gathered out of the Holie Scriptures* (London, 1603), A6 v.

6. H. C. White, *English Devotional Literature (Prose) 1600–1640* (Madison, 1931), 19.

7. L. B. Campbell, *Divine Poetry and Drama in Sixteenth-Century England* (Cambridge, 1959).

8. I. MacCaffrey, "The Meditative Paradigm," *English Literary History* 32 (1965): 392ff.

9. P. Janelle, "English Devotional Literature in the Sixteenth and Seventeenth Centuries," *English Studies Today* 2 (N.S.) (1961): 160–62.

10. J. R. Roberts, *A Critical Anthology of English Recusant Devotional Prose, 1558–1603* (Pittsburgh, 1966).

11. A. F. Allison, and D. M. Rogers eds., "A Catalogue of Catholic Books in English Printed Abroad or Secretly in England 1558–1640" *Recusant History [RH]* 3 (1956).

12. A. C. Southern, *Elizabethan Recusant Prose 1559–1582* (London, 1950), ix.

13. J. X. Evans, "The Art of Rhetoric and the Art of Dying in Tudor Recusant Prose," *RH* 10 (1970): 247.

14. Southern, *Prose,* 205.

15. J. J. Dwyer, "Robert Southwell," *The Month* 16 (N.S.) (1956): 14.

16. Bossy, *Community,* 3.

17. A. F. Allison, and D. M. Rogers, "Ten Years of *Recusant History,*" *RH* 6 (1961): 10; Allison and Rogers, "Twenty-five Years of *Recusant History,*" *RH* 13 (1976): 155.

18. J. S. Phillimore, "Blessed Thomas More and the Arrest of Humanism in England," *Dublin Review* cliii (1913): 7; Southern, *Prose,* 5.

19. Southern, *Prose,* 4; R. W. Chambers, *On the Continuity of English Prose from Alfred to More and his School* (London, 1932), clxxi.

20. Southern, *Prose,* 5.

21. Evans, "Rhetoric," 248.

22. Southern, *Prose,* xii.

23. *The Tatler* (London, 1709–11), ed. D. F. Bond (Oxford, 1987), 3: 195.

24. W. R. Maurer, "Spee, Southwell and the Poetry of Meditation," *Comparative Literature* 15 (1963): 16.

25. R. Barthes, "The Old Rhetoric: an aide-memoire," *The Semiotic Challenge*, trans. R. Howard (Oxford, 1988), 29.

26. B. Oxley, "'Simples are by compounds farre exceld: Southwell's Longer Latin Poems and 'St Peters Complaint'" *RH* 17 (1985): 330.

27. C. S. Lewis, *English Literature in the Sixteenth Century* (Oxford, 1954), 441.

28. R. Janelle, *Robert Southwell the Writer. A study in religious inspiration* (London, 1935), 205.

29. Granada, *Memoriall*, 569.

30. D. Crane, "Catholicism and Rhetoric in Southwell, Crashaw, Dryden and Pope," *RH* 15 (1980): 240.

31. Oxley, "Southwell"; Evans "Rhetoric"; R. V. Caro, "William Alabaster: Rhetor, Meditator, Devotional Poet"["Alabaster"], *RH* 19 (1988).

32. Augustine, *De doctrina Christiana (Christian Instruction)*, trans. J. J. Gavigan (New York, 1947), 169.

33. W. Allen, *A True Sincere and Modest Defence of English Catholiques* ([Rouen, 1584]), *2 v.

34. R. Southwell, *A Short Rule of Good Life* ([England, 1596–97]), C6 r.

35. Persons to Acquaviva, 21 October 1581, CRS 39 (1942): 114.

36. R. Southwell, *An Humble Supplication to Her Majestie* ([London], 1595 [1600–1601]), ed. R. C. Bald (Cambridge, 1953), xii. This is Southwell's mild and loyal answer to William Cecil's charge of treachery made in the November 1591 Proclamation, enjoining further vigilance against the entry of priests.

37. A. Copley, *An Answere to a Letter of a Iesuited Gentleman* ([London], 1601), Pl r.

38. CRS 54 (1962). The responses concerned are listed below. The numbers attached are those given by Anthony Kenny. I have expanded the title of recognizable books. The dates given are those of the first edition.

341 William Alabaster: "Catholic book of Rainolds's" [probably William Rainolds's *Refutation of Sundry Reprehensions*, 1583].

346 Robert Walker: Persons's *Directorie*, 1582.

354 Henry Chaderton: Bristow's *Briefe Treatise . . . [of] Motives*, 1574.

355 Alexander Bradshawe: Persons's *Briefe Censure Uppon Two Bookes . . . in Answere to . . . Campion*, 1581.

357 Thomas Newman: Campion's *Rationes decem*, 1581.

358 Edward Cottington: "Bellarmine on Purgatory."

360 John Faulkner: "Catholic books."

366 Henry Lanman: "Rastell and Harding against Jewell" [between them, Rastell and Harding wrote fourteen books against Jewel's Paul's Cross sermon and his *Apologia*. See *AR*, 69ff., 133ff.].

372 Charles Yelverton: *De contemptu mundi*.

393 John Jackson: "Office of the B.V.M. and a Jesus Psalter" [possibly the *Manual of Prayers*, 1583].

396 Henry Clyffe: "many Catholic books."

398 John Grosse: Lawrence Vaux, *A Catechisme*, 1568.

39. R. Bristow, *A Briefe Treatise of Divers Plaine and sure waies to finde out the truth* (1574; Antwerp [England], 1599), T8 v.

40. *The New Testament of Iesus Christ*, trans. G. Martin (Rheims, 1582), 3H2 r.

41. A. Hyperius, *The Practise of preaching, Otherwise Called The Pathway to the Pulpet,* trans. J. Ludham (London, 1577), Gii v.

42. W. J. Ong, *Rhetoric, Romance and Technology* (New York, 1971), 63.

43. R. Persons, *A Christian Directorie Guiding Men to their Salvation* (Louvain, 1598), chap. 2. Initially issued as *The First Booke of the Christian Exercise, Appertayning to Resolution* ([Rouen], 1582).

44. *A Manuall, or Meditation, and most necessary Prayers* ([1580–81; England, 1596]).

45. Cardinal William Allen to Dr. Vendeville, 16 September 1578, quoted in Southern, *Prose,* 232; T. F. Knox, ed., *The First and Second Diaries of the English College, Douay* (London, 1878), xl.

46. H. C. White, *The Tudor Books of Saints and Martyrs [Saints]* (Madison, 1963), 203–4.

47. T. H. Clancy, *Papist Pamphleteers* (Chicago, 1964), 10.

48. D. Shuger, *Sacred Rhetoric. The Christian Grand Style in the English Renaissance* (Princeton, 1988), 76–80.

49. *Rhetorica ad Herennium,* trans. H. Caplan (London, 1954), 4: iv.

50. Quintilian, *Institutio oratoria,* trans. H. E. Butler (London, 1920), 2: xiii, 16.

CHAPTER 2. PRODUCING RECUSANT DEVOTIONAL TEXTS

1. Luis de Granada, *Of Prayer, and Meditation [Of Prayer],* trans. Richard Hopkins (Paris, 1582). This text was first published as *De la oracion y meditacion* (Salamanca, 1554) and enlarged in 1556 with a third book as the *Guia de pecadores* (the *Sinner's Guide*). It was the latter version which Hopkins used to produce the recusant translation. The *Guia de pecadores* was placed on the Index in 1559 because of suspicion that it might favor the *alumbrados'* methods of prayer. It was revised by Granada and reissued in the same year, though Granada's biographer, J. A. Moore, minimizes the extent of any change. "He clarified a few passages to remove any language suggesting the 'sterile quietism' of which it had been accused."[J. A. Moore, *Fray Luis de Granada* (Boston, 1977), 32–34].

2. Granada, *A Spiritual Doctrine, Conteining A Rule To live wel,* trans. Richard Gibbons (Louvain, 1599), from the *Compendio de la doctrina espiritual.*

3. L. Scupoli, *The Spiritual Conflict,* trans. [John Gerard] (1598; [Douay, 1603–10]). This was a translation of *Il Combattimento Spirituale* (Venice, 1589).

4. Diego de Estella, *The Contempte of the World and the Vanitie thereof,* trans. G. C. [George Cotton] ([Rouen], 1584). This translation of *De la Vanidad del Mundo* (Toledo, 1562) appeared in three English editions before 1640.

5. G. Loarte, *The Exercise of a Christian Life,* trans. I.S. [Stephen Brinkley] (1579; [Rouen, 1584]). The *Exercise* is a translation of Loarte's *Exercitium vitae christianae* (Barcelona, 1569) and was translated into English four times before 1640.

6. G. Loarte, *Meditations, of the Life and Passion of our Lord and Saviour Iesus Christ,* trans. anon. ([England, 1596–98]). This text is a translation of Loarte's *Meditationes de Passione Domini* (Bolognia, 1576) and was first published in English as *The Godlie Garden of Gethsemani* in 1576.

7. *A Manual of Prayers Newly Gathered Out of Many and divers famous authours,* as compiled by G. F. [George Flinton] ([Rouen], 1583).

8. J. Bucke, *Instructions for the use of the beades* (Louvain, 1589).

9. *A Methode, to meditate on the Psalter, or great Rosarie of our blessed Ladie* (Antwerp [England], 1598).

10. T. Worthington, *The Rosarie of our Ladie*, (Antwerp, 1600).

11. H. Garnet, *The Societie of the Rosary* ([England, 1596–97]), first issued in 1593–94.

12. C. N., *Our Ladie Hath A New Sonne* (Douay [England], 1595).

13. I. C., *Saint Marie Magdalens Conversion* ([England, 1603]).

14. R. Verstegan, *Odes. In Imitation of the Seaven Penitential Psalmes* ([Antwerp], 1601).

15. R. Chambers, *Palestina* (Florence [England], 1600).

16. T. a Kempis, *The Folowing of Christ, Translated Out of Latin into Englishe* ([Rouen], 1585). I follow the Allison and Rogers's suggestion about the translator of this text, W. Whytford.

17. *A Breefe Collection Concerning the Love of God towards Mankinde.* (Douay, 1603).

18. *The Primer, or Office of the Blessed Virgin Marie*, trans. [R. Verstegan] (Antwerp, 1599); J.M. Blom, *The Post-Tridentine English Primer* (CRS Monographs 3, 1982), 14, 17.

19. *The New Testament of Iesus Christ* (Rheims, 1582) and *The Holie Bible Faithfully Translated into English* [*Douay Old Testment*] (Douay, 1609–10), both translated by G. Martin according to Allison and Rogers.

20. P. Holmes, *Resistance and Compromise. The Political Thought of the Elizabethan Catholics* (Cambridge, 1982).

21. CRS 39 (1942): 321.

22. R. Persons, *Confessio fidei* written 1581. Latin original and translation in CRS 39 (1942): 28–41; E. Campion, *Rationes decem: quibus fretus certamen adversariis obtulit in causa fidei, Edmundus Campianus* ([England, 1581]). These texts described the purpose of the mission, and were composed by Persons and Campion before they separated in July 1580. The manuscripts were given to Thomas Pounde, a lay recusant, to keep until one of the two men was taken by pursuivants, when they were to be used to frustrate any traitorous interpretation which the authorities might put on their activities. Pounde was so delighted with the tone of Campion's apologia that he leaked the document before either Jesuit was captured. The term "Bragge" was given to it by Meredith Hanmer's rejoinder to Campion, in *The Great Bragge . . . of M. Champion a Iesuite* of 1581 [Southern, *Prose*, 150; CRS 39 (1942), 35].

23. Aside from political maneuvers, there may also have been a greater supply of writers emerging from the better-regulated education system for recusants overseas toward the end of the decade.

24. Worthington, *Rosarie*, *4 r.

25. T. Alfield, *A true reporte of the death & martyrdome of M. Campion, Iesuite and preiste, & M. Sherwin, & M. Bryan preistes* ([England, 1582]); W. Allen, *A Briefe Historie of the Glorious Martyrdom of XII. Reverend Priests* ([Rheims], 1582); T. Worthington, *A Relation of Sixtene Martyrs* (Douay, 1601). I have followed A. C. Southern's attribution of *Campion* to Alfield, though the poems prefacing the text have also been variously assigned to Henry Walpole, Richard Verstegan, and Stephen Vallenger.

26. G. Martin, *A Treatyse of Christian Peregrination* ([Paris], 1583).

27. H. Garnet, *[A] Treatis[e of Chri]stia[n Renunciation]* ([England, 1593]).

28. *Manual of Prayers*, Q2 r (1st signature ser.).

29. Clancy, *Papist Pamphleteers*, 136.

30. G. Martin, *Roma Sancta*, ed. G. B. Parks (Rome, 1969), 47.

31. Persons, *Conversions*, 3: 367–68 (1st signature ser.).

32. R. Persons, *An Epistle of the Persecution of Catholickes in Englande*, trans.

G.T. (Douay [Rouen], 1582), 76. The quotation is from the translation of Persons's *De persecutione Anglicana libellus* (1581; Rome, 1582) by G.T. in 1582, but there are no engravings in the translation. The Latin original was also translated into French, German, and Italian.

33. R. Verstegan, *Theatrum crudelitatum haereticorum* (Antwerp, 1587). This work ran through several French and Latin editions but was never translated into English. The illustration facing p. 105 is taken from the French edition, the *Theatre des Cruautez des Heretiques de nostre temps* (Antwerp, 1588).

34. J. Gibbons, *Concertatio ecclesiae Catholicae in Anglia* (1583; Trier, 1588), ed. D. M. Rogers (Farnborough, 1970). The introduction to this edition notes that later editions were supplemented by eyewitness accounts of executions which were published nowhere else.

35. Holmes, *Resistance*, 47ff.

36. H. More, *The English Jesuits*, trans. F. Edwards (London, 1981), 35. This is a translation of the *Historia missionis Anglicanae societatis Jesu* (St. Omers, 1660).

37. CRS 39 (1942): 344. Instructions to various Provincials about the collection to be raised for Rheims in 1582.

38. A. G. Petti, "Richard Verstegan and Catholic Martyrologies of the Later Elizabethan Period." *RH* 5 (1959): 65; Petti, "A Study of the Life and Writings of Richard Verstegan, (ca. 1550–1640)." (MA. Diss: University of London, 1957), 90.

39. W. Cecil, *The Execution of Iustice Against Certeine Stirrers of Sedition, and Adherents to the Traytors and Enemies of the Realme, Without Any Persecution of Them for Questions of Religion* (London, 1583), Civ v, Dii r.

40. L. Vaux, *A Catechisme or Christian Doctrine necessarie for Children and ignorante people* (1568; [Rouen, 1583]), intro. T. G. Law (Manchester, 1885).

41. Garnet translated Peter Canisius's *Summe of Christian Doctrine* into English. Verstegan translated Peter of Lucca's *Dialogue of Dying Well* (Antwerp, 1603) from French.

42. R. Bellarmine, *A Shorte Catechisme of Cardinall Bellarmine illustrated with the Images* (Npp, 1614), 4. A translation of the *Dottrina cristiana breve* (Rome, 1597) by [R. Gibbons].

43. R. Bellarmine, *An Ample Declaration of the Christian doctrine* (Rouen, [England, 1602–5]). Translated by Richard Haydock from the *Dichiarazione piu copiosa della dottrina cristiana* (Rome, 1598).

44. P. Canisius, *A Summe of Christian Doctrine*, trans. [H. Garnet] ([London, 1592–96]) from the *Summa doctrina Christianae* (Vienna, 1555).

45. T.H. D., *Nine Rockes To Be Avoided of those which sayle towards the Port of Perfection* (Douay [England], 1600), B3 r, B1 r, A8 r.

46. Alphonso de Madrid, *A Breefe Methode or Way Teachinge all sortes of Christian People, how to serve God*, trans. I.M. ([London, 1602–05]), A2 v.

47. J. Gee, *The Foot out of the Snare* (London, 1624), D3 r.

48. H. S. Bennett, *English Books & Readers 1558–1603* (Cambridge, 1965), 112, 271.

49. CRS 39 (1942): xxxii.

50. Allen to Agazzari, 15 January 1582. CRS 9 (1911): 41.

51. Gee, *Snare*, N2 r ff.

52. W. Fulke, *The Text of the New Testament . . . by the Papists . . . Whereunto is added the Translation . . . used in the Church of England* (London, 1589), A1 r.

53. Southern, *Prose*, 231; *Douay Old Testament*, i + 2 r.

54. Persons to Agazzari, August 1581. CRS 39 (1942): 84.

55. Southern, *Prose*, 156.

56. Persons to Agazzari, August 1581. CRS 39 (1942): 85.

57. CRS 39 (1942): xxxviii.

58. Quoted by E. Arber, *A Transcript of the Registers of the Company of Stationers of London; 1554–1640 A.D.* (London, 1875–94), 4:18; G. Wither, *Schollers Purgatory* (London, 1625), 123.

59. F. S. Siebert, *Freedom of the Press in England 1476–1776* (Urbana, 1952), 40.

60. W. W. Greg, "Licensers for the press, etc. to 1640. A Biographical Index Based Mainly on Arber's *Transcript*," in *Oxford Bibliographical Society* N.S. 10 (1962): 1.

61. *Manual of Prayers,* + +4v–5 r.

62. Persons, *Directorie,* a2 v.

63. Lewis, *English Literature in the Sixteenth Century,* 544.

64. Granada, *Memoriall,* 12 (1st signature ser.).

65. Granada, *Of Prayer,* aiii v.

66. Ibid., avi r–v.

CHAPTER 3. MEDITATION AS DELIBERATIVE RHETORIC

1. Granada, *Of Prayer,* Aiii r.

2. Ibid., Bii v.

3. Scupoli, *Conflict,* B3 v.

4. Persons, *Directorie,* A4 r–v.

5. Scupoli, *Conflict,* A7 v.

6. Loarte, *Exercise,* + +iii r.

7. Estella, *Contempte,* A1 v.

8. Granada, *Of Prayer,* [A]aii r.

9. Estella, *Contempte,* D4 r.

10. Granada, *Of Prayer,* Bvi v.

11. Ibid., Aviii r, Aiv r.

12. Ibid., Bv v ff.

13. Lewalski, *Protestant Poetics,* 16.

14. Estella, *Contempte,* D9 r, T9 v.

15. Ibid., I12 r.

16. Granada, *Of Prayer,* Cii r, quoting Ps. 102.

17. Estella, *Contempte,* S11 v.

18. Scupoli, *Conflict.* F11 v.

19. Ibid., B10 v, B12 v.

20. Loarte, *Meditations,* Ki r.

21. Estella, *Contempte,* Z8 r.

22. Loarte, *Meditations,* Iiv r.

23. *Breefe Collection,* A9 v.

24. *Manual of Prayers,* A2 v ff (1st signature ser.).

25. Granada, *Spiritual Doctrine,* M6 r–v.

26. Loarte, *Meditations,* Bii r.

27. *Manual of Prayers,* E2 v (3rd signature ser.).

28. Persons, *Directorie,* B2 r.

29. Loarte, *Meditations,* Kiii r.

30. Ibid., Bii r–Bv v.

31. Granada, *Of Prayer,* biv v.

32. Ibid., Nnv v.

33. Scupoli, *Conflict*, B6 v–B7 r.

34. Granada, *Of Prayer*, Oovi r.

35. *NT*, 3Eiv r.

36. Ibid., 3Miv r.

37. *Manual of Prayers*, + +5 r.

38. Garnet, *Rosary*, M11 r.

39. Alphonso, *Breefe Methode*, A6 v–A7 r.

40. A. Fraunce, *The Lawiers Logike* (London, 1588), + +2r.

41. *NT*, ciii v.

42. *Campian Englished. Or A Translation of the Ten Reasons, in which Edmund Campian . . . insisted in his Challenge* ([?Rouen], 1632), 27.

43. CRS 67 (1981):49. The answer is never, if done for the sake of curiosity, otherwise only when read to stop the Church from being brought into scandal. Even then, it is necessary (except in cases of urgency) to request permission from your confessor. The concept of browsing does not exist in these manuals.

44. Instructions to Persons and Campion, 14 April 1580. CRS 39 (1942):320.

45. A. Copley, *Another Letter of Mr. A.C. to his Dis-Iesuited Kinseman* ([London], 1602), C2 v.

46. For example, the preface of the *Manuall, or Meditation* boasts that it is a comprehensive collection of prayers and instructions which reduces the number of books to be bought.

47. D. Crane, "Studies in Recusant Prose: The English Translations of the *Imitatio Christi* in the Sixteenth and Seventeenth Centuries." (D. Phil. diss., University of Oxford, 1968), 102.

48. J. Ledisma, *The Christian Doctrine in manner of a Dialogue betweene the Master and the Disciple*, trans. anon. ([England], 1597), B2 r.

49. T.H.D., *Nine Rockes*, B2 r.

50. *NT*, Siii v.

51. T. Harding, *An Answere to Maister Iuelles Chalenge* (Louvain, 1564), Vi v.

52. *NT*, bii v.

53. W. Fulke, *A Defense of the sincere and true Translations of the holie Scriptures . . . against . . . Gregorie Martin.* (London, 1583), dedicatory epistle.

54. R. Persons, *A Temperate Ward-word, to the Turbulent and Seditious Wach-word of Sir Francis Hastinges* ([Antwerp], 1599), B3 v.

55. *NT*, aiv r.

56. P. Martyr, *The Common Places of . . . Peter Martyr* [*Common Places*] ([London, 1583]), Aii v–Aiii r.

57. W. Allen, *A True Report of . . . Iohn Nicols* (Rheims, 1583), D2 r.

58. Shugar, *Sacred Rhetoric*, 79.

59. Granada, *Of Prayer*, Dviii v–Ei r.

60. *Manuall, or Meditation*, A2 r.

61. Loarte, *Meditations*, Kv r.

62. Granada, *Of Prayer*, NNiiii r.

63. *Manual of Prayers*, a3 r. These are prayers that are taken straight from Scripture.

64. *Methode*, B4 r.

65. H. C. White, *The Tudor Books of Private Devotion* (Madison, 1951), 49.

66. Augustine, *De doctrina Christiana* [*DDC*], 23.

67. Worthington, *Rosarie*, E2 r.

68. Loarte, *Exercise*, L5 r.

69. Granada, *Of Prayer*, Nni v.

70. *Manual of Prayers*, B5 v (1st signature ser.).

71. I.C., *Magdalen*, B3 v–B4 r.

72. Estella, *Contempte*, V7 v.

73. Ibid., A4 r.

74. Loarte, *Meditations*, [Avii r].

75. Granada, *Of Prayer*, Di v.

76. *NT*, aii r.

77. Bucke, *Beades*, Fii v–Fiii r.

78. *Breefe Collection*, A2 r; Loarte, *Meditations*, [Aii v].

79. *ad Herennium*, I ix.

80. Ascham, *Schoolmaster*, 68.

81. Cicero, *De partitione oratoria*, trans. H. Rackham (London, 1942), iv 15.

82. Persons, *Directorie*, a3 v.

83. Granada, *Of Prayer*, Ci v.

84. P. Sidney, "A Defence of Poetry," in *Miscellaneous Prose of Sir Philip Sidney* (London, 1595), eds. K. Duncan-Jones and J. van Dorsten (Oxford, 1973), 91.

85. *Manual of Prayers*, title page.

86. a Kempis, *Folowing*, Biv v.

87. Quintilian, *Institutio oratoria*, trans. H. E. Butler (London, 1920), 8:iii, 5.

88. *Manual of Prayers*, A2 r (1st signature ser.).

89. Southwell, *Magdalen*, A2 v, A4 r.

90. Ibid., A3 r–A4 v.

91. Puttenham, "Arte of English Poesie" (London, 1589), ed. G. Smith, *Elizabethan Critical Essays* (Oxford, 1904), 2:30.

92. *Manuall, or Meditation*, A4 r. The adaptation in this text is suitable for independent use. The *Exercises* themselves were designed as a manual for spiritual directors to use with exercitants, and may have been considered inappropriate for the circumstances of the mission, where priests were scarce.

93. I. Loyola, *The Spiritual Exercises of Saint Ignatius*, trans. T. Corbishley (1963; Wheathampstead, 1973), 12; *NCE*, "Spiritual Exercises," xiii 580.

94. J. Harington, "Orlando Furioso" (London, 1591), Smith, *Essays*, 2:220.

95. L. Cox, *The Arte or Crafte of Rhethoryke* (London, ca. 1530), ed. F. I. Carpenter (Chicago, 1899), 68.

96. S. Harsnet, *A Declaration of egregious Popish impostures in casting out of Devils* (London, 1603), D2 v; Gee, *Snare*, C2 v. Gee describes his escape from Catholicism and waspishly relates scandalous aspects of Church practice.

97. *NT*, bi v.

98. Quintilian, *Institutio*, 2:xvii, 26–28.

99. C. Soarez, "*De arte rhetorica*" (1562; Venice, 1568), trans. L. J. Flynn (Ph.D. diss., University of Florida, 1955), 113–14. The *Rhetorica* went through fourteen editions between 1557 and 1675 [J. J. Murphy, *Renaissance Rhetoric. A Short-Title Catalogue . . . to A.D. 1700* (New York, 1981)].

100. Soarez, *Rhetorica*, 120.

101. Quintilian, *Institutio*, 12:i, 3–13.

102. Ibid., 1:ii, 3.

103. Cicero, *De oratore*, trans. H. Rackham and E. Sutton (London, 1942), 1:viii, 30–31.

104. Southwell, *Magdalen*, A5 r.

105. Hyperius, *Pathway*, Giii r.

106. Cicero, *De oratore*, 2:xlvi, 191.

107. Ascham, *Schoolmaster*, 68.

108. Granada, *Of Prayer*, Bvii r.
109. Estella, *Contempte*, E7 v.
110. Soarez, *Rhetorica*. 261.
111. Southwell, *Short Rule*, B6 r.
112. Granada, *Memoriall*, 447.
113. Garnet, *Rosary*, A6 r.
114. Vaux, *Catechisme*, 23–25.
115. Fraunce, *Logike*, Hhiii r.
116. G. Herbert, "Jordan 2", *The Works of George Herbert*, ed. F. E. Hutchinson (Oxford, 1941), 102.
117. Verstegan, "Preface," in *Odes*, A2 v.

CHAPTER 4. *INVENTIO* AND *MEMORIA*
IN ENGLISH MEDITATIONS

1. The terms *loci* and *topoi* are used here without distinction.
2. W. J. Ong, *Ramus, Method, and the Decay of Dialogue* (Cambridge, Mass., 1958), 63.
3. *The Constitutions of the Society of Jesus*, trans. G. E. Ganss (St. Louis, 1970), pt. 4, chap. 6, declaration 8 (p. 194).
4. Quintilian, *Institutio*, 3:vi, 9.
5. Ibid., 5:i, 2.
6. Cicero, *De partitione*, iii 8.
7. Cicero, *Topica*, trans. H.M. Hubbell (London, 1949), 377.
8. Cicero, *De partitione*, ix, 33.
9. Ibid., xx 70, xxix 101.
10. Cicero, *De oratore*, 2:xxxix 166.
11. Quintilian, *Institutio*, 3:vi 66.
12. Ibid., 5:i 1.
13. Ibid., 5:viii, 4–6.
14. Ibid., 5:x 23.
15. Ibid., 5:x 94.
16. *ad Herennium*, 1:ii.
17. Ibid., 2:xxx.
18. Soarez, *Rhetorica*, 169.
19. Ibid., 257.
20. W. J. Ong, *Orality and Literacy: The Technologizing of the Word* (1982; London, 1988), 41. For example, H. Peacham, *The Garden of Eloquence* (1577; London, 1593), intro. W. G. Crane (Gainesville, Fla.: 1954), Si r.
21. Peacham, *Garden of Eloquence*, Riv v.
22. Erasmus, *De copia*, 635.
23. W. S. Howell, *Logic and Rhetoric in England, 1500–1700* (Princeton, 1956), 23.
24. L. Sterne, *The Life and Opinions of Tristram Shandy, Gentleman* (York, 1760–67), ed. I. Campbell Ross (Oxford, 1983), 323, 329.
25. Ascham, *Schoolmaster*, 107.
26. S. Johnson, "Waller." *Lives of the English Poets* (1779–81; London, 1783), ed. G. Birkbeck Hill (Oxford, 1905), 1:291–92.
27. Lewalski, *Protestant Poetics*, 218.
28. *NT*, 4Tii r.

29. Erasmus, "De duplici copia verborum ac rerum commentarii duo" (1512; Basel, 1534), trans. B. I. Knott (Toronto, 1978), 572.

30. Granada, *Of Prayer*, Biii r.

31. Ibid., Nniv v.

32. Hyperius, *Pathway*, Cii v.

33. C.N., *Our Ladie*, B3 v–B4 r.

34. R. Southwell, *An Epistle of Comfort, to the Reverend Priestes . . . & other of the Laye sort* (Paris [England, 1587–88]), E4 r.

35. Chambers, *Palestina*, + +4 r.

36. Verstegan, "Our Blessed Ladies Lullaby," in *Odes*, D4 r.

37. *Manuall, or Meditation*, C5 v.

38. E. Beilin, *Redeeming Eve. Women Writers of the English Renaissance* (Princeton, 1987), xix, 70.

39. *Holy Churches Complaint, for her childrens disobedience* [London, 1598–1601].

40. *Manuall, or Meditation*, A8 r ff.

41. C.N., *Our Ladie*, B2 v.

42. Southwell, *Magdalen*, C6 v.

43. T. Nashe, *Christs Teares Over Ierusalem* (London, 1593) in *The Works of Thomas Nashe*, ed. R. B. McKerrow (1904; London, 1910), 2:21, 60.

44. Chambers, *Palestina*, O1 r, O4 v. Emphases mine.

45. I.C., *Magdalen*, B3 r.

46. Ibid., C4 r.

47. Chambers, *Palestina*, Aa2 v.

48. *Breefe Collection*, C1 v–C2 r.

49. P. Howard, *A Foure-Fould Meditation, of the foure last things* (London, 1606), B4 v.

50. Loarte, *Meditations*, Iviii r.

51. Garnet, *Renunciation*, title page, A6 r.

52. Ibid., B3 v. The names of authorities give support to a cause, though they may not clarify what is said; they are there to frank the text with their ethos. Garnet's use of "genuine" also implies that a redaction of the saints' words through himself could lead to misrepresentation. Presumably, since he is writing the text, he is not worried about deceiving himself, but about a perceived tendency to distortion by words.

53. Persons, *Directorie*, Yy8 v.

54. *Manual of Prayers*, A1 r, C3 v–C6 v (1st signature ser.).

55. *Breefe Collection*, A10 r.

56. Bucke, *Beades*, Di v.

57. Ibid., Ciii v, [D]iii v.

58. Janelle, *Southwell*, 95.

59. Fraunce, *Logike*, Civ v.

60. Hyperius, *Pathway*, Jii r.

61. Granada, *Of Prayer*, Rviii r, Si r.

62. Hyperius, *Pathway*, Bi r.

63. W. S. Howell, *Logic and Rhetoric in England, 1500–1700* (Princeton, 1956), 3.

64. J. Hall, *The Arte of Divine Meditation* (1606; London, 1607), 149.

65. Granada, *Of Prayer*, Mmvi r.

66. Persons, *Directorie*, Zz3 v.

67. R. V. Caro, "William Alabaster: Rhetor, Meditator, Devotional Poet," RH 19 (1988):67.

68. U. Eco, "An *Ars Oblivionalis?* Forget it!" *PMLA* 103, no. 1 (1988): 255–57.

69. Loarte, *Meditations*, [Avii v].

70. T. Wilson, *Arte of Rhetorique* (London, 1553), intro. R. H. Bowers (Gainesville, Fla., 1962), Ffiv v.

71. R. Persons, *A Relation of the King of Spaines Receiving in Valliodolid* ([Antwerp], 1592), [B]5 v. This text describes the brilliance of learning fostered in the English college, and Philip's support of the foundation.

72. *Methode*, G2 r.

73. Loarte, *Exercise*, Y1 r ff.

74. T. Elyot, *The Boke Named The Governour* (London, 1531), ed. H. H. Croft (London, 1880), 2:253.

75. F. Yates, *The Art of Memory* (London, 1966), 300 n.

76. F. Yates, *The Art of Memory*, (London, 1966), 20.

77. Puttenham, "Arte of English Poesie," in Smith, *Essays*, 2:40–41. Emphases mine.

78. Garnet, *Rosary*, L3 v.

79. *Methode*, B3 v.

80. Granada, *Of Prayer*, Ppv r.

81. Martin, *Roma sancta*, 165.

82. Chambers, *Palestina*, A3 r.

83. Verstegan, "Saint Peeters Comfort," in *Odes*, F4 v.

Chapter 5. Hagiography and Catechism: Producing a Saint

1. Cicero, *De partitione*, xx, 69; Cicero, *De oratore*, 2:xi, 47.

2. Persons, *Conversions*, i: 2*8 v.

3. Quintilian, *Institutio*, 5:i, 2; 5:ix, 1.

4. Aristotle, *The "Art" of Rhetoric*, trans. J. Freese (London, 1926), 1: xv, 13.

5. Martin, *Peregrination*, B5 v.

6. Quintilian, *Institutio*, 5:xi, 37.

7. R. Bristow, *Demaundes to bee Proponed of Catholickes to the Heretickes* (1576; [England, 1596–97]), C5 r.

8. Persons, *Conversions*, 2: 53 (2nd signature ser.).

9. Quintilian, *Institutio*, 5:xii, 9.

10. Ibid., 6:ii, 8.

11. *NT*, Bii r.

12. Persons, *Conversions*, 2: 51 (2nd signature ser.).

13. Ibid., 2: 365–66.

14. T. Wright, *A Treatise, Shewing the possiblitie . . . of the reall presence* (Antwerp [England], 1596), R2 r.

15. Soarez, *Rhetorica*, 246.

16. *ad Herennium*, 3:vi.

17. Puttenham, "Arte of English Poesie," in Smith, *Essays*, 2: 43.

18. Granada, *Of Prayer*, bi v.

19. Persons, *Conversions*, 3: 40 (1st signature ser.).

20. Allen, *Defence*, C7 r–v.

21. Ibid., C8 r.

22. Evans, "Rhetoric," 249.

23. Bossy, *Community*, 12, 415.

24. Allen, *XII. Reverend Priests*, av v. Emphases mine.

25. Persons to Agazzari, August 1581. CRS 39 (1942): 83.

26. Gee, *Snare*, G3 v–G4 r.

27. Ascham, *Schoolmaster*, 68.

28. Southwell, *Supplication*, 60.

29. Quintilian, *Institutio*, 5: vii, 16.

30. Southwell, "I dye without desert," in *Poems*, 48.

31. Persons, *Conversions*, 2: 239 (1st signature ser.).

32. A. Nowell, *A Catechisme or First Instruction and Learning of Christian Religion*, trans. T. Norton (London, 1570), intro. F. V. Occhiogrosso (New York, 1975), Aiii r–v.

33. Bristow, *Briefe Treatise*, B6 v.

34. Persons, *Conversions*, 1: 3*2 r.

35. Granada, *Memoriall*, 7 (2nd signature ser.).

36. Persons, *Directorie*, a2 v.

37. Persons, *Conversions*, 2: 1 (1st signature ser.).

38. Persons, *The Warn-word to Sir Francis Hastinges Wast-word* ([Antwerp], 1602), Ll4 r.

39. Augustine, *The City of God [De civitate Dei]*, trans. J. Healey (1610; Edinburgh, 1909), 1: 315.

40. Persons, *Conversions*, 3: 19–20 (2nd signature ser.).

41. Clancy, *Papist Pamphleteers*, 153.

42. Persons, *Conversions*, 2: 26 (2nd signature ser.); 3: 228 (1st signature ser.).

43. Persons, *Conversions*, 3: 10, 16 (1st signature ser.).

44. *NT*, Biii r.

45. Quintilian, *Institutio*, 5: x, 11.

46. Canisius, *Summe*, *4 r.

47. *Campian Englished*, 155.

48. Verstegan, "Triumphe of feminyne Saintes," in *Odes*, E6 r, E7 r.

49. *NT*, 3Miii r.

50. Persons, *Conversions*, 1: 3*5, r.

51. Alfield, *Campion*, B2 v.

52. Persons, *Conversions*, 1: 101.

53. Allen, *Nicols*, Aiv v.

54. Persons, *Conversions*, 2: 11 (2nd signature ser.).

55. Alfield, *Campion*, E2 v; A. Munday, *A breefe aunswer made unto two seditious Pamphlets* (London, 1582), D7 v.

56. Alfield, *Campion*, B1 v.

57. Southwell, *Supplication*, 40.

58. Allen, *Defence*, title page.

59. Allen, *XII. Priests*, aiv v; W. Cecil, *A Declaration of the favourable dealing of her Maiesties Commissioners* (London, 1583) [A]iii r.

60. Allen, *XII. Priests*, di v; Alfield, *Campion*, A4 v.

61. Persons to Agazzari, 3 January 1582. CRS 4 (1907): 45.

62. Birkhead to Agazzari, undated. CRS 4 (1907): 153.

63. *Campian Englished*, 16, 19.

64. Alfield, *Campion*, E4 v.

65. *Campian Englished*, 20.

66. Southwell, *Short Rule*, A10 v.

67. W. Alabaster, *The Sonnets of William Alabaster*, eds. G. M. Story and H. Gardner (Oxford, 1959), 13.

68. R. Corthell, "'The secrecy of man": Recusant Discourse and the Elizabethan Subject." *English Literary Renaissance* 19 (1989):272.

69. Worthington, *Martyrs*, B8 v.

70. T. Pounde, T., "The Cheerer,", in MS only, in L. I. Guiney, *Recusant Poets* (London, 1938), 182.

71. Augustine, *DCD*, 1: 17.

72. Martin, *Peregrination*, B5 r, B8 v. Following Augustine, *DCD*, 2: 336.

73. Martin, *Peregrination*, D8 r.

74. Harsnet, *Impostures*, KK2 r.

75. J. Harington, Preface to *Orlando Furioso* (London, 1591). In Smith, *Elizabethan Essays*, 2: 220. Martin, *Peregrination*, C5 r.

76. Allen, *XII. Priests*, Diii r; Worthington, *Martyrs*, B5 r.

77. J. Donne, *Ignatius His Conclave* (London, 1611), ed. T. S. Healy (Oxford, 1969), 19.

78. Martin, *Peregrination*, A6 r–v.

79. *Manual of Prayers*, B5 r (1st signature ser.).

80. Martin, *Roma sancta*, 27.

81. A. Munday, *The English Romane Life* (London, 1582), ed. P. J. Ayres (Oxford, 1980), 61.

82. Southwell, *Short Rule*, F5 r–F6 r.

Chapter 6. Hagiographies as Examples to Clarify the Faith

1. Puttenham, "Arte of English Poesie," in Smith, *Essays*, 2:41.

2. *ad Herennium*, 4:iii, 5. The *ad Herennium* does, however, contradict itself by following Aristotle in warning that examples in deliberative rhetoric require a greater degree of historical veracity than the two other causes, because as a rule the future resembles the past.

3. P. Sidney, "A Defence of Poetry," (London, 1595), *Miscellaneous Prose of Sir Philip Sidney*, eds. K. Duncan-Jones and J. van Dorsten (Oxford, 1973), 89.

4. Ibid., 89.

5. H. C. White, *Tudor Books of Saints and Martyrs* (Madison, 1963), 17.

6. R. Southwell, "Decease release," in *The Poems of Robert Southwell*, S. J., eds. J. H. McDonald and N. P. Brown (Oxford, 1967), 47.

7. Southwell, *Triumphs over Death*, xvi, 21.

8. Janelle, *Southwell*, 237.

9. Worthington, *Martyrs*, A5 r, A7 r.

10. Alfield, *Campion*, B4 v; Allen, *XII. Priests*, dv r.

11. Persons, *Directorie*, Qq7 v.

12. Alfield, *Campion*, A2 r.

13. Ibid., G1 v, A2 v.

14. Worthington, *Martyrs*, F4 v–F5 r.

15. Alfield, *Campion*, E2 v–E3 r.

16. A. Munday, *A breefe aunswer made unto two seditious Pamphlets* (London, 1582), C1 v.

17. L. I. Guiney, *Recusant Poets* (London, 1938), 264, 287.

18. Alfield, *Campion*, F2 v.

19. Southwell, "Decease, release," in *Poems*, 47.

20. Alfield, *Campion*, A2 r, B3 v. Alfield says that Campion quoted 1 Cor.4 on the cart.

21. Bellarmine, *Ample Doctrine*, B3 r.

22. Verstegan, "Visions of the worlds instabillitie," in *Odes*, H1 r.

23. S. Harsnet, *A Declaration of egregious Popish impostures in casting out of Devils* (London, 1603), B2 r.

24. Persons to Agazzari, 3 January 1582. CRS 39 (1942): 133.

25. More, *The Elizabethan Jesuits*, 265.

26. Holmes, *Resistance*, 60.

27. Persons, *Conversions*, 3: 189 (1st signature ser.).

28. Ibid., 3: 258 (1st signature ser.).

29. E. Beilin, *Redeeming Eve. Women Writers of the English Renaissance* (Princeton, 1987), 30.

30. Allen, *XII. Reverend Priests*, evii v; Worthington, *Martyrs*, C1 r.

31. Augustine, *DCD*, 2: 339–40, 344.

32. Persons, R. and others, *A Conference About the Next Succession* ([Antwerp], 1594), 121; Persons, *A Relation of the King of Spaines Receiving in Valliodolid* ([Antwerp], 1592), A2 r. It may be that Persons distrusted the effect of any sort of drama. Despite the importance of establishing good relations with the Roman Curia for funding reasons, there were no plays produced at the English College between 1598 and 1610, while Persons was its Rector.

33. Ledisma, *The Christian Doctrine*, A2 r.

34. Southwell, *Short Rule*, F2 v; Southwell, "Saint Peters Complaint." *Poems*, 75.

35. Persons, *Conversions*, iii *2r ff.

36. White, *Saints*, 28. The *Golden Legend* is a translation of the thirteenth-century *Legenda aurea*, compiled by Jacobus de Voragine.

37. Persons, *Conversions*, i 2*8 v; Southwell, *Short Rule*, F3 v.

38. E. Auerbach, *Mimesis. The Representation of Reality in Western Literature*, trans. W. R. Trask (Princeton, 1953), 19.

39. Southwell, "I dye without desert," in *Poems*, 48.

40. J. Gennings, *The Life and Death of Mr. Edmund Geninges Priest* (St. Omers, 1614).

41. *ad Herennium*, 3: iv.

42. Quintilian, *Institutio*, 3: vii, 13.

43. Soarez, *Rhetorica*, 187ff. Surprisingly, neither Soarez nor Protestant writers on rhetoric such as Cox include religious fervor as one of these virtues.

44. *ad Herennium*, note to 3: vi. Emphases mine.

45. Quintilian, *Institutio*, 9: iii, 102.

46. T. Eagleton, *Literary Theory* (Oxford, 1983), 206.

47. Loarte, *Exercise*, L6 r.

48. Canisius, *Summe*, Mmi v–Mmii r. Comment by Henry Garnet.

49. "Trent 1545–1563," trans. P. McIlhenny and J. Coventry, in *Decrees of the Ecumenical Councils* ed. N. P. Tanner (London, 1990), 2: 775–76.

50. Bellarmine, *Ample Declaration*, I1 r.

51. Granada, *Memoriall*, 45.

52. Allen, *A True Report of Iohn Nicols*, D1 r.

53. *Campian Englished*, 66.

54. H. Garnet, *An Apology Against the Defence of Schisme* ([England, 1593]), 91. This text is another of Henry Garnet's "place" texts, bringing together material from the Fathers and Church Councils to prove that it is not lawful to attend heretical services.

55. J. Foxe, *The Acts and Monuments of John Foxe* (London, 1563), ed. J. Pratt (London, 1877), 1:xix.

56. Persons, *Conversions*, 1:459, 1:439.

57. Ibid., 1:290, 3:196 (both 1st signature ser.).

58. *Campian Englished*, 67–68.

59. M. Aston, *England's Iconoclasts* (Oxford, 1988), 347, 454.

60. Martyr, *Common Places*, Mmvi r.

61. Gee, *Snare*, C3 r.

62. Persons, *Directorie*, Qq3 v. Design by Pomerancio.

63. CRS 4 (1907):113.

CHAPTER 7. CATECHISMS: AUDITING THE SELF

1. Granada, *Memoriall*, 1–2 (2d signature ser.).

2. R. Lanham, *The Motives of Eloquence* (New Haven, 1976), 14.

3. Quintilian, *Institutio*, 10:iii, 15.

4. Lanham, *Motives*, 4.

5. Auerbach, *Mimesis: The Representation of Reality in Western Literature*, 15.

6. Southwell, *Short Rule*, B6 r, B7 r, B5 v–B6 v.

7. Scupoli, *Conflict*, A8 r.

8. *Manual of Prayers*, F3 r (1st signature ser.).

9. Southwell, "Saint Peters Complaynte," in *Poems*, 29, 76, 81.

10. Granada, *Memoriall*, 139.

11. *Breefe Collection*, A6 v.

12. For example, Canisius, *Summe*, S5 v; Southwell, *Short Rule*, D7 v.

13. S. Fish, *Self-Consuming Artifacts. The Experience of Seventeenth-Century Literature* (1972; Berkeley, 1974), 156 ff.

14. Clancy, *Papist Pamphleteers*, 143, 146.

15. R. Persons, *A Brief Discours contayning certayne Reasons Why Catholiques refuse to goe to Church* (Douay [London], 1580), ++iiiv–++ivr.

16. Augustine, *Confessions*, trans. H. Chadwick (Oxford, 1991), 69.

17. Loarte, *Exercises*, A1 r.

18. Alphonso, *Breefe Methode*, A5 v, A6 v.

19. Martz, *Meditation*, 16.

20. E. A. Peers, *Studies of the Spanish Mystics* (London, 1951–60), 1:34.

21. Estella, *Contempte*, L4 v.

22. Garnet, *Renunciation*, A4 r.

23. Moore, *Fray Luis de Granada*, 85.

24. Persons, *Directorie*, V3 v–V4 r.

25. Southwell to Persons, probably early 1582. CRS 5 (1908):302–3.

26. Bossy, *Community*, 20.

27. R. Southwell, *Spiritual Exercises and Devotions of Blessed Robert Southwell, S.J.* trans. P. E. Hallett, ed. J.-M. de Buck (London, 1931), 64.

28. L. B. Wright, *Middle Class Culture in Elizabethan England* (1935; New York, 1958), 167.

29. Southwell, *Short Rule*, E3 v.

30. Granada, *Spiritual Doctrine,* O3 v; *Memoriall*, 33.

31. Southwell, *Short Rule*, E1 v ff; Persons, *Directorie*, 542, in 1607 edition only.

32. Persons, *Valliodolid*, A7 r–v.

33. Munday, *English Romane Lyfe*, 43.

34. Martz, *Meditation*, 321.

35. C. W. Slights, *The Casuistical Tradition* (Princeton, 1981), 6.

36. Granada, *Memoriall*, 167.

37. Southwell, *Spiritual Exercises*, 36.

38. Gennings, *Geninges*, A4 r.

39. Southwell, *Short Rule*, a6 r. The Bodleian copy of Bellarmine's *Shorte Catechisme* (8*B180Th) illustrates this neatly, with a child's writing exercise bound in to protect the title page. This is on the theme of "The first stepp to vertue, is to imitate godly men."

40. P. Martyr, *The Common Places of . . . Peter Martyr* (London, 1587), Gi r.

41. A. Fraunce, *The Lawiers Logike* (London, 1588), Bii r.

42. Ascham, *Schoolmaster*, 114.

43. Aristotle, *The Poetics*, iv 2.

44. G. Harvey, *Ciceronianus* (London, 1577), trans. C. A. Forbes, ed. H. S. Wilson (Nebraska, 1945), 73.

45. A. P. Farrell, *The Jesuit Code of Liberal Education* (Milwaukee, 1938), 290ff.

46. Aristotle, *Rhetoric*, 1:xi, 3.

47. Augustine, *Confessions*, 140.

48. I.C., *Magdalen*, B1 r, A4 v.

49. Alphonso, *Breefe Method*, C5 r–v.

50. Puttenham, "Arte of English Poesie," in Smith, *Essays*, 2:41.

51. F. Meres, *Palladis tamia* (London, 1598), intro. D. C. Allen (New York, 1938), Mm1 r–v.

52. Bennett, *English Books & Readers 1558–1603*, 135.

53. Allen, *Nicols*, Dii v–Diii r; Persons, *Directorie*, a5 r.

54. R. Greene, "The Repentance of Robert Greene" (London, 1592). *The Life and Complete Works . . . of Robert Greene*, ed. A. B. Grosart (London, 1881–86), 12:165.

55. Rogers, *Seven Treatises, Containing Such Direction as is Gathered out of the Holie Scriptures*, A6 r.

56. E. Sandys, *Europae Speculum or, a View or Survey of the State of Religion in the Westerne parts of the World* (1605; Hagae-Comitis, 1629), Kiv r. This is from the preface, dated 1599.

57. Lewalski, *Protestant Poetics*, 457 note 6.

58. Southern, *Prose*, 150.

59. A. Petti, "Stephen Vallenger (1541–1591)," *RH* 6 (1962):258.

60. P. Milward, *Religious Controversies of the Elizabethan Age. A Survey of Printed Sources* (London, 1977), 2.

61. Bossy, *Community*, 15.

62. Persons, *Warn-word*, Ll8 r ff; *Conversions*, 1:439.

63. Persons, *Directorie*, b3 v, a8 r.

64. Persons, *Conversions*, 2:44 (2d signature ser.).

65. Persons, *The First Booke of the Christian Exercise*, A2 r ([Rouen], 1582); E. Bunny, *A Booke of Christian exercise . . . Perused, and accompanied now with a Treatise tending to Pacification* (1584; London, 1585), A2 r, A3 v; Persons, *Directorie*, b4 r; Bunny, *A Briefe Answer, unto those idle and frivolous quarrels of R. P. against the late edition of the Resolution* (London, 1589).

66. Janelle claimed to have compared the two versions, but his statement that "they are identically the same" is incorrect; the 1585 *Directorie* even gives the page numbers to the Bunny alterations (Janelle, "English Devotional Literature in the Sixteenth and Seventeenth Centuries," 160). For instance, the very first of the alter-

ations which Persons lists in the 1585 *Directorie*, the 1582's "Those which attend in the Catholique Churche, to deale with soules in the holie sacrament of confession" [L4 v] becomes "those which are known to be skilful, and to deal so sincerely withal, that others disburden their consciences unto them for their comfort" in Bunny's version [O6 v].

67. R. Loomis, "The Barrett Version of Robert Southwell's *Short Rule of Good Life*," RH 7 (1964):239–48.

68. Constable, "Spirituall Sonnettes," 189, 192.

69. Southwell, *Short Rule*, a6 v.

70. C.N., *Our Ladie*, F4 r; Verstegan, "Triumphe of feminyne Saintes," in *Odes*, D7 v.

71. Allen, *Nicols*, Cviii v.

72. CRS 5 (1908):118–19.

73. H. Garnet, *An Apology Against the Defence of Schisme*, 70.

74. Persons, *Reasons Why Catholiques refuse to goe to Church*, Bvii v, Ci r.

75. Quoted in Janelle, *Southwell*, 82 (Stonyhurst MS. Anglia A III 1, *A Brefe Discourse*, 5–11).

76. Garnet, *A Treatise of Equivocation* ed. D. Jardine (London, 1851), 52.

77. Janelle, *Southwell*, 81.

78. Holmes, *Resistance*, 123; *Constitutional Documents of the Reign of James I*, ed. J. R. Tanner (Cambridge, 1930), 91.

79. Persons, *Reasons*, + + iii r.

80. J. Halley, "The Family of Love," in *Representing the English Renaissance*, ed. S. Greenblatt, (Berkeley, 1988), 305.

81. Garnet, *Equivocation*, 13.

82. *NT*, dii v.

83. Granada, *Memoriall*, 518–19; *Spirituall Doctrine*, S8 v.

84. Persons, *Directorie*, B2 r.

85. Southwell, *Short Rule*, C6 r.

86. W. H. McCabe, *An Introduction to the Jesuit Theater*, ed. L. J. Oldani (St. Louis, 1983), chap. 15.

Chapter 8. Conclusion

1. R. Switzer, *The Ciceronian Style in Fr. Luis de Granada* (New York, 1927), 149.

Appendix: The Rhetorical Education of Recusant Writers

1. J. Gillow, *A . . . Bibliographical Dictionary of the English Catholics* (London, 1885–1902); G. Anstruther, *The Seminary Priests. A Dictionary of the Secular Clergy of England and Wales, 1558–1850* (Ware, 1968); D. Bellenger, *English and Welsh Priests 1558–1800* (Bath, 1984); J. Venn, and J. A. Venn, *Alumni Cantabrigienses . . . to 1751* (Cambridge, 1922–27); J. Foster, *Alumni Oxonienses . . . 1500–1714* (Oxford, 1891–92).

2. Vaux, *Catechisme*, viii.

3. Evans, "Rhetoric," *RH* 10 (1970):249.

4. L. Jardine, "The Place of Dialectic Teaching in Sixteenth-Century Cambridge," *Studies in the Renaissance* 21 (1974): 44, 50.

5. T. W. Baldwin, *William Shakspere's Small Latine & Lesse Greeke* (Urbana, 1944), 2:70, 1:299–300, 1:349, 1:417, 1:413.

6. Ibid., 2:17; T. Elyot, *The Boke Named The Governour* (London: 1531), 72–74.

7. Baldwin, *Shakspere*, 2:25–26; J. Sturm, *De literarum ludis recte aperiendis liber* (Argentorati, 1557), D2 r.

8. Baldwin, *Shakspere*, 1:197; W. Kempe, *The Education of Children* (London, 1588), Di v.

9. Baldwin, *Shakspere*, 1:101; D. Erasmus, "De ratione studii" (1511; Strasbourg, 1514), trans. B. McGregor; *Collected Works of Erasmus*, ed. C. R. Thompson (Toronto, 1978), 24:672, 679, 681, 687.

10. W. H. Curtis, *Oxford and Cambridge in Transition 1558–1642* (Oxford, 1959), 86–87, 101.

11. A. C. Beales, *Education Under Penalty. English Catholic Education . . . 1547–1689* (London, 1963), 131, 133.

12. A. P. Farrell, *The Jesuit Code of Liberal Education* (Milwaukee, 1938), 344–345, 235; Society of Jesus, *Ratio atque institutio studiorum societatis Iesu* (1599; Rome, 1606), H4 v, I2 r.

Bibliography

Section A. *Primary works.*
  1. Rhetorical texts.
  2. Meditations and devotional texts.
  3. Catechisms and "rules of life."
  4. Hagiographies and antihagiographies.
  5. Other primary texts (Protestant and Catholic).
Section B. *Secondary works.*

Note: Conjectural publishing dates and names are those suggested in *AR* and are indicated by square brackets.

A. *Primary works*

1. *Rhetorical texts*

Aristotle. *The "Art" of Rhetoric.* Translated by J. Freese. London: William Heinemann Ltd., Loeb Classical Library, 1926.

———. *The Poetics.* Translated by W. Hamilton Fyfe. London: William Heinemann Ltd., Loeb Classical Library, 1927.

———. "On Memory and Recollection." In *Parva Naturalia,* translated by W. S. Hett. London: William Heinemann Ltd., Loeb Classical Library, 1936.

Blundeville, T. *The Art of Logike.* London, 1599. Menston, Great Britain: Scolar Press, 1967.

Cicero. *De partitione oratoria.* Vol. 2 of *De oratore,* translated by H. Rackham. London: William Heinemann Ltd., Loeb Classical Library, 1942.

———. *De oratore.* Translated by E. Sutton and H. Rackham. 2 vols. London: William Heinemann Ltd., Loeb Classical Library, 1942.

———. *Topica.* In *De inventione,* translated by H. M. Hubbell. London: William Heinemann Ltd., Loeb Classical Library, 1949.

Cox, L. *The Arte or Crafte of Rhethoryke.* London, ca. 1530. Edited by F. I. Carpenter. Chicago: University of Chicago Press, 1899.

Erasmus, D. "De duplici copia verborum ac rerum commentarii duo," 1512. Basel, 1534. Translated by B. I. Knott. "De ratione studii," 1511. Strasbourg, 1514. Translated by B. McGregor. Vol. 24 of *Collected Works of Erasmus,* edited by C. R. Thompson. Toronto: University of Toronto Press, 1978.

Fraunce, A. *The Lawiers Logike.* London, 1588.

———. *The Arcadian Rhetorike.* London, 1588.

Harvey, G. *Ciceronianus* (London, 1577). Translated by C. A. Forbes. Edited by H. S. Wilson. Lincoln: University of Nebraska Studies, 1945.

Hoskyns, J. *Direccions for Speech and Style.* In *The Life, Letters, and Writings of John Hoskyns 1566–1638,* edited by L. B. Osborn. New Haven: Yale University Press, 1937.

Hyperius, A. *The Practise of preaching, Otherwise Called The Pathway to the Pulpet.* Translated by J. Ludham. London, 1577.

Peacham, H. *The Garden of Eloquence,* 1577; London, 1593. Introduction by W. G. Crane. Gainesville, Fla.: Scholars' Facsimiles & Reprints, 1954.

Plato, *Gorgias.* Translated by W. R. Lamb. London: William Heinemann Ltd., Loeb Classical Library, 1925.

———. *Phaedrus,* Translated by H. N. Fowler. London: William Heinemann Ltd., Loeb Classical Library, 1914.

Quintilian. *Institutio oratoria.* Translated by H. E. Butler. 4 vols. London: William Heinemann Ltd., Loeb Classical Library, 1920.

Rainolde, R., *The Foundacion of Rhetorike.* London, 1563. Introduction by F. R. Johnson. New York: Scholars' Facsimiles & Reprints, 1945.

Rhetorica ad Herennium. Translated by H. Caplan. London: William Heinemann Ltd., Loeb Classical Library, 1954.

Sherry, R. *A Treatise of Schemes and Tropes.* London, 1550. Introduction by H. W. Hildebrandt. Gainesville, Fla.: Scholars' Facsimiles & Reprints, 1961.

Sidney, P. "A Defence of Poetry," In *Miscellaneous Prose of Sir Philip Sidney.* London, 1595, edited by K. Duncan-Jones and J. van Dorsten. Oxford: Clarendon Press, 1973.

Smith, G., ed. *Elizabethan Critical Essays.* 2 vols. Oxford: Oxford University Press, 1904.

Soarez, C. *The "De arte rhetorica" (1568) . . . A Translation* (1562; Venice, 1568). Translated by L. J. Flynn. University of Florida: unpublished Ph.D., 1955.

Tommai, P. *The Art of Memory, that otherwyse is called the Phenix.* Translated by R. Coplande. London, ca. 1545.

Wilson, T., *Arte of Rhetorique.* London, 1553. Introduction by R. H. Bowers. Gainesville, Fla.: Scholars' Facsimiles & Reprints, 1962.

Wright, T. *The Passions of the Mind in General.* London, 1601. Edited by W. W. Newbold. New York: Garland Publishing, Inc., 1986.

2. Meditations and Devotional Texts

A Breefe Collection Concerning the Love of God towards Mankinde. (Douay, 1603). Vol. 170 of ERL. Menston, Great Britain: Scolar Press, 1973.

Bucke, J. *Intructions for the use of the beades.* (Louvain, 1589). Vol. 77 of ERL. Menston, Great Britain: Scolar Press, 1971.

C., I. *Saint Marie Magdalens Conversion* ([England, 1603]). Vol. 85 of ERL. Menston, Great Britain: Scolar Press, 1972.

Chambers, R. *Palestina* (Florence [England], 1600). Vol. 100 of ERL. Menston, Great Britain: Scolar Press, 1972.

Diego de Estella. *The Contempte of the World, and the Vanitie thereof.* Translated by G. C. [George Cotton] ([Rouen], 1584). Vol. 242 of ERL. Ilkley, Great Britain: Scolar Press, 1975.

Garnet, H. *The Societie of the Rosary.* [1593–94; England, 1596–97].

Hall, J. *The Arte of Divine Meditation.* 1606; London, 1607.

The Holie Bible Faithfully Translated into English [Douay Old Testament]. Translated by [G. Martin] (Douay, 1609–10). Vol. 265–66 of ERL. Ilkley, Great Britain: Scolar Press, 1975.

Howard, P. *A Foure-Fould Meditation, of the foure last things.* London, 1606.

a Kempis, T. *The Folowing of Christ, Translated Out of Latin into Englishe.* Translated by [W. Whytford]. [Rouen], 1585.

Loarte, G. *The Exercise of a Christian Life.* Translated by I.S. [Stephen Brinkley]. 1579; [Rouen], 1584.

———. *Meditations, of the Life and Passion of our Lord and Saviour Iesus Christ.* Translated anon. ([1576; England, 1596–98]). Vol. 352 of ERL. Ilkely, Great Britain: Scolar Press, 1977.

Luis de Granada. *Of Prayer, and Meditation.* Translated by R. Hopkins. (Paris, 1582). Vol. 64 of ERL. Menston, Great Britain: Scolar Press, 1971.

———. *A Spiritual Doctrine, Conteining A Rule To live wel.* Translated by R. Gibbons. (Louvain, 1599). Vol. 204 of ERL. Ilkley, Great Britain: Scolar Press, 1974.

A Manuall, or Meditation, and most necessary Prayers. [1580–81; England, 1596].

A Manual of Prayers Newly Gathered Out of Many and divers famous authours. Compiled G. F. [George Flinton]. [Rouen], 1583.

A Methode, to meditate on the Psalter, or great Rosarie of our blessed Ladie. Antwerp [England], 1598.

N., C., *Our Ladie Hath A New Sonne* (Douay [England], 1595). Vol. 78 of ERL. Menston, Great Britain: Scolar Press, 1971.

The New Testament of Iesus Christ. Translated by G. Martin. (Rheims, 1582). Vol. 267 of ERL. Ilkley, Great Britain: Scolar Press, 1975.

Persons, R. *A Christian Directorie Guiding Men to their Salvation.* Louvain, 1598.

———. *The First Booke of the Christian Exercise, appertayning to resolution.* [Rouen], 1582.

The Primer, or Office of the Blessed Virgin Marie. Translated by R.V. [R. Verstegan]. Antwerp, 1599.

Scupoli, L. *The Spiritual Conflict.* Translated by [J. Gerard] (1598; [Douay, 1603–10]). Vol. 8 of ERL. Menston, Great Britain: Scolar Press, 1968.

Southwell, R. *Marie Magdalens Funerall Teares.* 1591; London, 1594.

———.*Spiritual Exercises and Devotions of Blessed Robert Southwell, S.J.* Translated by P. E. Hallett. Edited by J.-M. de Buck. London: Sheed & Ward, 1931.

Verstegan, R. *Odes. In Imitation of the Seaven Penitential Psalmes* ([Antwerp], 1601). Vol. 53 of ERL. Menston, Great Britain: Scolar Press, 1970.

Worthington, T. *The Rosarie of our Ladie* (Antwerp, 1600). Vol. 329 of ERL. Ilkley, Great Britain: Scolar Press, 1977.

3. *Catechisms and "rules of life"*

Alphonso de Madrid. *A Breefe Methode or Way Teachinge all sortes of Christian People, how to serve God.* Translated by I.M. ([London, 1602–05]). Vol. 109 of ERL. Menston, Great Britain: Scolar Press, 1972.

Bellarmine, R. *A Shorte Catechisme of Cardinall Bellarmine illustrated with the Images.* Translated by [R. Gibbons]. Npp, 1614.

An Ample Declaration of the Christian doctrine. Translated by R. Haydock (Rouen [England, 1602–5]). Vol. 341 of ERL. Ilkley, Great Britain: Scolar Press, 1977.

Broughton, R. *The First Part of the Resolution of Religion* (1603; Antwerp [England, 1603]). Vol. 281 of ERL. Ilkley, Great Britain: Scolar Press, 1976.

Canisius, P., *A Summe of Christian Doctrine.* Translated by [H. Garnet] ([London, 1592–96]). Vol. 35 of ERL. Menston, Great Britain: Scolar Press, 1971.

D.,T.H. *Nine Rockes To Be Avoided, of those which sayle towards the Port of Perfection* (Douay [England], 1600). Vol. 9 of ERL. Menston, Great Britain: Scolar Press, 1969.

Ledisma, J. *The Christian Doctrine in manner of a Dialogue betweene the Master and the Disciple.* Translated anon. ([England], 1597). Vol. 2 of ERL. Menston, Great Britain: Scolar Press, 1969.

Luís de Granada, *A Memoriall of a Christian Life.* Translated by R. Hopkins (Rouen, 1586).

Nowell, A. *A Catechisme or First Instruction and Learning of Christian Religion.* Translated by T. Morton (London, 1570). Introduction by F. V. Occhiogrosso. New York: Scholars' Facsimiles & Reprints, Inc., 1975.

Southwell, R. *A Short Rule of Good Life* ([England, 1596–97]). Vol. 78 of ERL. Menston, Great Britain: Scolar Press, 1971.

Vaux, L. *A Catechisme or Christian Doctrine necessarie for Children and ignorante people* ([1568; Rouen], 1583). Introduction by T. G. Law. Vol. 4, new series of publications of The Chetham Society. Manchester, Great Britain: 1885.

4. Hagiographies and antihagiographies

Alfield, T. *A true reporte of the death & martyrdome of M. Campion Iesuite and preiste* ([London, 1582]). Vol. 56 of ERL. Menston, Great Britain: Scolar Press, 1970.

Allen, W., *A Briefe Historie of the Glorious Martyrdom of XII. Reverend Priests* ([Rheims], 1582). Vol. 55 of ERL. Menston, Great Britain: Scolar Press, 1970.

—. *A True Sincere and Modest Defence of English Catholiques.* [Rouen, 1584].

"Awfeeld," *The Life and end of Thomas Awfeeld a Seminary Preest.* [England], 1585.

Cecil, W. *The Execution of Iustice . . . Against Certaine Stirrers of Sedition, and Adherents to the Traytors and Enemies of the Realme, Without Any Persecution of Them for Questions of Religion.* London, 1583.

———. *A Declaration of the favourable dealing of her Maiesties Commissioners.* London, 1583.

Foxe, J. Vol. 1 of *The Acts and Monuments of John Foxe* (London, 1563). Edited by J. Pratt. 4th ed. London: The Religious Tract Society, 1877.

Garnet, H. *[A] Treatis[e of Chri]stia[n Renunciation]* ([England, 1593]). Vol. 47 of ERL. Menston, Great Britain: Scolar Press, 1970.

Gennings, J. *The Life and Death of Mr. Edmund Geninges Priest* (St. Omers, 1614). Vol. 69 of ERL. Menston, Great Britain: Scolar Press, 1971.

Gibbons, J. *Concertatio ecclesiae Catholicae in Anglia* (1583; Trier, 1588). Edited by D. M. Rogers. Farnborough, Great Britain: Gregg International Publishers Limited, 1970.

Martin, G. *A Treatyse of Christian Peregrination.* [Paris], 1583.

Munday, A. *A breefe aunswer made unto two seditious Pamphlets.* London, 1582.

Persons, R. *A Treatise of Three Conversions of England* ([St. Omers], 1603–4). Vols. 304–6 of ERL. Ilkley, Great Britain: Scolar Press, 1976.

———. *An Epistle of the Persecution of Catholickes in Englande*. Translated by G.T. (Douay [Rouen, 1582]). Vol. 125 of ERL. Menston, Great Britain: Scolar Press, 1973.

———. *De persecutione Anglicana libellus*. 1581; Rome, 1582.

Southwell, R. *Triumphs over Death* (London, 1596). Edited by J. W. Trotman. London: Manresa Press, 1914.

———. *An Epistle of Comfort, to the Reverend Priestes . . . & other of the Laye sort* (Paris [England, 1587–88]). Vol. 211 of ERL. Ilkley, Great Britain: Scolar Press, 1974.

Stapleton, T. *The Life and Illustrious Martyrdom of Sir Thomas More*. Translated by P. E. Hallett. Edited by E. E. Reynolds. 1928; London: Burns & Oates Limited, 1966.

Verstegan, R. *Theatre des Cruautez des Hereticques de nostre temps*. Antwerp, 1588.

———. *Theatrum crudelitatum haereticorum nostri temporis*. 1587; Antwerp, 1592.

Wilson, J. *The English Martyrologe*. [St. Omer], 1608.

Worthington, T. *A Relation of Sixtene Martyrs* (Douay, 1601). Vol. 350 of ERL. Ilkley, Great Britain: Scolar Press, 1977.

5. Other primary texts (Protestant and Catholic).

Alabaster, W. *The Sonnets of William Alabaster*. Edited by G. M. Story and H. Gardner. Oxford: Oxford University Press, 1959.

Allen, W. *A True Report Of . . . Iohn Nicols* (Rheims, 1583). Vol. 63 of ERL. Menston, Great Britain: Scolar Press, 1971.

———. *The Copie of a Letter . . . Concerning the Yeelding Up, of the Citie of Daventrie* (Antwerp, 1587). Vol. 51 of ERL. Menston, Great Britain: Scolar Press, 1970.

———. *An Admonition to the Nobiltity and People of England and Ireland* (Npp, 1588). Vol. 74 of ERL. Menston, Great Britain: Scolar Press, 1971.

Ascham, R. *The Schoolmaster* (London, 1570). Edited by L. V. Ryan. New York: Cornell University Press, 1967.

Augustine, *The Teacher [De magistro]*. Translated by R. P. Russell. Vol. 59 of The Fathers of the Church ser., ed. R. J. Deferrari. Washington, D.C.: Catholic University of America Press, Inc., 1968.

———. *The City of God [De civitate Dei]*. Translated by J. Healey (London, 1610). 2 vols. Edinburgh: John Grant, 1909.

———. *Confessions*. Translated by H. Chadwick. Oxford: Oxford University Press, 1991.

———. *Christian Instruction [De doctrina Christiana]*. Translated by J. J. Gavigan. Vol. 2 of The Fathers of the Church ser., ed. R. J. Deferrari. New York: Fathers of the Church, Inc., 1947.

Bagshaw, C. *A True relation of the faction begun at Wisbich* ([London], 1601). Vol. 24 of ERL. Menston, Great Britain: Scolar Press, 1970.

Bristow, R. *Demaundes to bee Proponed of Catholickes to the Heretickes*. 1576; [England, 1596–97].

———. *A Briefe Treatise of Divers Plaine and sure waies to finde out the truth.* 1574; Antwerp [England], 1599.

Bunny, E. *A Briefe Answer, unto those idle and frivolous quarrels of R.P. against the late edition of the Resolution.* London, 1589.

———. *A Booke of Christian exercise . . . Perused, and accompanied now with a Treatise tending to Pacification.* 1584; London, 1585.

Campion, E. *Rationes decem: quibus fretus certamen adversariis obtulit in causa fidei, Edmundus Campianus.* [England, 1581].

Campian Englished. Or A Translation of the Ten Reasons, in which Edmund Campian . . . insisted in his Challenge ([?Rouen], 1632). Vol. 71 of ERL. Menston, Great Britain: Scolar Press, 1971.

Castiglione, B. *The Book of the Courtier.* Translated by T. Hoby (London, 1561). Edited by W. Raleigh. London: The Tudor Translations, 1900.

Catholic Record Society. *Miscellanea.* Vol. 2. 1906.

———. *Miscellanea.* Vol. 4. 1907.

———. *Unpublished Documents Relating to the English Martyrs,* ed. J. H. Pollen. Vol. 5. 1908.

———. *Miscellanea.* Vol. 9. 1911.

———. *Letters and Memorials of Father Robert Persons, S.J.,* ed. L. Hicks. Vol. 39. 1942.

———. *The Letters and Despatches of Richard Verstegan (ca. 1550–1640),* ed. A. G. Petti. Vol. 52. 1959.

———. *The Responsa Scholarum of the English College, Rome (1598–1621).* Edited by A. Kenny. Vol. 54. 1962.

———. *Elizabethan Casuistry.* Edited by P. J. Holmes. Vol. 67. 1981.

Constable, H. *A Discoverye of a Counterfecte Conference.* [Paris], 1600. Vol. 6 of ERL. Menston, Great Britain: Scholar Press, 1969.

———. *The Poems of Henry Constable.* Edited by J. Grundy. Liverpool: Liverpool University Press, 1960.

Coote, E. *The English Schoole-Maister* (London, 1596). Menston, Great Britain: Scolar Press, 1968.

Copley, A. *An Answere to a Letter of a Iesuited Gentleman* ([London], 1601). Vol. 31 of ERL. Menston, Great Britain: Scolar Press, 1970.

———. *Another Letter of Mr. A.C. to his Dis-Iesuited Kinseman* ([London], 1602). Vol. 100 of ERL. Menston, Great Britain: Scolar Press, 1972.

Donne, J. *Devotions Upon Emergent Occasions* (London, 1624). Edited by J. Sparrow. Cambridge: Cambridge University Press, 1923.

———. *Ignatius His Conclave* (London, 1611). Edited by T. S. Healy. Oxford: Clarendon Press, 1969.

Elyot, T. *The Boke Named The Governour* (London, 1531). Edited by H. H. Croft. 2 vols. London: C. Kegan Paul & Co., 1880.

Fulke, W. *The Text of the New Testament . . . by the Papists . . . Whereunto is added the Translation . . . used in the Church of England.* London, 1589.

———. *A Defense of the sincere and true Translations of the holie Scriptures . . . against . . . Gregorie Martin.* London, 1583.

Garnet, H. *An Apology Against the Defence of Schisme* ([England, 1593]). Vol. 167 of ERL. Menston, Great Britain: Scolar Press, 1973.

————. *A Treatise of Equivocation*. Edited by D. Jardine. London: Longman, Brown, Green and Longmans, 1851.

Gee, J. *The Foot out of the Snare: With a Detection of Sundry Late practices and Impostures of the Priests and Iesuits in England*. London, 1624.

Gerard, J. *John Gerard. The Autobiography of an Elizabethan*. Translated by P. Caraman. London: Longmans, Green and Co., 1951.

Greene, R. "The Repentance of Robert Greene." London, 1592. Vol. 12 of *The Life and Complete Works . . . of Robert Greene*, ed. A. B. Grosart. London: from the Huth Library, 1881–86.

Guiney, L.I. *Recusant Poets*. London: Sheed & Ward, 1938.

Haddon, W. and J. Foxe, J. *Against Ierome Osorius . . . and against his slaunderous Invectives*. Translated by J. Bell. London, 1581.

Harding, T. *An Answere to Maister Iuelles Chalenge*. Louvain, Belgium: 1564.

Harsnet, S. *A Declaration of egregious Popish impostures in casting out of Devils*. London, 1603.

Herbert, G. *The Works of George Herbert*. Edited by F. E. Hutchinson. Oxford: Clarendon Press, 1941.

Holy Churches Complaint, for her childrens disobedience ([London, 1598–1601 in Scolar Press facsimile, not catalog]). Vol. 236 of ERL. Ilkley, Great Britain: Scolar Press, 1975.

Jerome. *The Letters of St. Jerome*. Translated by C. C. Mierow. Vol. 33 of the Ancient Christian Writers' Series. London: Longmans, Green and Co., 1963.

Kempe, W. *The Education of Children*. London, 1588.

Loyola, I. *The Spiritual Exercises of Saint Ignatius*. Translated by T. Corbishley. 1963; Wheathampstead, Great Britain: Anthony Clarke Books, 1973.

Martin, G. *Roma Sancta*. Edited by G. B. Parks. Rome: Edizioni di Storia e Letteratura, 1969.

Martyr, P. *The Common Places of . . . Peter Martyr*. [London, 1583].

Meres, F. *Palladis tamia* (London, 1598), Introduction by D. C. Allen. New York: Scholars' Facsimiles & Reprints, 1938.

More, H. *The Elizabethan Jesuits [Historia missionis Anglicanae societatis Jesu]* (St. Omers, 1660). Translated by F. Edwards. London: Phillimore & Co. Ltd., 1981.

Munday, A. *The English Romane Lyfe* (London, 1582). Edited by P. J. Ayres. Oxford: Clarendon Press, 1980.

Nashe, T. "Christs Teares Over Ierusalem" (London, 1593). Vol. 2 of *The Works of Thomas Nashe*. Edited by R. B. McKerrow. 1904; London: Sidgwick & Jackson, Ltd., 1910.

Persons, R. *A Relation of the King of Spaines Receiving in Valliodolid* ([Antwerp], 1592). Vol. 351 of ERL. Ilkley, Great Britain: Scolar Press, 1977.

————. *Newes from Spayne and Holland* ([Antwerp], 1593). Vol. 365 of ERL. Ilkley, Great Britain: Scolar Press, 1977.

————. *A Temperate Ward-word, to the Turbulent and Seditious Wach-word of Sir Francis Hastinges* ([Antwerp], 1599). Vol. 31 of ERL. Menston, Great Britain: Scolar Press, 1970.

————. *A Briefe Apologie, or Defence of the Catholike Ecclesiastical Hierarchie* [Antwerp, 1601]. Vol. 273 of ERL. Ilkley, Great Britain: Scolar Press, 1975.

————. *The Warn-word to Sir Francis Hastinges Wast-word*. [Antwerp], 1602.

————.*A Manifestation of the Great Folly & Bad Spirit of . . . secular priestes* [Antwerp], 1602. Vol. 169 of ERL. Menston, Great Britain: Scolar Press, 1973.

————. *The Jesuit's Memorial, For the Intended Reformation of England.* Edited by E. Gee. London, 1690.

————. *A Brief Discours contayning certayne Reasons Why Catholiques refuse to goe to Church* [Howlett, I., psued.]. Douay [London], 1580.

Persons, R. and others. *A Conference About the Next Succession* [Doleman, R., psued.] ([Antwerp], 1594). Vol. 104 of ERL. Menston, Great Britain: Scolar Press, 1972.

Plutarch. *The Education or bringinge up of children, translated oute of Plutarche.* Translated by T. Elyot (London, 1530). New York: Da Capo Press, 1969.

Rogers, R. *Seven Treatises, Containing Such Direction as is Gathered out of the Holie Scriptures.* London, 1603.

Sandys, E. *Europae Speculum or, a View or Survey of the State of Religion in the Westerne parts of the World.* 1605; Hagae-Comitis, 1629.

Sixtus V. *A Declaration of the Sentence and deposition of Elizabeth.* Npp, [1588].

Society of Jesus. *The Constitutions of the Society of Jesus.* Translated by G. E. Ganss. St. Louis: The Institute of Jesuit Sources, 1970.

————. *Ratio atque institutio studiorum societatis Iesu* (Rome, 1606).

Southwell, R. *The Poems of Robert Southwell, S.J.* Edited by J. H. McDonald and N. P. Brown. Oxford: Clarendon Press, 1967.

————. *An Humble Supplication to Her Maiestie* ([London], 1595 [1600–1601]). Edited by R. C. Bald. Cambridge: Cambridge University Press, 1953.

Sturmius, J. *De literarum ludis recte aperiendis liber* (1538; Argentorati, 1557).

Tanner, J. R. ed. *Constitutional Documents of the Reign of James I.* Cambridge: Cambridge University Press, 1930.

"Trent 1545–1563", translated by P. McIlhenny and J. Coventry. Vol. 2 of *Decrees of the Ecumenical Councils.* Edited by N. P. Tanner. London: Sheed and Ward Limited, 1990.

Weston, W. *William Weston. The Autobiography of an Elizabethan.* Translated by P. Caraman. London: Longmans, Green and Co., 1955.

Wither, G. *Schollers Purgatory.* London, 1625.

Wright, T. *A Treatise, Shewing the possibilite . . . of the reall presence.* Antwerp [England], 1596.

B. SECONDARY WORKS

Allison, A. F. "The Writings of Fr. Henry Garnet, S.J. (1555–1606)." *RH* 1 (1951): 7–21.

Allison, A. F. and D. M. Rogers, eds. "A Catalogue of Catholic Books in English Printed Abroad or Secretly in England 1558–1640." *RH* 3 (1956): 119-[319].

————. *The Contemporary Printed Literature of the English Counter-Reformation between 1558 and 1640.* Aldershot, Britain: Scolar Press, 1989.

————. "Review of A.C. Southern, *Elizabethan Recusant Prose 1559–1582.*" *Library* 5th ser. 6 (1951): 48–57.

————. "Ten Years of *Recusant History.*" *RH* 6 (1961): 2–11.

————. "Twenty-five Years of *Recusant History.*" *RH* 13 (1976): 153–56.

Anstruther, G. *The Seminary Priests. A Dictionary of the Secular Clergy of England and Wales, 1558–1850*. 4 vols. Ware, Great Britain: St. Edmund's College, 1968.

Antona-Traversi, D. A., "Devotional Prose in English Written on the Continent During the Reign of Elizabeth." B.Litt., University of Oxford, 1937.

Arber, E. *A Transcript of the Registers of the Company of Stationers of London; 1554–1660 A.D.* 4 vols. London: Privately printed, 1875–94.

Aston, M. *England's Iconoclasts*. Oxford: Clarendon Press, 1988.

Auerbach, E. *Mimesis: The Representation of Reality in Western Literature*. Translated by W. R. Trask. Princeton: Princeton University Press, 1953.

Baldwin, T. W. *William Shakspere's Small Latine & Lesse Greeke*. 2 vols. Urbana: University of Illinois Press, 1944.

Barthes, R. "The Old Rhetoric: An Aide-Memoire." In *The Semiotic Challenge*, translated by R. Howard. Oxford: Basil Blackwell Ltd., 1988.

Baumer, F. A. "Toward the Development of Homiletic as Rhetorical Gesture: a Critical Study of Roman Catholic Preaching in the United States Since Vatican Council II." P.D. diss., Northwestern University, Illinois, 1985.

Bayley, P. *French Pulpit Oratory 1598–1650*. Cambridge: Cambridge University Press, 1980.

Beal, P. ""Notions in Garrison." The Seventeenth-Century Commonplace Book." Newberry lecture to the Renaissance English Text Society, 1987.

Beales, A. C. *Education Under Penalty. English Catholic Education . . . 1547–1689*. London: University of London, The Athlone Press, 1963.

Beilin, E. *Redeeming Eve. Women Writers of the English Renaissance*. Princeton: Princeton University Press, 1987.

Bellenger, D. *English and Welsh Priests 1558–1800*. Bath, Great Britain: Downside Abbey, 1984.

Bennett, H. S. *English Books & Readers 1558–1603*. Cambridge: Cambridge University Press, 1965.

Blom, J. M. *The Post-Tridentine English Primer*. Vol. 3 of the Monograph Series. CRS Publications, 1982.

Bolgar, R. R. *The Classical Heritage and its Beneficiaries*. 1954; London: Cambridge University Press, 1973.

Bossy, J. *The English Catholic Community 1570–1850*. London: Darton, Longman & Todd, 1975.

Brennan, G. E. "Papists and Patriotism in Elizabethan England." *RH* 19 (1988): 1–15.

Briggs, J. *This Stage-Play World*. Oxford: Oxford University Press, 1983.

Brogan, K. M. "The Religious and Moral Poetry in the Ellizabethan Miscellanies." Ph.D. diss., University of Tennessee, 1979.

Brown, P. *Augustine of Hippo*. London: Faber & Faber Limited, 1967.

Campbell, L. B. *Divine Poetry and Drama in Sixteenth-Century England*. Cambridge: Cambridge University Press, 1959.

Caro, R.V. "William Alabaster: Rhetor, Meditator, Devotional Poet." *RH* 19 (1988): 62–79, 155–70.

———. "Rhetoric and Meditation in the Sonnets of William Alabaster." Ph.D. diss., University of Washington, 1977.

Carruthers, M. J. *The Book of Memory. A Study of Memory in Medieval Culture.* Cambridge: Cambridge University Press, 1990.

Carter, M. F. "The Ritual Functions of Epideictic Rhetoric: the Case of Socrates' Funeral Oration." *Rhetorica* 9 (1991): 209–32.

Chambers, R. W. *On the Continuity of English Prose from Alfred to More and his School.* London: Early English Text Society, Oxford University Press, 1932.

Chandos, J. "Recusant Poets of the English Renaissance". *The Month* 3 (N.S.) (1950): 5–18.

Chanoff, D. "Donne's Anglicanism." *RH* 15 (1980): 154–67.

Clancy, T. H. *Papist Pamphleteers.* Chicago: Loyola University Press, 1964.

———. "Notes on Persons's *Memorial for the Reformation of England* (1596)." *RH* 5 (1959): 17–34.

Corthell, R. "'The secrecy of man': Recusant Discourse and the Elizabethan Subject." *English Literary Renaissance* 19 (1989): 272–90.

Crane, D. "Studies in Recusant Prose: the English Translations of the *Imitatio Christi* in the Sixteenth and Seventeenth Centuries." B.Litt., University of Oxford, 1968.

———. "Catholicism and Rhetoric in Southwell, Crashaw, Dryden and Pope." *RH* 15 (1980): 239–58.

Crane, W. G. *Wit and Rhetoric in the Renaissance. The Formal Basis of Elizabethan Prose Style.* New York: Columbia University Press, 1937.

Cross, F. L., and Livingstone, E. A., eds., *The Oxford Dictionary of the Christian Church.* 1958; London: Oxford University Press, 1974.

Curtis, M. H. *Oxford and Cambridge in Transition 1558–1642.* Oxford: Clarendon Press, 1959.

Dures, A. *English Catholicism 1558–1642: Continuity and Change.* Harlow, Great Britain: Longman Group UK Limited, 1983.

Dwyer, J. J. "Robert Southwell." *The Month* 16 (N.S.) (1956): 13–21.

Eagleton, T. *Literary Theory.* Oxford: Basil Blackwell Publisher Limited, 1983.

Eco, U. "An *Ars Oblivionalis?* Forget It!" *PMLA* 103, no. 1 (1988): 254–61.

Evans, J. X. "The Art of Rhetoric and the Art of Dying in Tudor Recusant Prose." *RH* 10 (1970): 247–72.

Evetts-Secker, J. "Consolatory Literature of the English Recusants." *Renaissance and Reformation* 6 (N.S.) (1982): 122–41.

Ezell, M. J. *The Patriarch's Wife. Literary Evidence and the History of the Family.* Chapel Hill: University of North Carolina Press, 1987.

Farrell, A. P. *The Jesuit Code of Liberal Education.* Milwaukee: The Bruce Publishing Company, 1938.

Fish, S. *Self-Consuming Artifacts. The Experience of Seventeenth-Century Literature.* 1972; Berkeley: University of California Press, 1974.

Foster, J. *Alumni Oxonienses . . . 1500–1714.* Oxford: Parker & Co., 1891–92.

Fullenwider, H. F. "The Loving Arrow: Pointed Diction in God's Word." *Rhetorica* 8 (1990): 255–74.

Gardner, H. *Religion and Literature.* London: Faber and Faber Limited, 1971.

Gillow, J. *A . . . Bibliographical Dictionary of the English Catholics.* 5 vols. London: Burns and Oates, 1885–1902.

Gossett, S. "Drama in the English College, Rome, 1591–1660." *English Literary Renaissance* 3 (1973): 60–93.

Grafton, A., and L. Jardine. *From Humanism to the Humanities. Education and the Liberal Arts in Fifteenth-and Sixteenth-Century Europe.* London: Gerald Duckworth & Co. Ltd., 1986.

Green, L. "Aristotelian Rhetoric, Dialectic, and the Traditions of [Analogue]." *Rhetorica* 8 (1990): 5–27.

Greenblatt, S. *Renaissance Self-Fashioning. From More to Shakespeare.* Chicago: University of Chicago Press, 1980.

——, ed. *Representing the English Renaissance.* Berkeley: University of California Press, 1988.

Greg, W. W. "Licensers for the Press, etc. to 1640. A Biographical Index Based Mainly on Arber's *Transcript.*" *Oxford Bibliographical Society* N.S. 10 (1962).

Haigh, C. "The Fall of a Church or the Rise of a Sect?" *The Historical Journal* 21 (1978): 181–86.

Hannay, M. P., ed. *Silent But for the Word.* Kent, Ohio: Kent State University Press, 1985.

Holmes, P. *Resistance and Compromise. The Political Thought of the Elizabethan Catholics.* Cambridge: Cambridge University Press, 1982.

Howell, W. S. *Logic and Rhetoric in England, 1500–1700.* Princeton: Princeton University Press, 1956.

Hudson, E. K. "English Protestants and the *imitatio Christi,* 1580–1620." *Sixteenth-Century Journal* 19, no. 4 (1988): 541–58.

Hunter, G. "The Use of Sententia in the Tragedies of Senecca." D.Phil, University of Oxford, 1950.

Hunter, L., ed. *Toward a Definition of Topos.* Basingstoke, Great Britain: Macmillan Education Ltd., 1991.

Huntley, F. L. "*Macbeth* and the Background of Jesuitical Equivocation." *PMLA* 79, no. 1 (1964): 390–400.

Janelle, P. *Robert Southwell the Writer. A study in religious inspiration.* London: Sheed and Ward, 1935.

——. "English Devotional Literature in the Sixteenth and Seventeenth Centuries." *English Studies Today* 2 (N.S.) (1961): 159–71.

Jardine, L. "The Place of Dialectic Teaching in Sixteenth-Century Cambridge." *Studies in the Renaissance* 21 (1974): 31–62.

Johnson, S. "Waller." Vol. 1 of *Lives of the English Poets* (1779–81; London, 1783). Edited by G. Birkbeck Hill. Oxford: Clarendon Press, 1905.

Knox, T. F. *The First and Second Diaries of the English College, Douay.* London: David Nutt, 1878.

Koelb, C. *Inventions of Reading. Rhetoric and the Literary Imagination.* Ithaca: Cornell University Press, 1988.

Lanham, R. *A Handlist of Rhetorical Terms.* 1968; Berkeley: University of California Press, 1969.

——. *The Motives of Eloquence.* New Haven: Yale University Press, 1976.

Leff, M. C. "The Topics of Argumentative Invention in Latin Rhetorical Theory." *Rhetorica* 1 (1983): 23–44.

Legarda-Carrion, C. "Robert Southwell." B.Litt., University of Oxford, 1967.

Levine, R. "Prudentius" *Romanus:* The Rhetorician as Hero, Martyr, Satirist, and Saint." *Rhetorica* 9 (1991): 5–38.

Lewalski, B. *Protestant Poetics and the Seventeeth-Century Religious Lyric*. Princeton: Princeton University Press, 1979.

Lewis, C. S. *English Literature in the Sixteenth Century*. Oxford: Clarendon Press, 1954.

Loades, D. M. "The Press Under the Early Tudors. A Study in Censorship and Sedition." *Cambridge Bibliographical Society Transactions* 4 (1964): 29–50.

Loomis, R. "The Barrett Version of Robert Southwell's *Short Rule of Good Life*." *RH* 7 (1964): 239–48.

MacCaffrey, I. "The Meditative Paradigm." *English Literary History* 32 (1965): 388–407.

Manamon, J. M. "Renaissance Preaching . . . [and] Aurelio Brandolini." *Viator* 10 (1979): 355–73.

Martin, J. W. "The Marion Regime's Failure to Understand the Importance of Printing." *Huntingdon Library Quarterly* 44 (1981): 231–47.

Martz, L. *The Poetry of Meditation*. 1954; New Haven: Yale University Press, 1962.

Maurer, W. R. "Spee, Southwell and the Poetry of Meditation." *Comparative Literature* 15 (1963): 15–22.

Mazzeo, J. A. *Renaissance and Seventeenth-Century Studies*. New York: Columbia University Press, 1964.

McGrath, P. "The Bloody Questions Reconsidered." *RH* 20 (1991): 305–19.

McCabe, W. H. *An Introduction to the Jesuit Theater*. Edited by L. J. Oldani. St. Louis: Institute of Jesuit Sources, 1983.

Milward, P. *Religious Controversies of the Elizabethan Age. A Survey of Printed Sources*. London: Scolar Press, 1977.

Moore, J. A. *Fray Luis de Granada*. Boston: Twayne Publishers, 1977.

Mullaney, S. "Lying Like Truth: Riddle, Representation and Treason in Renaissance England." *English Literary History* 47 (1980): 32–47.

Murphy, J. J. *Renaissance Rhetoric. A Short-Title Catalogue . . . to A.D. 1700*. New York: Garland Publishing, Inc., 1981.

New Catholic Encyclopedia, ed. The Catholic University of America, Washington. 18. vols. New York: McGraw-Hill Book Company, 1967–.

Nuttall, A. D. *Overheard By God. Fiction and Prayer in Herbert, Milton, Dante and St John*. 1980; London: Methuen & Co. Ltd., 1983.

O'Malley, J. W. "Erasmus and the History of Sacred Rhetoric." In *Erasmus of Rotterdam Society Yearbook Five* (1985), 1–29.

———. *Catholicism in Early Modern History. A Guide to Research*. St. Louis, Missouri: Center for Reformation Research, 1988.

Ong, W. J. *Rhetoric, Romance and Technology*. New York: Cornell University Press, 1971.

———. *Orality and Literacy. The Technologizing of the Word*. 1982; London: Routledge, 1988.

———. *Ramus, Method, and the Decay of Dialogue*. Cambridge, Mass.: Harvard University Press, 1958.

———. "Tudor Writings on Rhetoric." *Studies in the Renaissance* 15 (1968): 39–69.

Oxley, B. "'Simples are by compounds farre exceld': Southwell's Longer Latin Poems and 'St Peters Complaint'" *RH* 17 (1985): 330–40.

Parker, P. *Literary Fat Ladies*. London: Methuen & Co. Ltd, 1987.

Parkin-Speer, D. "Freedon of Speech in Sixteenth-Century English Rhetorics." *Sixteenth-Century Journal* 12, no. 3 (1981):65–72.

Peers, E. A. *Studies of the Spanish Mystics*. 2 vols. London: S.P.C.K., 1951–60.

Petti, A. G. "Richard Verstegan and Catholic Martyrologies of the Later Elizabethan Period." *RH* 5 (1959):64–90.

———. "A Study of the Life and Writings of Richard Verstegan, (ca. 1550–1640)." M.A., University of London, 1957.

———. "Stephen Vallenger (1541–1591)." *RH* 6 (1962):248–64.

Phillimore, J. S. "Blessed Thomas More and the Arrest of Humanism in England." *Dublin Review* 153 (1913):1–26.

Pollen, J. H. *Acts of English Martyrs*. London: Burns and Oates Limited, 1891.

———. "The Politics of the English Catholics during the Reign of Queen Elizabeth." *The Month* 99 (1902):394–411, 600–18; 100 (1903): 71–87, 176–88.

Praz, M. *Studies in Seventeenth-Century Imagery*. 1939; Rome: Edizioni di Storia e Letteratura, 1964.

Price Zimmerman, T. C. "Confession and Autobiography in the Early Renaissance." In *Renaissance Studies in Honor of Hans Baron*, edited by A. Molho and J. A. Tedeschi. Florence: Biblioteca Storica Sansoni, 1971, 119–40.

Raspa, A. *The Emotive Image. Jesuit Poetics in the English Renaissance*. Fort Worth: Texas Christian University Press, 1983.

Richards, I. A. *The Philosophy of Rhetoric*. 1936; New York: Oxford University Press, 1965.

Roberts, J. R. *A Critical Anthology of English Recusant Devotional Prose, 1558–1603*. Pittsburgh, PA: Duquesne University Press, 1966.

Rollins, H. E. "An Analytical Index to the Ballad-Entries in the Registers of the Company of Stationers of London." *Studies in Philology* 21 (1924):1–324.

Ross, M. M. *Poetry & Dogma*. New Brunswick, N.J.: Rutgers University Press, 1954.

Scarisbrick, J. J. *The Jesuits and the Catholic Reformation*. 1988; London: The Historical Association, 1989.

Sharratt, P. "Recent Work on Peter Ramus (1970–1986)." *Rhetorica* 5 (1987):7–58.

Shuger, D. *Sacred Rhetoric. The Christian Grand Style in the English Renaissance*. Princeton: Princeton University Press, 1988.

Siebert, F. S. *Freedom of the Press in England 1476–1776*. Urbana: University of Illinois Press, 1952.

Slights, C. W. *The Casuistical Tradition*. Princeton: Princeton University Press, 1981.

Smith, A. J. "An Examination of Some Claims for Ramism." *Review of English Studies* 7 (N.S.) (1956):348–59.

Sonnino, L. A. *A Handbook to Sixteenth-Century Rhetoric*. London: Routledge and Kegan Paul Limited, 1968.

Sorabji, R. *Aristotle on Memory*. London: Gerald Duckworth & Company Limited, 1972.

Southern, A. C. *Elizabethan Recusant Prose 1559–1582*. London: Sands and Co. (Publishers), Limited, 1950.

Sterne, L. *The Life and Opinions of Tristram Shandy, Gentleman* (York, 1760–67). Edited by I. Campbell Ross. Oxford: Clarendon Press, 1983.

Switzer, R. *The Ciceronian Style in Fr. Luis de Granada*. New York: Instituto de las Espanas, 1927.

The Tatler (London, 1709–11). Edited by D. F. Bond. 3 vols. Oxford: Clarendon Press, 1987.

Thomas, K. *Religion and the Decline of Magic*. London: Weidenfeld and Nicolson, 1971.

Thurston, H. "Catholic Writers and Elizabethan Readers." *The Month* 83 (1895):230–45, 383–99.

Tinkler, J. F. "Renaissance Humanism and the *genera eloquentiae*." *Rhetorica* 5 (1987):279–309.

Trimpi, W. "The Quality of Fiction: the Rhetorical Transmission of Literary Theory." *Traditio* 30 (1974):1–118.

———. "The Meaning of Horace's *Ut pictura poesis*." *Journal of the Warburg and Courtauld Institutes* 26 (1973):1–34.

Tuve, R. *Elizabethan and Metaphysical Imagery*. Chicago: University of Chicago Press, 1947.

Venn, J., and J. A. Venn, *Alumni Cantabrigienses . . . to 1751*. 4 vols. Cambridge: Cambridge University Press, 1922–27.

Vickers, B. *In Defence of Rhetoric*. Oxford: Clarendon Press, 1988.

———, ed. *Rhetoric Revalued*. New York: International Society for the History of Rhetoric Monograph 1, 1982.

———. "Valla's Ambivalent Praise of Pleasure." *Viator* 17 (1986):271–319.

———. "Rhetorical and anti-rhetorical tropes." *Comparative Criticism* 3 (1981).

Wallace, W. A. "Aristotelian Science and Rhetoric in Transition: the Middle Ages and the Renaissance." *Rhetorica* 7 (1989):7–21.

Whigham, F. *Ambition and Privilege. The Social Tropes of Elizabethan Courtesy Theory*. Berkeley: University of California Press, 1984.

White, H. C. *The Tudor Books of Private Devotion*. Madison: University of Wisconsin Press, 1951.

———. *Tudor Books of Saints and Martyrs*. Madison: University of Wisconsin Press, 1963.

———. *English Devotional Literature (Prose) 1600–1640*. Madison: University of Wisconsin Press, 1931.

Wittkower, R. *Art and Architecture in Italy 1600 to 1750*. 1958; Harmondsworth, Great Britain: Penguin Books Ltd., 1980.

Wright, L. B. *Middle Class Culture in Elizabethan England*. 1935; New York: Cornell University Press, 1958.

Yates, F. *The Art of Memory*. London: Routlege and Kegan Paul Ltd., 1966.

Index